GENIUS AT WORK

Peter Freeth

CGW PUBLISHING

2015

Genius at Work

First Edition   October 2012

Second Edition   May 2014

Third Edition   June 2015

ISBN 978-1-9082930-2-2

CGW Publishing 2015

© Peter Freeth 2000 - 2015

Peter Freeth has asserted his rights under the Copyright, Designs and Patents act 1988 to be identified as the author of this work.

All rights reserved in all media. This book may not be copied, stored, transmitted or reproduced in any format or medium without specific prior permission from the author. Contact CGW Publishing for information about wholesale orders and review copies.

CGW Publishing

B1502

PO Box 15113

Birmingham

B2 2NJ

www.cgwpublishing.com

mail@cgwpublishing.com

www.geniuslearning.co.uk

www.genius-at-work.co.uk

For Dad, Millie and Isobel

So much to explore
and so little time

A Model of Genius at Work

    How This All Started......1

1 Setting the Scene......3

2 In Pursuit of Excellence......7

3 We Are Simulators......17

4 Brainy People......31

5 Development......53

    How Do We Know What Children Think?......55

    Learning by Doing......56

    The Sensorimotor Stage, 0 - 2 Years......57

    Pre-Operational Stage, 2 - 7 Years......57

    Learning by Talking......59

    Concrete Operations Stage, 7 - 11 Years......59

    Formal Operations Stage, 12+ Years......60

6 Learning......61

    Honey and Mumford......65

7 Modelling......71

    We are models......78

    Recognising Models......80

    A Context for Modelling......85

    Meta Model......88

    Isomorphism......91

    Strategies and the TOTE Model......94

    Strategy elicitation......111

8 The Meta Model......117

    The Meta Model......128

9 Beyond Simple Strategies..133
    Changing Context..137
    Well Formed Outcomes..139
    It's Broken..143
    Incongruence..146
    Strategies, Programs and Simulations................................151

10 Metaprograms...155
    Metaprograms and Modelling..160
    Sensory Preference..163
    Motivation Direction..166
    Reference Source..167
    Choice..170
    Sorting and Comparison..171
    Scope Level...173
    Metaprograms - an Alternative View..................................179
    Alternatives..183

11 Modelling Systems...185
    Success Factor Modelling..187
    Modelling Belief Systems..188
    Coaching with Beliefs..195

12 Logical Levels...201

13 Neurologic..211

14 Creativity..221

15 Installation...225
    Rituals and Incantations..228
    A Worked Example...238

16 Instructional Design..243

Nesting the Model...245
Naming..248
Mnemonics...248
Multiple Methods..250
Kolb's Experiential Learning..259
Other Learning Theories...261

17 Recruitment..263

18 Testing...267
Unexpected Results..275

19 Evaluation...279

20 The Beginning..291

21 Appendices...295

22 A Talent Modelling Methodology..297
Methodology...299
Benchmarking..303
The people cycle..306

23 Case Study: Retail Managers..309
Project Overview..312
Modelling Results...313
Role 3: Retail...317
Results and Behaviour..317
Beliefs, Rules and Perceptions...332
Culture..337
Retail - the Difference...338
Overall Observations...341
Recommendations..353

24 Case Study: Facilitators..........359

Project Overview..........361
Culture & Environment..........365
Analysis..........369
The Difference..........409
Recommendations..........414
Workshop Outlines..........418
Overview..........418
Level 1 – Presenting with Confidence..........420
Level 2 – Chairing Meetings Effectively..........423
Level 3 – Achieving Consensus in Challenging Situations....425

25 Further Reading..........427

Books..........429
Articles and Papers..........429
Websites..........429
Reader's Offer..........431

Exercises

7.1 Every Model is a Generalisation................................81

7.2 Every Model Has a Purpose...................................83

7.1 Sequences..101

7.2 Eye Accessing Part 1..103

7.3 Eye Accessing Part 2..110

7.4 Model a Decision Strategy.....................................113

7.5 Model a Skill or Talent..114

7.6 Model a Problem...115

9.1 Set an Outcome..141

9.2 Work Back From an Outcome...............................142

9.3 What Is It Supposed To Do?..................................144

9.4 What Is Supposed To Happen?.............................145

9.5 But..150

10.1 Understanding Profiles...162

10.1 Metaprogram Profiling...177

11.1 Complex Strategies..189

12.1 Logical Levels Modelling......................................209

13.2 Designing Logic 1..219

13.3 Designing Logic 2..220

15.1 Modelling Solutions..236

15.2 Custom Technique Design...................................236

How This All Started

From the earliest time that I can remember, my father was a DIY fanatic. He would have a go at anything; plumbing, electrics, decorating, gardening, car maintenance, brickwork, wine and beer making and almost anything else that could be built, fixed or formulated. Sometimes, the results were something of a disaster, like tea wine that you could only use to clean paint brushes. And sometimes, he achieved results through sheer brute force, will power and little regard for whether the thing he was trying to fix was now more smashed up than it was before. But on the whole, and over many years of trial and error, he taught himself to fix machinery as a maintenance engineer for a newspaper printing works, to French polish doors and to grow the most glorious selection of vegetables I've ever seen.

As I got older, I found myself emulating my father's behaviour, having a go at all kinds of jobs around the house and learning slowly through my own mistakes as I lost various quantities of blood and sweat along the way. No matter how much we pretend we're nothing like our parents, our earliest influences always find their way through our carefully crafted adult persona.

At the age of 86, my father still periodically redesigned his back garden, designing ingenious mechanisms to keep slugs off his strawberries and building mini greenhouses out of plastic sheeting attached to the fence with string, producing the most abundant and succulent tomatoes. He could tell you how to grow and care for just about any plant or vegetable, and he continued to be fascinated by new ideas and new technologies.

He got his first job as a maintenance engineer in a factory that used a steam engine to drive overhead belts to operate sewing machines – the kind of thing that you will see in an industrial museum. One of the pulleys was out of alignment, causing the machines to stop working. The foreman said that if my father could fix it, he could have the job. And that really sums him up – his belief that he could probably have a go at anything.

Very recently, I realised that my father's attitude that he could have a go at anything, and his fascination with how things work has driven me along the journey that led to this book. I too believed that I could have a go at anything, and I too have always been fascinated with how things work. Whilst my father kept to machines, I also became interested in how people work.

I don't think that my father would ever have described himself as a brave man, yet he always stood up for what was right, even getting himself into trouble to protect others. Yet so many people lack the confidence to try new things, to have a go at something, to risk getting it wrong.

So when you mix together the principles of doing the right thing, working hard and having a go at anything, you really can't go wrong in life, can you?

Therefore, I would like to acknowledge the significant part that my father has played in developing this methodology and this book, and I would also like to thank all of the people who are directly indirectly mentioned here, for sharing their Genius at Work with me.

In memory of Philip D Freeth, 1926 - 2013

1 Setting the Scene

I wanted to set the scene for the book, and I thought long and hard about how I could do that without giving the exciting conclusion away.

Recently, the RSA held a 'challenge' entitled 'Valuing your Talent', described as, "...a major new research and engagement programme ... to help employers understand how to measure the impact their people have on the performance of their organisation."

After I wrote my own response for this challenge, I realised that I'd described the essence of Genius at Work, so I hope that this will help to put the rest of the book into its proper perspective for you.

> Talent is, in itself, irrelevant
>
> Everyone's focusing on talent; nurturing talent, the war for talent etc. and forgetting a very important point; that talent, in itself is irrelevant. If that talent cannot express itself in a which which creates value, it's a waste. In fact, we can only ever identify talent in light of an organisation's goals. Do we analyse an investment banker's talent for playing the trumpet? Or a production manager's talent for creating hybrid roses in his garden? Whether you think we should or shouldn't, the reality is that we don't. When we think of nurturing talent, there is therefore an implication that the talent is aligned with the organisation's goals. So, if we don't also look at an organisation's culture then that talent means nothing, because the culture will define what constitutes talent, and what doesn't.
>
> A culture can be disabling, where organisational and tacit rules inhibit the expression of rules, or it can be

enabling, where those rules allow or even reinforce the expression of talent.

A culture is simply a set of rules (plus a language) which adapts as quickly as the people who make those rules. When managers talk about culture as an ethereal, intangible concept, they're talking about tacit rules - rules that aren't written down anywhere and which are passed on through experience. My Genius at Work approach maps these rules as they connect with a person's behaviours and beliefs to create an interaction which either makes it difficult for that person to express their talents or easy.

We already know, intuitively, that you can have the best candidate in the world, on paper, but if they don't 'fit in', they won't perform. What we lack is a way to quantify and predict this. On the other hand, a group of average performers, working as a close-knit team to achieve shared, inspiring goals, will achieve more than a team of superstars, each fighting for the limelight.

My insight is therefore that talent is irrelevant, in itself, and you must look at the relationship between talent and culture to see how to improve performance, which is ultimately what we're aiming for.

Genius at Work, then, is simply a framework and a method for codifying talent within the context of an organisational culture so that the talent can be better understood, refined and copied, so that both individual and organisational performance improve.

Sounds simple! Let's see how it works in practice...

2 In Pursuit of Excellence

A few years ago, I listened to a program on BBC Radio 4 about the time and motion men of the 1950s. Time and motion was a study of efficiency, concluding that much time was lost in movement. By rearranging the stages of a manufacturing process, the process would work more efficiently, productivity would improve, production costs would fall and profits would increase.

The program focused on a British engineering company where craftsmen fabricated turbine blades for jet engines.

This was an incredibly delicate operation, because even the slightest error would cause a vibration which could literally tear the engine apart.

The time and motion men observed the craftsmen carefully, comparing their actions to the company's written procedure. The craftsman took the blade from the foundry, checked it with a micrometer, corrected the blade's width by a fraction of an inch, checked again, corrected again, and so on.

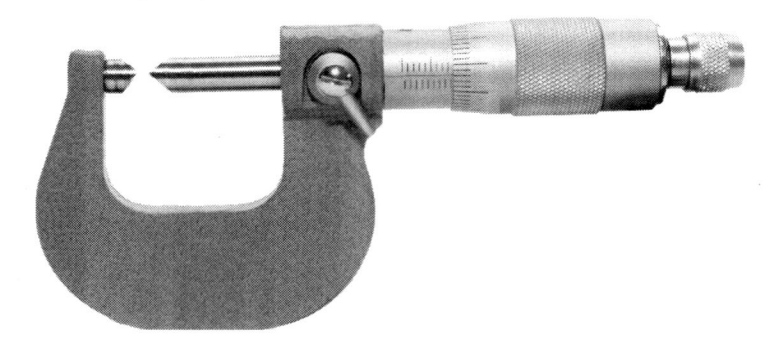

Hundreds of micrometer measurements were required to produce blades that met the strict quality requirements, and the entire process took one whole working day.

The time and motion men went away and reported that the craftsman was working exactly 'by the book', and that the time required to fabricate one blade was, indeed, one day.

Everyone was very happy with this result.

Once the time and motion men had left, the craftsman put away his micrometer and went back to his real method - checking the blade by touch. Running his fingers along the length of the blade, he could detect surface irregularities and other casting defects that were far beyond the capability of a micrometer. The micrometer could only measure the width of the blade at a specific point, and hundreds of measurements were required to 'map' the surface of the blade. The craftsman could essentially feel the entire surface in one movement, and his sense of touch had become very much attuned to the 'right' dimensions, much like a classic car owner knows when something is wrong, simply because the engine's sound changes to such a small degree that no-one else can hear the difference. Even today, craftsmen at Steinway shape the components of a piano by touch rather than by measurement, such is their experience in discriminating the smallest imperfections.

At least in the way that we process sensory signals, our brains are 'difference engines', like the early computers, attuned to changes. The more accustomed we become to something, the more easily we can detect even the slightest variation from the norm.

Using his sense of touch only, the craftsman could produce a finished blade, not in a day, but in half an hour.

Did he use this remarkable talent to increase productivity by 1600%?

No, he spent the rest of the day fishing in the local canal.

As was popular at the time, the company had a well established apprenticeship scheme, where young, inexperienced engineers worked alongside the craftsmen to learn their skills.

Did the apprentice go fishing too?

No, he stayed in the workshop in case the foreman came down to see what was going on.

Did he use that time to reflect on what he had learned from the craftsman?

No, because he didn't know what the craftsman could feel. He knew that the craftsman was feeling something, but it would take him years to learn the skill. That was why apprenticeship schemes were so popular. The philosophy was that you can't teach someone to be a craftsman in five minutes, and there are lots of things that craftsmen do that are very difficult to quantify. Since human beings are outstanding natural learners, the apprenticeship system was an excellent way to train new craftsmen.

The apprenticeship system does have one major flaw.

Have you noticed what happens when a parent says something they shouldn't in front of a young child? The child picks up on it straight away and repeats it, over and over, much to the parent's embarrassment.

Similarly, apprentices didn't only learn the craftsman's technical skills, they learned all of their work avoidance skills too.

I served a three year apprenticeship in the telecoms industry. During that time, I learned how to run cables through a factory or office, I learned to memorise a colour scheme for 200 wires, I learned to solve various technical and mechanical problems and I learned about the theory of communication technologies.

I also learned how to hide private mileage on a company van, what time to expect the area manager, where to get the best bacon sandwiches and how to do 'foreigners', private jobs, using company materials and equipment.

The problem is that you get all or nothing; you can't select only the skills and knowledge that you want to pass on.

Or can you?

Part of the problem is that what we might call 'low value skills' are passed on very easily and can therefore be isolated and taught. The series of steps to connect up a cable, for example.

A public telecoms operator had a written, twelve step procedure for connecting up a cable, however someone noticed that an experienced engineer only performed nine of these steps. Should they therefore rewrite the procedure?

No. The experienced engineer still performed all twelve steps. The difference was that he carried out three of them *inside his head*.

Learning the nine visible steps is easy. What makes the difference between a properly connected cable that will withstand corrosion is contained within those three hidden steps. Those three steps lead to excellence, and you can't see it just by watching. What's more frustrating is that when you ask the person how they are able to excel, they say, "I don't know, I just do it. It's obvious, isn't it?"

The difference between average performance and excellence seems hidden, innate, tacit, impenetrable.

Yet if that were true, this book would not exist.

One of the greatest challenges in businesses today is the protection of tacit knowledge. As competitive pressures increase and a more rapidly changing workforce needs to rely more and more on knowledge that has taken a lifetime to acquire, the ability of HR and L&D professionals to protect an organisation's culture and replicate that unique knowledge has become vital to a business' survival.

Part of a company's market value is defined as its unique knowledge, its "know-how", and as each new generation of graduates spends less and less time in a job, that knowledge must be protected and preserved if its value is to be retained.

For example, one of the UK's oldest and most respected engineering companies had a rapidly ageing workforce in a rapidly changing global market. Their most senior technical staff had designed the first nuclear power stations, military installations and materials handling systems, but within the next five years, 50% of that experience would be lost through retirement.

Attracting new talent was not an issue; the biggest problem was getting the right people into the right places as quickly as possible to 'absorb' that knowledge before it was lost forever.

A British High Street retailer launched a new graduate program, and I used the performance modelling methodology contained within this book to figure out what the highest performers were doing. The results were something of a surprise to the HR team, because the highest performing store managers, buyers and finance managers, in both hard business metrics and staff satisfaction surveys, weren't doing what they were 'supposed' to be doing.

For example, the company had invested considerably in teaching fashionable new 'coaching skills' to the store managers. I discovered that the average store managers relied heavily on their coaching skills, but the high performers used a rather different set of skills.

The HR team adopted my recommendations, with the result that the new graduate program delivered operationally ready staff into the business in just 9 months instead of 12; a 25% saving in time and cost.

The retention of people is a key issue for HR managers and business leaders, but the real, underlying issue isn't the retention of people, it's the retention of tacit knowledge. Abstracting this hard-earned experience from the people who acquired it first hand means that you can develop new talent more quickly and more efficiently, and it means that you can build business processes that automatically favour and align with high performers.

Genius at Work explains the methodology behind these outstanding results and shows you how to identify and model your high performers and then use the results in the design and delivery of everything from recruitment and selection processes, interviewing and induction training to performance management, talent management, succession planning, mentoring schemes and knowledge management processes.

With a curiosity to understand excellence and the tools to capture its essence, you really will discover genius at work.

3 We Are Simulators

You have probably been on a motion simulator at a funfair. It might have featured a roller-coaster ride, or a runaway train, or a jet fighter performing aerobatics. The machine itself is just a combination of two things; a video, taking from the participant's eye view, and a 'motion platform' that shakes you about in time with the movie.

However enjoyable these rides may be, you're very unlikely to believe that you actually were on a real roller-coaster. However, what is most fascinating about these machines is that they can simulate so many different activities. The operator just puts in a different DVD and a spaceship is transformed into an airboat, skimming over Florida's Everglades. The simulation is good enough for most people to suspend reality just long enough to enjoy the ride.

Professional flight simulators are something quite different. They take an actual cockpit from the aircraft in question and place it within the motion platform. Incredibly complex and detailed graphics simulate any airport, complete with the right aircraft and vehicles on the ground, weather, terrain and feedback through the aircraft's cockpit displays. These simulators are so accurate that when a pilot crashes one, the stress is as severe as if the aircraft were real, and time in a simulator is equivalent to time in the air, as far as licensing is concerned.

After half an hour in a flight simulator, you would definitely be forgiven for forgetting that you were never more than thirty feet from the ground.

Meteorologists spend much of their time gathering data from weather stations. On top of buildings, at airports and out on remote hillsides, monitoring stations collect data on wind speed and direction, rainfall, temperature and humidity. Why are they so interested in collecting such useless data? Is it just so that they can tell us that it's been the wettest July since 1903?

No. The reason that they collect this data is so that they can constantly refine and update their weather models. By comparing their simulations to actual conditions, they can increase their confidence in their predictions. The scientist Nikola Tesla was said to construct mental models that he ran alongside his physical experiments. He would lock his experiments in a room and after many days or even months, discover that the physical experiment matched his mental simulation perfectly.

This shouldn't be surprising, though, because you can do exactly the same thing. You can put some bread under the grill and go into another room. The phone rings, you end up chatting, you forget about the toast and when you start to smell smoke, you instantly know what you're going to find under the grill. How surprised would you be if you *didn't* find two smouldering squares of charcoal?

And when you return to a favourite restaurant or holiday destination, how do you feel when it's not how you remembered it?

Sometimes, you criticise yourself. It might be when you feel you have made an obvious mistake, or it might be when you knew you should have listened to your intuition but didn't.

We build simulations that mirror reality so that we can predict what will happen in reality and take action to achieve our goals and avoid danger.

Imagine that someone throws a snowball at you. Given enough time, you can intuitively compute the snowball's flight path and move your head out of the way, just in time.

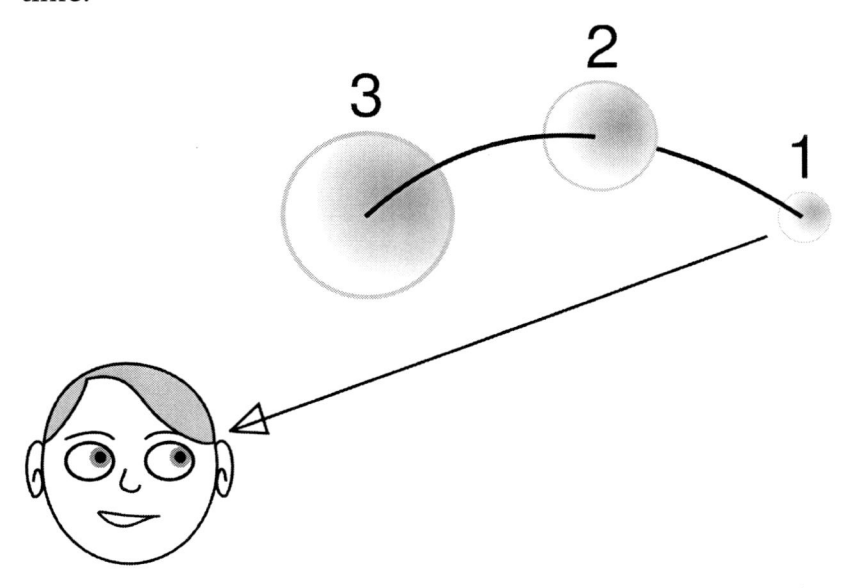

This is an incredibly complex thing to be able to do, and it cannot be achieved by reacting, because by the time you react, the snowball is no longer where it was when you saw it.

When the snowball is in position 1, the light reflected from it arrives at your eyes almost instantly, but the signal from your retinas takes a much longer period of time to reach your brain, by which time the snowball, which is moving at a fairly constant speed, is in position 2. Your brain takes time to process the visual information, compute the snowball's path, determine in which direction to move to avoid the snowball and begin signalling to your muscles through your motor cortex, by which time the snowball is in position 3.

By the time your muscles begin to respond, the snowball is now in this position:

After you have recovered, you will probably feel a little silly that you saw the snowball but couldn't get out of the way fast enough to avoid it. No matter how good your reactions are, you can never overcome this signal delay.

When you think about the computation required to recognise a fast moving object as an incoming icy missile, determine its path, calculate avoiding action and then translate that action into specific muscle movements, it's a wonder that you get to see the snowball at all.

Having a good reaction time simply means that you don't have to think about what to do for as long, but there is nothing that you can do about that signal delay. By the time you are processing the image of the snowball, it has already moved further along its flight path, and by the time your muscles begin contracting, it has moved further still.

At a very early age, you learned to simulate the laws of motion. Newton wrote them out in plain English for other people to understand, and from those laws we can now throw snowballs with some degree of accuracy, and we can also launch a spaceship with three men on board, land it on the moon and return it to Earth with only a few minutes of fuel to spare.

In 2005, NASA launched a probe called Deep Impact that, seven months later, crashed into the "Tempel 1" comet. The comet is essentially a lump of ice, 4 miles across and travelling at about 23,000 mph. The probe was about the size of a washing machine.

NASA's analogy is that the probe hitting the comet is like a pebble hitting a truck. A pebble that you threw seven months ago.

Just imagine that for a moment. You look through a telescope and see a comet, millions of miles away. You observe it every day and, accounting for the time it takes the light reflected from the comet to reach your telescope, you calculate the comet's path, using equations that were developed over 300 years ago in 1687. The Wright brothers didn't achieve sustained, heavier than air flight until more than 200 years later in 1903. Yet you can calculate the path of the comet with such confidence that you can take something the size of a washing machine, place it on top of a very large firework, light the blue touch paper and launch it out beyond Earth's atmosphere where it just floats along at its own pace, obeying Newton's first law of motion until, seven months later, the paths of the comet and the probe intersect.

A certain genre of film associated with martial arts often shows the hero shooting an arrow and knocking an enemy's arrow out of the air. It's utterly implausible, but no less impossible, technically, than a military anti-missile system that can hit something the size of a baguette travelling at 2,600 mph.

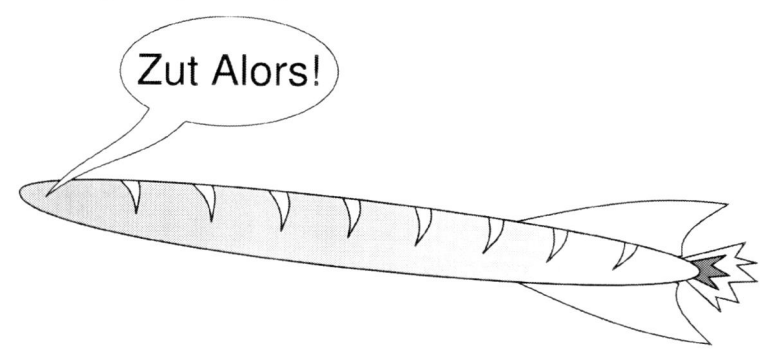

Zut Alors!

The only difference between the film and reality is that computers are much better at computing flight paths, quickly, than most humans are.

Remember, the purpose of a simulation is to be able to predict the future.

When people act inappropriately, or they act in a certain way because of the reaction that they hope to get, they are trying to control future events. If I want to open a door, I can predict the amount of force with which to push or pull it. I try to control the future behaviour of the door in order to achieve an outcome.

A child learns to control future events by asking for more pocket money when Daddy's watching the football, or Mummy's on the phone. But parents can "wise up" to these early attempts at manipulation, and the child has to revise its simulations.

We cannot ever get away from simulations because they literally make us who we are. However, what we can seek to do is narrow the gap between our simulations and reality, just like the meteorologists do.

Creating a simulation of an inanimate object, moving within the consistent and predictable 'laws' of physics isn't that difficult. We know this because we can program computers to make predictions based on the constants that govern the motion of objects, gravity, the behaviour of gases as their temperature changes and so on. But humans are quite different; their behaviour based on a far more complex set of rules and constants. Humans seem to change over time, they seem to make different choices in the same situation from one day to the next and they adapt to changes in the external environment.

Philosophers have, over many thousands of years, attempted to understand human behaviour, coming up with various theories to define this experience that we call "reality". Yet, intuitively, we have each mastered the ability to predict the complexities of "human nature". You walk into a bar to meet a friend and correctly order a drink for them, even when it's not what they normally have. A parent pre-empts their child's behaviour and prevents an embarrassing situation at a restaurant. You weigh up a dilemma and the mentor on your shoulder gives you exactly the advice that they would offer if they were sitting in front of you.

I'm sure you've had this latter experience. Your hand reaches for the chocolate and a voice in the back of your head reminds you of the promise you made to yourself. Whose voice is it? We build simulations of people close to us that are so lifelike that they often seem to take on a life of their own, giving direction, advice and criticism as if the person was there in the room with you.

Children need to acquire their parents' experiences in order to stay safe. They need to learn boundaries and in order to operate independently as responsible adults, they need to live by those rules without they parent watching over their every move. But we often inherit more rules from our parents than we would like, and it can be difficult for some people to separate the useful rules from those which have become outdated.

One of the aspects of mental simulation that is most often cited in the self-help world is mental rehearsal. The idea is that by running through a scenario in your mind, you can develop the same level of skill as if you were really practising it. Taken to extremes, some celebrity self-help gurus talk about the "law" of attraction, which means that by harbouring positive thoughts, you can 'manifest' wealth and happiness into your life. Sadly, such claims discredit the underlying science which is regularly used by athletes when they rehearse for races. They can't control what their opponents will do on the day, but they can rehearse the track in their minds until every twist and turn is 'second nature' to them.

What is the reality of mental rehearsal? Does it simply build a memory of a task, or does it affect the body too? When people are asked to imagine a task while in a MRI scanner, the results show that many brain areas are engaged just as they would be in the physical performance of that task. But surely, this doesn't affect someone's muscles. How could it? Yet research conducted by Alvaro Pascual-Leone indicates that practice not only reinforces a person's memory of a task, it also enlarges the brain's motor area for the muscles that control that task. More output neurons means stronger muscles and better muscle control. Pascual-Leone used a technology called TMS (Transcranial Magentic Stimulation) to map brain activity in great detail. In a study of people learning to play the piano, he compared people practising at a real keyboard with people who were simply *imagining* playing. After five days, the 'mental' players required only a two hour live practice session to acquire the same level of skill as the people who had practised on a real keyboard.

In another study, Drs Yue and Cole compared a group of people undertaking physical exercise with a group who just imagined exercising. At the end of the four week study, the people who had physically exercised had increased their muscle strength by 30%. Surprisingly, the people who had only *imagined* the same exercise increased their muscle strength by 22%.

We mustn't get carried away with such news; while mental rehearsal can strengthen the brain's connections to muscles, the muscles themselves don't change, and you certainly won't 'think yourself thin'. However, when learning fine motor tasks such as are involved in sports or music, mental rehearsal clearly benefits the learning process. Your muscles are, of course, activated by motor nerves, and so mental rehearsal refines the connections in your motor cortex to more accurately control the contraction of muscle fibres.

In 2000, I worked as a teacher for a 'gifted and talented' project, running weekend and holiday courses for young children. On one course, a number of the children said that they wanted to be able to use a computer keyboard more quickly, so I tried an experiment. Their starting level of ability was to type with the index finger of their dominant hand, with a few seconds delay between key presses while they searched around the keyboard for the key they wanted. I theorised that, once they had found a letter, they didn't forget where it was. The reason that they searched for each letter was that they only *thought* they didn't know which letters were in which location, when at some unconscious level, they intuitively knew. In fact, young children can easily acquire 'procedural knowledge', enabling them to learn a task, but only when their brains have further developed can they articulate that knowledge in an abstract form. So intuitively knowing the location of a letter on a keyboard but not being able to translate that into the sound or word would probably make sense.

I gave the children a series of very simple, repetitive tasks to perform. First, I had them typing rows and rows of letters in the order that they appear on the keyboard; QWERTY... After a few minutes, the children's' typing got faster and settled into a comfortable rhythm, so I changed the task to typing the letters in alphabetical order; ABCDE... Again, their typing was slow at first but soon accelerated and settled into a rhythm. I then changed the task to 'the quick brown fox...' and this time, as they practised typing, I distracted them by saying the alphabet backwards, counting and so on. What happened was quite remarkable; the more I distracted them, the faster they could type.

I then let the children rest for a moment, and then had them imagine typing, and asked them to imagine themselves in different scenarios; at school, at home, with friends, typing letters, emails, and perhaps most importantly, receiving positive comments, praise and supportive feedback. Finally, I had them physically practice again. All of the children, a group of about 15, showed a measurable increase in the speed and accuracy of their typing and, perhaps most importantly, their confidence that they *could* type.

Clearly, the more accurate and challenging the mental simulations we can build, the more we can achieve the ultimate goal of all self-help gurus; *to fulfil our potential.*

Brainy People

You are a very brainy person. In fact, we could even go so far as to say that you are one big brain. Every part of your body has evolved to serve the needs of your brain. Your senses gather external information and your muscles enable your brain to modify external events so that your sensory experience aligns with your desires.

Imagine, for a moment, a drink. Something that you want, perhaps a cup of tea or coffee. As you imagine it, you know exactly what to do in order to get it. By conjuring up that mental simulation, your entire neurology and physiology can spring into action to close the gap between desire and reality.

Most 'self help' books and training programs contain some descriptions of neurology and brain organisation. Perhaps the creators of such systems wanted to hijack some real science in order to lend their work some credibility, just like some alternative therapists maintain that the law of attraction is based on the real science of quantum mechanics.

Seriously, it's utter nonsense. And you know it, don't you?

The problem with writers and trainers who talk about neurology is that they are regurgitating knowledge that is decades old, and of course they are largely regurgitating a rather one sided account of that knowledge which has more to do with brand image than any real science.

I don't want you thinking that you only get upset because your amygdala takes over, or that your ancient reptilian brain is where all of your base desires live. This model of brain function is closer to the Victorian art of phrenology than to any modern understanding of brain science, even though it is still being taught on self-styled accelerated learning courses. By the way, why does it take three days to learn about accelerated learning? And why is there a book entitled, "Speed reading in a week". Shouldn't that be "Speed reading in five minutes"?

Even twenty years ago, a theory of 'holographic' brain function was emerging, where functions are spread across the brain rather than localised in particular areas. Even those localised areas are named, not after any understanding of their function, but after the person who first dissected them or the animal that they remind someone of. Your hippocampus is so named because it looks a bit like a seahorse. I suppose we should think our selves lucky that our neural structures are not shaped like anything more embarrassing.

We cannot figure out how the mind works by dissecting it, however there is another approach that we can learn from, and that is the approach taken by the people who are trying not to figure out how the brain *works* but to reproduce what it *does*.

Artificial Intelligence is one goal of computer research, however there seems to be some disagreement over what intelligence is, even though we can be fairly certain what the 'artificial' part refers to. Or can we? Robots have been built that use cells from rat brains to make navigational decisions, and electronic components have been inserted into peoples' bodies, and I'm not just talking about the assistant at the local electrical retailer who told me that they couldn't replace the mobile phone that I bought last week because it's already obsolete. No, I'm talking about people who have had artificial retinas and ear drums wired into their brains.

One of the most interesting people in this field of research is Steve Grand, who set out to build an artificial orangutan called Lucy. His goal was to have Lucy point at a banana.

Now, this in itself is a very simple task. We can easily program a computer to recognise the characteristic shape and colour of a banana, under controlled conditions, and we can easily have that computer control a robotic arm to 'point' at that banana. You might have a digital camera that has 'face recognition' so that the camera can focus on the nearest face, even if it isn't centred in the frame. But that does not make your camera intelligent, it merely emulates one tiny aspect of your abilities, and that idea is central to the way that Steve Grand is approaching the problem. He built Lucy 'from the ground up', from first principles. Rather than building a robot to *do* something, such as paint a car or mow your lawn, he built Lucy to emulate the way that our brains are wired up, and in doing so, he figured out some very interesting functions that relate to our simulation theory of mind.

For a long time, there has been a theory of brain function that represents the brain as a number of discrete functional areas. Visual processing here, right index finger there, sense of self awareness down in that corner. This model essentially developed from the study of one man, Phineas Gage, who we'll discuss later on. In short, he suffered a serious brain injury but survived, minus some aspects of his personality. This demonstrated that the bits of mental facility that he lost were resident in the bits of brain that were blown out of the top of his head by a large metal rod, and fitted very nicely with the observation that the rest of the human body is also made up of clearly delineated functional areas called organs.

However, as medical science has progressed, we no longer need to remove parts of the brain in order to deduce function, we can watch the brain in action in real time by giving people tasks and observing which parts of their brain draw more oxygen from blood flow, indicating increased activity and therefore functional significance.

I should point out that the latest neurological old wives' tale that is doing the rounds is that when you connect an EEG machine to a strawberry jelly, it shows the same signs of consciousness as are observed in the human brain. Therefore, to deduce brain function by observing brain operation is misleading at best. By the way, I cannot find any evidence of this supposed research, and it seems likely that it's an urban myth, like the early experiments into subliminal messaging. By the time you read this, it will probably be 'common knowledge' that strawberry jelly is sentient, according to the neurologists whose statistical analysis of random electrical activity leaves them clutching at straws in an effort to prove that they can determine a person's thoughts from the electrical activity in their brains. You can mock them now, but when the fruit trifles move in and take all our women and jobs, you'll be laughing on the other side of your face.

We now know that the brain is made up, not of functional organs, but of layers. Every sensory nerve ending in your body arrives, through your brain stem, into a primary input area, and every motor nerve leaves your brain through a primary output area.

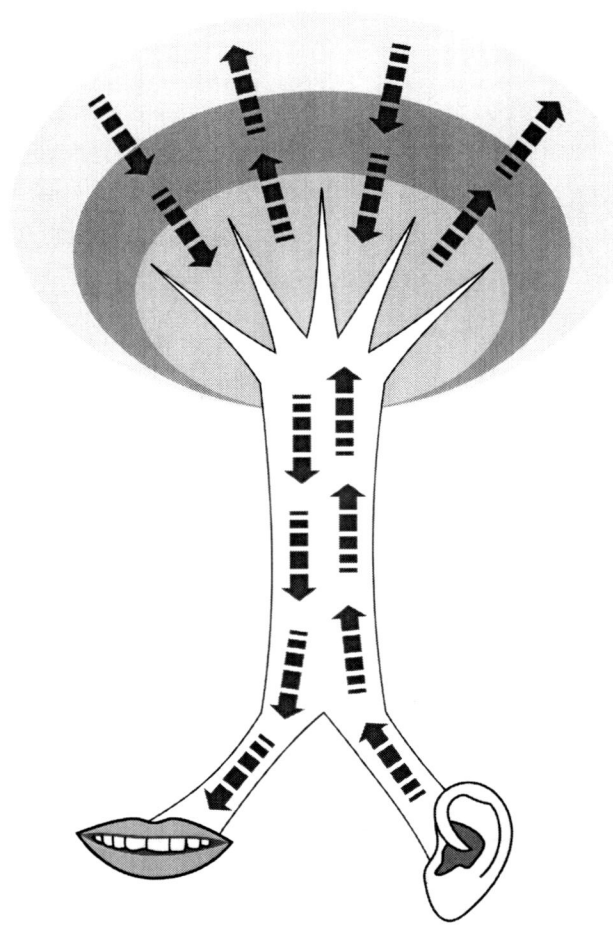

In that regard, we humans are no different, neurologically, from any other animal; from earthworms to orang-utans. The key difference between ourselves and other animals is not the number of brain cells that we have, nor the number of chromosomes in our DNA; it is the number of processing steps that a signal goes through in between reception and action. Each of these processing steps could introduce an extra layer of finesse or detail into the overall decision process.

When a shadow passes over a frog, it dives for cover. It doesn't differentiate between a kestrel and a pigeon, as it simply reacts to a pattern of changing light levels. This means that a frog can react much faster than a human because there are fewer layers of processing in between 'shadow' and 'jump'. Similarly, if you have ever tried to swat a fly, you'll know that they excel at moving out of the way, just when you think you have them cornered. This isn't because the fly 'thinks' any faster than you do, it's simply to do with those previously mentioned signal delays.

An external observer will see that the fly has already moved out of the way before your hand is anywhere near it, thanks to its short reception to action delay, and you're unable to adjust your action because you don't even know that the fly has moved. When you swat a fly with a rolled up newspaper, it's smaller than your hand but it's also moving a lot faster, and as long as you attack the fly from the same direction as it is flying towards, the result will be bad news for the fly.

Whilst frogs and flies can react faster than humans, they lack our versatility, and most importantly they lack our ability to understand and predict possible future events. If a predator approached you, you would have a number of choices available; freeze, run, grab a stick, try to distract it or even negotiate with it if the predator in question is a sales assistant in a furniture store. This versatility requires complex computational power, and that comes at the expense of raw speed.

Probably the most recognisable part of the human brain is the cortex, which is essentially a folded sheet of nerve tissue wrapped around the central parts of the brain. It's as if those original parts grew more and more layers, so those layers became folded in order to pack them inside your skull, much like a folded umbrella manages to pack a large surface area into an apparently small volume.

At the centre of all of this is a structure called the Superior Colliculus, through which all incoming and outgoing nerve connections are routed. One important observation which reinforces the theories that I'm covering here is that the more complex the behavioural response, the further into the cortex are the connections that drive that behaviour.

For example, fundamental behaviours such as breathing and regulating a heart beat are driven from within the brain stem itself. Our version of the frog's "Leg it!" response is called our 'orienting response', and it automatically points your eyes in the direction of movement.

Crucially, the computational work required to achieve this feat never gets any further than the Superior Colliculus, so by the time you are consciously aware of what you are looking at, your eyes have already been pointing at it for some time. A similar response orients your eyes in the direction of new sounds. Just imagine for a moment the calculations required to achieve that, and remember that all of that takes place in the most basic area of your brain. Your brain takes two images or sounds which arrive at different angles, tracks changing signal levels across a two dimensional surface (your retina), computes a three dimensional location, translates that into a two dimensional muscle movement and then continues to track that changing signal over time as the object in question moves across your visual field.

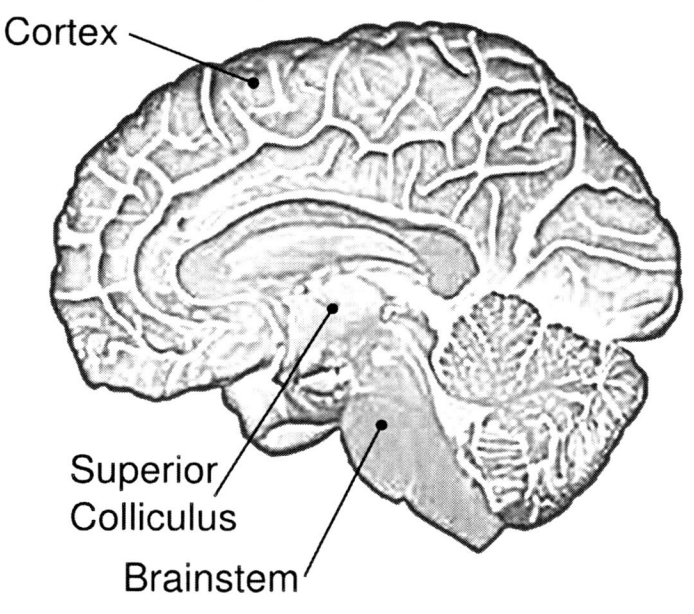

Cortex

Superior Colliculus

Brainstem

In the image above, you can see the folded or 'convoluted' cortex, wrapped around the central areas of the brain. Those layers are pretty much the same, regardless of which part of the cortex we look at, which is very interesting indeed, and certainly fits with what we know of the brain's 'plasticity'; its ability to reorganise itself in case of damage. Nerve tissue apparently never regrows, but the brain can move functions around in order to bypass areas that have been damaged by injury or perhaps a stroke.

A common simplified model that is often used to explain the process of perception is illustrated as follows:

Reception   Perception   Comprehension

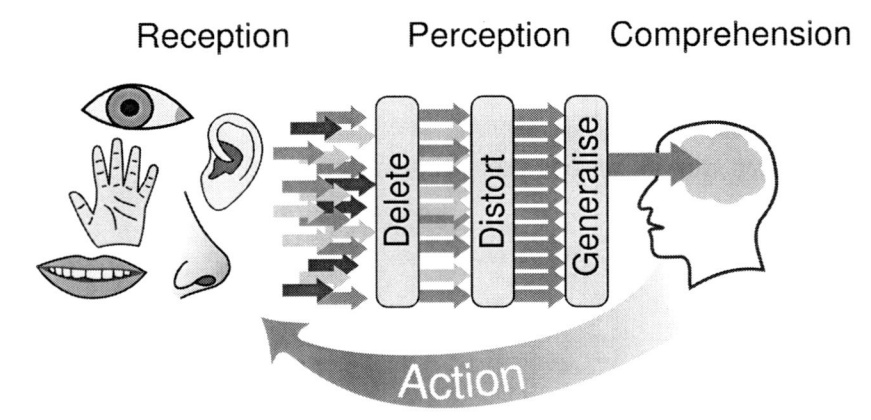

This model implies that perception happens in only one direction, and action also happens only in one direction. If we mapped this simplified model onto the structure of the brain, we might represent the chain of connections as follows:

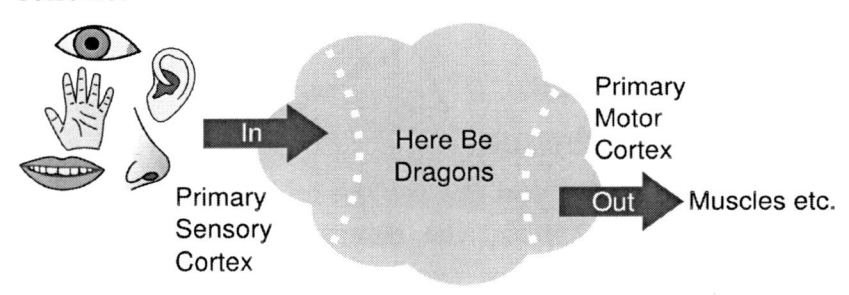

However, our brains are not wired up that way; there are connections running back in the opposite direction too.

The cortex is made up of a number of distinct layers, distinct in that they look different when studied under a microscope. Traditionally, there are six layers, and in some regions of the brain, those six layers are further divided into sub-layers.

Connections can be traced between the layers, and if we take a functional view of the brain rather than a structural one, it would appear that there are in fact four functional layers. A structural view would be to say that because something is built differently, it must be different. A functional view says that because something functions differently, it must be different.

A horse and a car are structurally different but functionally similar. A telephone directory and a romantic novel are structurally similar but functionally different.

A cross section, grouping the six traditional layers into four functional layers, looks like this:

Each layer of the brain looks like some kind of transport interchange, not with a simple 'in' and 'out' but with connections both in and out at both the 'top' and the 'bottom'. But what purpose could these extra connections possibly serve?

The answer might be found within the mysterious region of the model where 'thinking' happens, whatever that means.

Unlike frogs and earthworms, we do not react to the outside world directly, we react to a simulation of it, and that simulation contains what we could call our 'desired state'. Whilst our eyes may orient themselves automatically towards movement, our 'higher functions' such as being able to identify a moving object, determine if it poses a threat and decide what to do about

Brainy People 42

it are most definitely influenced by factors such as past experiences and current emotional state. A very simplified description of the theory is as follows.

Within our brains, nerve cells hold a copy of what is happening in the outside world, as sampled through our sensory organs. They work like an old fashioned cathode ray tube television screen, holding a complete, apparently moving image which at any given instant really only comprises a single tiny dot of light, moving quickly across the screen in carefully organised and synchronised rows.

Other nerve cells hold a copy of what we would like to be happening in the outside world, as defined by our needs and desires. More nerve cells compare the two 'maps' and try to reduce the differences between the two by modifying their outputs to motor systems such as muscles and the endocrine system.

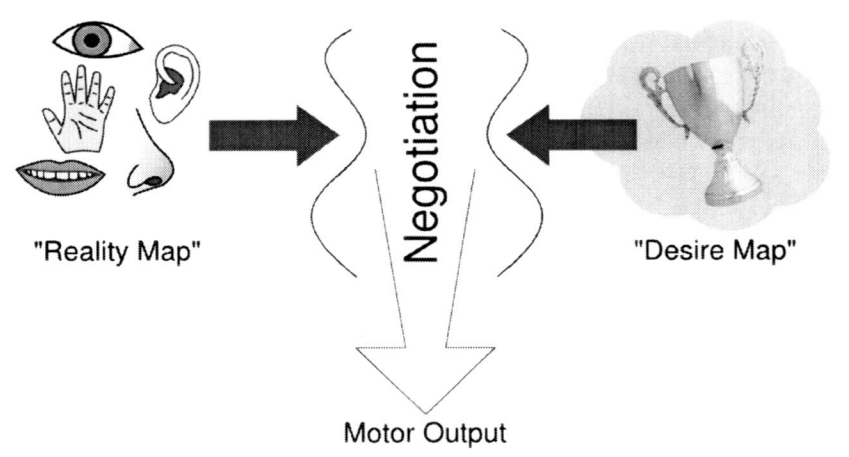

"Reality Map" → Negotiation ← "Desire Map"

Motor Output

At each layer of processing, the cells and connections in the cortex seek to minimise the difference between the incoming 'present state' signals and the internally connected 'desired state' signals. Just like the thermostat on your central heating, the system takes action to achieve a specific goal, and when that goal has been achieved, the output of the system reduces. This is known as a 'servo system', where the operator sets an output and the system modifies itself to achieve that output. A servo system needs its current state and target state to be reasonably close to each other – too far apart and the system swings out of control because the feedback gap is too great, or is unstable, like setting your car's air conditioning target temperature and then opening all the windows.[1]

Our brains, like many of the automated systems that you use in your home or office, are 'servo systems', they direct behaviour towards a goal. Imagine a toy car which has a very simply arrangement of a motor, wheels and some kind of sensor to direct it towards a target. The car's guidance system doesn't need to be accurate, it only needs to keep focus on the target. The car's path will look something like this:

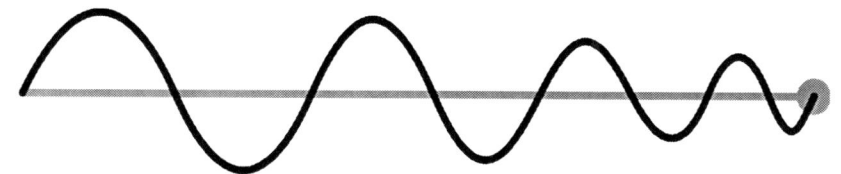

The car is 'off course' for most of its journey, yet it still gets there. That's what your behaviour is like as you direct yourself towards your goals. Sometimes, it will feel like you're moving backwards, but that doesn't matter. What matters is that you are moving.

---

[1] This has important implications for personal and organisational change which I'll be exploring in the new release of my book Change Magic, It turns out we don't have to force people through the Kubler-Ross grief roller-coaster, after all.

It's hard to imagine such complexities and subtleties of human behaviour working in such a simple way, until you take into account the fact that, in your brain, there is a nerve 'map' for every nerve ending, every cell on your retina, every taste bud, every muscle and every hair follicle, to name but a few. Those external connections are combined and integrated through these successive layers of processing, until a complex behaviour such as 'drive to the shops' can be de-constructed into a script of muscle movements, sensory inputs and rational decisions that begins with hearing an advert on the radio for a delicious new chocolate bar.

I believe that not only is this the most realistic, practical and accurate model of brain function, it also happens to fit very neatly with other models and theories which are equally practical, such as Gallese and Goldman's Simulation Theory and even Eric Berne's Transactional Analysis.

Steve Grand's work is fascinating because he is not a neurologist and he has not arrived at his design for Lucy by trying to understand the mind but instead by trying to replicate the brain. Coincidentally, the test of a model is similar; can you reproduce the results of the person whose talent you have modelled?

Another important aspect of these 'backwards' connections is their ability to modify input. As babies develop their neural wiring, they become accustomed to certain inputs, learning to prioritise the importance of different stimuli. We are extremely economical and efficient machines, so neural connections which are not used are erased. A chemical called Oxytocin allows synaptic connections to 'dissolve' and be replaced with new ones, and it is the chemical of both learning and love. Neuroscientists have even theorised that the production of Oxytocin, which increases when we fall in love, allows us to forgive and forget, or at least to forget, by literally dissolving old memories and patterns of behaviour. If you want to change the habit of a lifetime, fall head over heels in love with someone who discourages it.

Our eyes and ears are receptive to a certain range of stimuli. For example, we can see light in a frequency range which we perceive as running from red through to violet. We see the colours of a rainbow, not because they are 'there' but because our eyes detect frequencies of light in a certain way. We know that some insects can see in what we would call the 'ultraviolet' range, and we know that dogs can hear in what we would call the 'ultrasound' range. Our sensory organs have evolved specifically for the purpose of living on Earth, so it's no surprise that both the retinal cells of our eyes and the chlorophyll in plants are optimised for working in sunlight.

When we start to build more complex structures on top of these basic sensory systems, something interesting happens. Language is a good example, because it is so incredibly complex. Our ability to convert an experience into an abstract set of symbols and then convey those symbols to another person – or even a dog – in such a way that the original experience, or something like it, is recreated in the mind of the receiver is nothing short of miraculous. Our ability to hear language is learned, and our ability to learn is influenced by the production of Oxytocin. If you want to learn a new language, go to classes with someone you love.

While our natural production of Oxytocin declines past childhood, we can restart it by choosing to try out new experiences, keeping our brains active, fit and healthy.

One of the hardest things about learning a new language is hearing the different sounds or phonemes that make up that language. Whilst English and French, for example, have many different words for the same things, the basic sounds of the vowels and consonants are quite similar, and certainly similar enough that you could get through a holiday with a phrase book. But what about English compared to Finnish or Japanese? Some of the phonemes are very different, a stereotypical example being that native Japanese speakers struggle with the sound of the letter 'R', pronouncing it as a 'L'. As a Japanese baby grows, it hears only Japanese language and so its remarkably economical brain develops only the necessary connections. A native Japanese speaker doesn't only struggle with 'R' because they're not used to saying it, they struggle because their brains are unable to process the sound of 'R', so they never develop the connections required to say it. As a baby, they never hear it, so they never develop the connections to make sense of and replicate it. Even within the UK, we struggle to pronounce place names in Scotland and Wales, simply because we're not used to the way that 'LL', 'DD' and 'GH' are used, and many of us struggle to understand the 'broadest' regional accents, simply because we're not used to hearing them.

The point here is that these reverse connections modify sensory input in order to simplify processing and cognition. If you were building a computer system to analyse images, such as a car number plate recognition system, you would want to reduce the amount of computational power required as much as possible, because that will optimise the system's response time and accuracy. If you could use a camera which only received light around the yellow range of the visible spectrum, it would emphasise the number plates on the back of British cars and reduce the amount of information for the computer to process.

The sensory capability of our eyes and ears is modified by our experiences so that we become more attuned to seeing and hearing what we expect.

Michael Merzenich is another name worth looking up; he has been working in the field of 'neuroplasticity' for many years and has pioneered a revolution in neurology; a revolution which has shaken the previously accepted model that brain functions are localised into functional areas that cannot be changed once a person leaves their childhood. Merzenich's work shows that the brain reorganises itself surprisingly quickly when recovering from damage or adapting to new experiences. Some of his experiments, and those of others in the field, have involved mapping the individual connections between sensory receptors and the cortex, showing that there is a one to one mapping between the various senses and the processing centres of the brain. For example, there is a topographical map of the skin within the brain, meaning that the map is the same overall shape as the real thing. The area of your brain where your right index finger tip connects to is next to the area where your right thumb tip connects to, however that won't be in precisely the same place as it is in my brain.

You can read more about Merzenich's research in any of his publications or papers, or in 'The Brain that Changes Itself' by Normal Doidge, a popular science book which collects a number of different fields of research to add weight to the argument that the brain never stops growing, changing and learning.

Personally, I find it more surprising that scientists ever believed the brain to be immutable. After all, you are learning from these words as you read them now. Could it really be possible that your brain is acquiring new knowledge *without* changing in some way? Why should learning from a new experience be significantly different to learning a new language or recovering the use of a limb after nerve damage?

Where, you may ask, does this research fit with cognitive or behavioural psychology? The 'desire map' is an obvious analogy for a goal, belief, value, outcome or need. It doesn't really matter which of those words we use, because the end result is the same - an intention to modify the world to meet our expectations. Whether I want an interviewer for a job to be scary, or whether I just know deep down that they will be, even though I don't want that, the result is the same; a scary interviewer. What this gives us is two important things:

1. A way to reveal and perhaps modify those hidden behavioural drivers
2. A way to modify the 'desire map' that directs our behaviour and the results that we achieve

We could say that the brain's purpose is to direct external behaviour so that the difference between present and desired state is minimised, but that then raises the question of where the desired state comes from. Sometimes, regardless of what long term plans we make, our short term behaviour seems to lead us round in the same circles.

Clearly, certain essential biological processes can drive the desire map; thirst or hunger, for example. But where does a desire map for a promotion or for recognition from one's peers come from?

Steve Grand proposed that our brains comprise layers upon layers of such maps which each have their own short term goals and form part of a larger, far more complex pattern of behaviour. Certainly, we could relate a need for food or security to a job promotion through a chain of connected beliefs. One role of coaching or counselling is to challenge those beliefs so that a person may meet their needs more effectively.

The goal of any living organism is homeostasis; an equilibrium that keeps the organism healthy and alive. Life is a delicate balance, for example between staying in the safety of the cave, risking starvation and heading out to forage, risking being eaten by a predator. Your body temperature, blood oxygenation and stomach acid level must all be maintained within carefully controlled ranges, and either too much or too little can be fatal.

While homeostasis is a good thing at a level of basic bodily functions, it's not so useful for humans with career aspirations and other long term goals, because it tends to keep you exactly where you are. Many psychotherapeutic approaches work with 'life scripts'; behaviours learned during our childhood that are no longer appropriate for us yet which repeat as if on autopilot. We know this when we act like our parents and promise to stop, yet we hear the same words coming out of our mouths as if someone else is in the driving seat.

We need to be able to break the connection between past experiences and future expectations, and having done that, we need to create a new desired state which is appropriate for the way that we want our lives to be.

To summarise, the purpose and function of a brain is to minimise the difference between an organism's present and desired states. Interventions such as coaching and counselling give us a set of tools for minimising the differences between that perceived present state and 'objective reality', and also for modifying the desired state so that it reflects our conscious, long term plans rather than our unconscious, learned, repetitive behaviours.

5 Development

Another valuable way of understanding how people learn is by understanding how our brains and mental abilities developed. Through experiment, we are able to deduce how children see the world differently to most adults, and we can therefore see the stages of learning from a different angle.

How Do We Know What Children Think?

Children take a relatively long time to develop to full mental maturity. Humans, as a species, are unusual in that our babies are unable to fend for themselves when born. Many other mammals can stand and walk within minutes of birth, but because humans have a relatively large head, a human baby is born with a brain that is not yet fully developed.

Our mental capacity comes at the cost of an extended development phase after we are born, when we are extremely vulnerable and need the protection of our parents and other adults. Many months of learning must pass before a human baby can do the things that a lamb or calf can do almost immediately after birth.

This extended developmental period gives psychologists an opportunity to study how children learn, how they perceive the world, how they think and how they develop.

The Swiss scientist Jean Piaget conducted extensive research and described a number of development stages that a child will normally progress through, and these form the basis for much of child psychology and developmental testing today.

Learning by Doing

Children live in a concrete, sensory world. If you have ever played a game of 'peek-a-boo' with a baby, you will have seen its surprise and delight when your face or the toy reappeared. Why is a baby so surprised by this? Surely, the baby or child must know the toy was still there, just hidden out of sight.

In fact, a young child's experience of the world is so concrete, so built upon its primary senses, that when the toy is hidden, it ceases to exist.

As a child gets older, it explores and begins to create abstract 'maps' of its surroundings. There comes an age when a child is no longer surprised by the reappearing toy, and you will see a different behaviour – when you hide the toy, the child will look for it.

There is a conflict between the data available to the child. Its senses say that the toy no longer exists, but its experience says the toy is just out of sight. The child then takes action to resolve this conflict.

Between 4 and 12 months old, the child has started to call upon its internal map, and is valuing its own internal data above external data.

Many years later, at a magic show, that early surprise and delight is rekindled when the child looks for the coin in the magician's hand, only to find it empty.

The more you expose a child to rich, sensory experiences, the more information it has to build new maps and develop new ways of thinking about the world.

The Sensorimotor Stage, 0 - 2 Years

At this time, the child is developing its sensory awareness and its motor skills. It is learning to sense the world around it and take action in order to meet its needs.

Age	Developmental stage
1-4 months	"Primary circular reactions" - an action, such as thumb sucking, becomes its own stimulus which leads to the same action.
4-12 months	"Secondary circular reactions" - an action, such as squeezing a toy, leads to an external stimulus such as a sound which leads to the same action.
12-24 months	"Tertiary circular reactions" - an action is repeated in different situations, such as hitting different objects to hear the different sounds they make.

Pre-Operational Stage, 2 - 7 Years

At this time, the child develops the ability to use symbols to represent objects and events in the 'real world'.

A symbol is used to represent something, and you can have many different symbols to represent the same thing.

The child develops a sense of past and future at this stage, and the ability to mentally manipulate symbols. This marks the child's progression to the next stage of development, and is what Jean Piaget called the ability to 'decentre', which he investigated with the following experiment, which you can try for yourself with a table, some household objects and a selection of children.

Piaget sat down at a table with a model mountain range on it. He asked a child to tell him which view of the mountain range Piaget could see. Younger children indicated their own point of view, older children indicated Piaget's point of view, demonstrating their ability to see the model from an imaginary angle.

Here is a top view of a version of Piaget's mountain range (two balls and a cube) showing the positions of Piaget and a child.

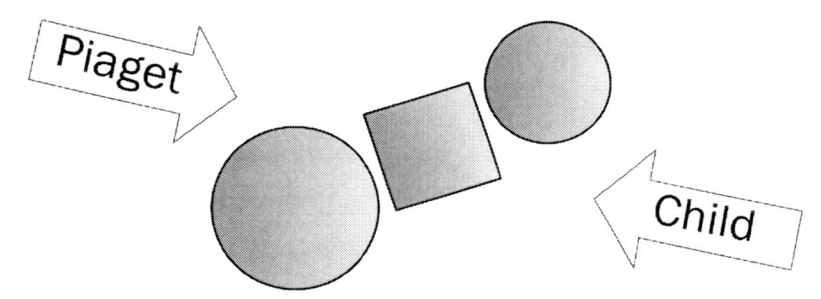

Which of the following views would the child see, and which would Piaget see?

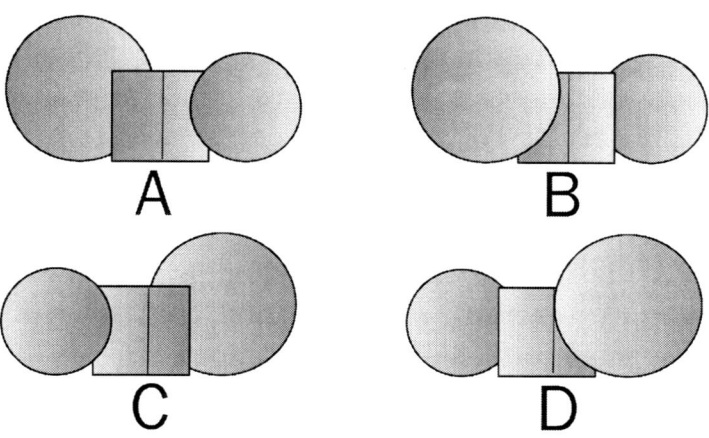

Learning by Talking

One of the most important abstract maps that a child learns to use is that of language. Language is a symbolic representation of the world, in that the word 'apple' is not an apple, it is a symbol that represents an apple. When the child learns to use the symbol, it can communicate its needs to a parent or carer.

Children learn to use many different types of symbol in order to communicate their needs, and parents have differing levels of success in interpreting those symbols.

Games such as charades are good ways to teach children to use different communication symbols.

At around 18 months old, you will see a child develop the use of other symbols too. For example, it will use objects as toys to represent other objects, such as play food or toy villages with cars and people.

Concrete Operations Stage, 7 - 11 Years

The word 'operations' refers to logical calculations or rules that are used in solving problems. At this stage, the child can understand symbols and can manipulate those symbols mentally to solve problems, although at first this will still need to be within the context of concrete, real world situations. Children learning maths at school still work with objects rather than purely abstract ideas.

Around the age of 6, most children will know that a quantity of something stays constant, even when it is a different shape or in a different container.

A   B

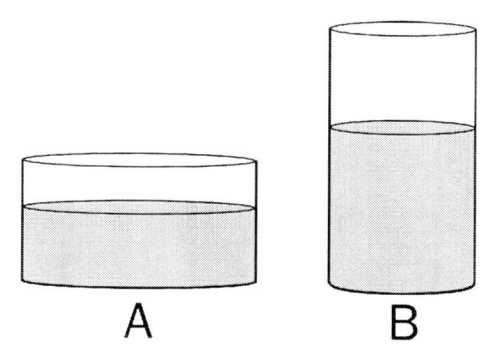

Prior to this stage, a child will tend to see glass B as being the most full because the level of liquid in it is higher, when in fact both have the same amount of liquid in, which a child at this stage will understand. The amount of liquid is 'conserved' regardless of how it is stored.

Having said that, many adults are similarly fooled by the shape of a glass, much to the joy of the owners of bars and restaurants who use glasses and other presentation methods to trick us into thinking that we're getting more for our money.

Formal Operations Stage, 12+ Years

At this point, the child is developing adult thinking abilities, particularly the ability to use logical and abstract operations and form theories about how things work.

...

When you appreciate how the mind develops, you'll begin to see how learning is a process which can be studied and copied. Regardless of our age, job or social status, we all have, quite literally, a lifetime of experience to share with each other.

6 Learning

Before we get into modelling, it's important to understand something about learning, because this is the natural process that we are trying to unpick and replicate through modelling. By understanding the learning process, you'll find it easier to implement the models that you create with the help of this book.

While a craftsman spends a lifetime mastering his craft, it needn't take a lifetime to master a specific skill within that craft. Much of the learning time is redundant; practising motor actions instead of learning decision criteria, or performing tasks which have no bearing on the particular skill that we want to model.

Whilst there are many theories about learning, representing the different ways that you can analyse the subject, the one I'd like to briefly discuss here is Kolb's theory because it relates to a cyclical learning process rather than a static learning preference or style.

David Kolb published his learning styles model in 1984 as Kolb's experiential learning theory (ELT). It divides the learning cycle into four stages, as follows.

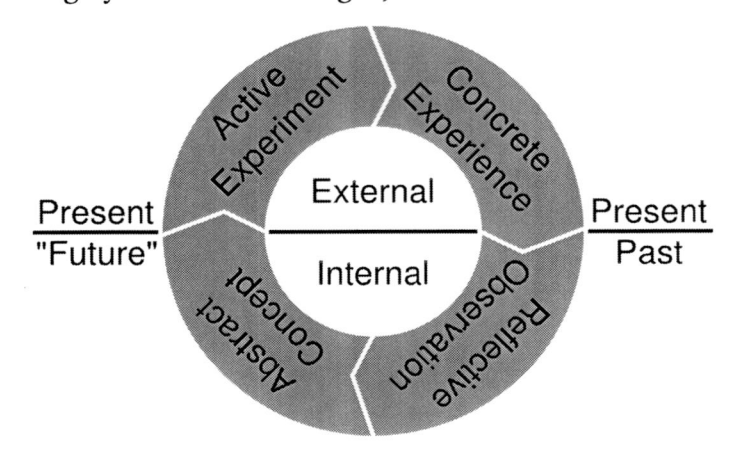

Concrete Experience

This stage is one of real, physical, direct, first hand, visceral sensory experience. An experience comprises a unique combination of sights, sounds, feelings, tastes and smells and, while all memories comprise all of these elements, some of them may be more or less prominent than others. A concrete experience is external to us and therefore always in the present.

Reflective Observation

Once we've had a concrete experience, we reflect on it. We cast our mind back, both consciously and unconsciously, and relive the experience so that we can make generalisations and draw conclusions. Research has shown that the structure within the brain known as the hippocampus creates a kind of 'action replay' of emotionally charged events, etching them forever in our long term memories. Reflective observation is internal to us and therefore always in the past, and the observation isn't necessarily visual, it features all of the sensory information which was present in the original experience.

Abstract Concept

Having relived the experience, we take those generalisations create an abstract concept, a set of rules or principles which govern the experience and others like it. When abstract conceptualisation involves mental rehearsal, it is internal and appears to be in the future, when in fact it is a replay of the past as we cannot internally represent the future; it doesn't yet exist.

Active Experiment

Finally, we take the abstract concept and test it by applying it to new situations. A child tests a range of household objects to find out if they float as well as his lost balloon. A father gives all of the house plants a close shave in order to 'try out' the new hedge trimmer that he received for his birthday. Active experimentation leads full circle to a new concrete experience which either affirms or contradicts the abstract concept. Active experimentation is always external and in the present.

Honey and Mumford

Onto Kolb's four learning stages, Peter Honey and Alan Mumford later mapped the four roles shown in the diagram; Activist, Pragmatist, Theorist and Reflector. In Kolb's model, there are four learning stages which we might paraphrase as Think, Do, Feel and Watch.

Activist

Activists need to do something and they learn by experimenting. They need to experience something for themselves and work out how they feel about it, so they make decisions based on their instincts more than on logic. Activists seek hands on experience and get bored with implementation.

Activists say, "Can I have a go?"

Pragmatist

Pragmatists like to do what works. They like to know what works in the real world. Pragmatists like to find practical applications for ideas.

Pragmatists say, "Does it work?"

Theorist

Theorists like to observe what's going on and then form a theory or opinion about it. Theorists like evidence, logical explanations, abstract models, facts and figures. They don't like subjectivity and exaggeration.

Theorists say, "How does it work?"

Reflector

Reflectors like to observe and reflect and turn things around from different points of view. They like to use their imagination to solve problems rather than diving in like the activists. They like to take time to ponder and don't rush into decisions until they think that they have covered all the angles.

Reflectors say, "Let me think about it."

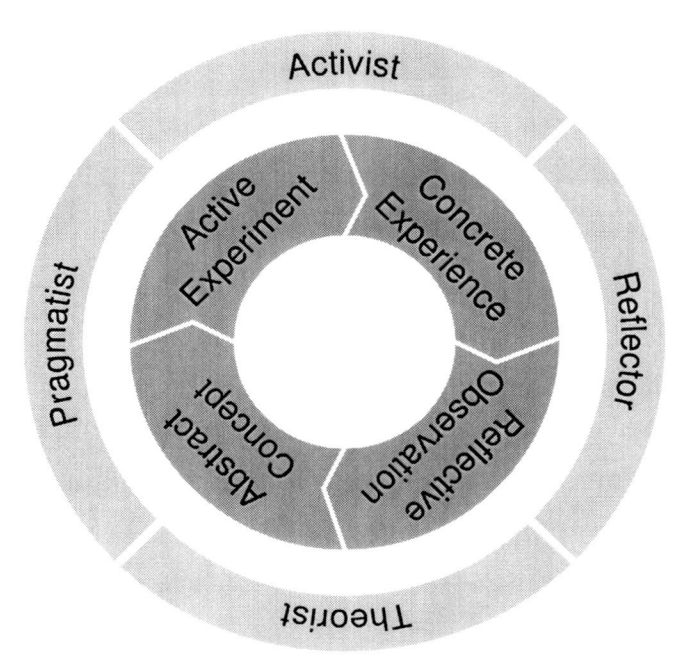

People are not fixed in these roles, they are preferences. We all need time to reflect, we all need to take part, we all need to create rules and we all need experience to confirm those rules. You could therefore think of the roles above as a bias towards a particular learning sequence or a tendency to spend longer in one part of the learning cycle.

You might even consider that the learning style is the point in the cycle at which a person prefers to begin, however a complete learning experience must always involve the full cycle because that reflects how our life experiences are formed. Life happens, we ponder on it, we wonder what it all means and then figure out what to do about it. We probably don't have a great deal of control over life as a learning experience which happens whether we like it or not, but Kolb's work gives us a language and a framework for understanding what happens when a person *intentionally sets out to learn something new*.

This probably calls to mind the idea of 'conscious incompetence'. When I know that I don't know something, I set out to learn it. I know that I want to record my favourite TV show, but I can't for the life of me remember how to program the video recorder.

However, when learning is not motivated by the individual, the idea of 'unconscious incompetence' is more relevant. I have no idea that there are such things as superconductors, or cytoblasts, or actuaries, and that's generally because I had no interest in them. Should I become interested, just because someone else thinks that it's important for me to know about such things?

Learning theories are important because the primary aim of modelling is to produce a model which can be replicated. In order to 'install' a model in someone else, you'll need to understand how they learn.

Studies of brain plasticity and learning show that a realistic time to master a new behaviour is about six months, with daily activity, reflection and integration. It's interesting that the most current and advanced work in neuroscience adds weight to what teachers have said for generations; that students need regular practice over a prolonged period of time together with proper rest in order to truly master a new skill. A good night's sleep really is part of the learning process.

A common approach to learning is to structure a sequence of activities as follows:

1. Present a theory
2. Find practical examples of the theory
3. Use the theory to build a personal concept
4. Apply that personal concept
5. Reflect on the experience to construct a new theory
6. Repeat the whole process with a new and perhaps contradictory theory

A psychology student might learn about Jung's theory of archetypes, looking at the descriptions and finding real examples of people who fit those descriptions. They might use a type indicator tool or psychometric instrument to bring their own personal experience into the learning process. They would then work out how they could apply the theory in their own work and practically try it out, perhaps using Jungian archetypes as a set of signposts for a coaching intervention. After spending some time working with this, they would reflect on what they had learned about the theory, its practical application and about their own preconceptions and experiences, abstracting those experiences and creating a new theoretical model.

The whole process can be repeated, and if that is done with a contradictory theory, the student will greatly open up their thinking on the subject and develop a richer, deeper understanding of it.

The ability to truly understand apparently contradictory explanations is the very basis of intellect and of science. To be able to explain the motion of the planets around the sun and, at the same time, to be open to the possibility that the sun comes up because sufficient sacrifices have been made to the Sun God is the basis of the scientific method; to reject no idea, no matter how incredible, and to test every theory, no matter how obvious.

The saying, "the exception proves the rule" is generally used to mean that an exception makes the rule correct:

"I'm always on time!"

"You were late this morning!"

"Well, the exception proves the rule..."

However, the origin of the word "prove" doesn't mean 'confirm', it means 'test'. The phrase actually means, "the exception tests the rule", which makes absolute sense.

Theoretical models can never, ever be 'true' or 'right' and your mindset must always be one of curiosity, of testing in order to prove the rule.

The approach to modelling that I am detailing in this book is not a replacement for a thorough learning process. If anything, it is a foundation for the instructional design process, where you can use a high performance model as the basis for the design of a learning intervention.

As you will see later, modelling is as much about transferring culture as it is about transferring specific behavioural skills.

7 Modelling

In the world of electronics, there are good engineers and there are average engineers. The average engineers will fix a problem by replacing all the components until they find the one that was causing the problem. A good engineer will locate the problem first before changing only the faulty component. A good engineer uses systemic knowledge to make very precise interventions; the proverbial bill for £100, comprising £1 for tapping and £99 for knowing where to tap.

Good engineers (in fact, all good professionals) observe behaviour. They know how something behaves when it is working normally, so they know where to start looking when it does not behave normally. Average engineers do not observe behaviour in the same way.

When I was an engineer, I learned to observe behaviour, because it was the only way to fix complex problems. If you don't know what the equipment does when it's working properly, how can you know what is wrong with it when it isn't working properly?

If you want to improve the performance of a sales team, it's no use focusing on the under-performers. We need to figure out what the over-performers are doing first. Our approach to modelling is inherently systemic and ecological. By modelling a successful sales person, we can understand the mindset that works for that team, in that company, in that market, with those products and those customers. Therefore, by teaching that mindset to other sales people in the same team, we have an instantly workable process.

By comparing the high performers to average performers, we are using the well established principle of the 'control group'.

Many people assume that this means the behavioural knowledge required to perform a complex task is locked away and is irretrievable. We get a glimpse of the knowledge through observing behaviour, but there is no way to extract the knowledge itself. Other people went on to guess at the behavioural programming, based on their observations, but they tried to guess 'why' the individual behaved that way instead of asking 'how'. 'Why' is irrelevant. If I want to copy your talent for writing music, or sticking to a diet, or remember people's names at a party, I don't need to know why you do it. I just need to know how, so I can learn to do it. If I decide to acquire this skill for myself, I will have my own, personal, unique "why".

Traditional 'body language' is an example of this, where a particular movement 'means' something specific such as arrogance or fear. Body movement is not a language in itself, it's a component of communication. The effects of 'body language' training are still with us today, lingering on in presentation skills courses that teach people how to stand so that they look confident. Isn't it better just to be confident, and let your body naturally communicate that?

We can say with some certainty that we just don't understand how the brain works, because there are many competing schools of thought. Behaviourists say that we can only observe behaviour, therefore whatever goes on inside is unknowable and therefore irrelevant. This philosophy leads us to the conclusion that other people might be zombies with no internal consciousness at all, and we would be unable to determine the difference.

Existentialists argue that we create our own experience and therefore we can only observe and think subjectively. There is no objectivity, and the human observer can never be removed from what is being observed. An apple is only red in relation to its human observer and a falling tree only makes a sound in the forest when an illegal logger cuts it down with his noisy chainsaw.

Modelling is as much a mindset of curiosity as an explicit set of tools. This mindset will help you to learn interesting things from experts, from people you admire and from yourself. It is an open mindedness, in which you suspend any questions about why someone is doing something and instead only observe how they are doing something. This initial observation is then followed up with detailed questions about *how they decided* what to do at each stage of the process.

For example, driving a car is a very complex set of behaviours which take many months to learn and years to thoroughly master. Yet the individual actions that a driver takes aren't new. A child can imitate the actions of a racing driver, but can they drive a car? Generally, no, but not because they don't know how to steer or operate the controls, but because they don't know *how* to steer and *when* to operate *which* controls.

When you watch your colleagues, clients and friends, you will notice that they do certain things in a certain order. You will be able to watch the process by which they individually behave in order to achieve their goals.

There seem to be a number of hallmarks of a talent:

- The person is able to get consistent results without having to think about the process or even being aware of it

- When asked, the person is a little surprised that the skill is worth modelling. They will often deny they are good at the task and will be surprised that everyone doesn't do it.

- When you first ask, "how do you do it?" they answer, "I don't know - I just do it"

The mechanic movements of driving a car are easy to master. You can observe your parent or driving instructor and you can copy the movements required to press a pedal or change gear. But how did they know when to change gear? How did they know which gear to turn into? How did they know how hard and for how long to depress the pedal? These are the internal decision processes that distinguish an average driver from a talented one. For most of us, this may not make a lot of difference, but for a racing driver, microseconds of efficiency at the decision level lead to the difference between starting out in pole position and ending up in the pits.

One of the other important aspects of modelling is that we analyse what is working rather than trying to classify what isn't working. Rather than researching people who have phobias, we look for people who used to have phobias but now don't and we figure out what they did to get rid of their phobias. Many self help and positive psychology 'experts' are highly critical of the therapeutic community for researching phobias and other conditions. I'd like to distance myself from their criticism, as I find it to be naïve and uniformed. My view is that studying a phobia has merit and studying the way in which a phobia can change has merit. In terms of modelling, the skill that we want to extract and teach to others is the skill of losing a phobia. There is generally less value in teaching someone to learn a phobia, although I sometimes think that learning a phobia of cream cakes wouldn't be a bad thing for someone who had trouble dieting.

This brings us to the issue of context. One of the common beliefs of coaches is that "There is a positive intention motivating every behaviour and a context in which it has value". These beliefs form layers which influence the end result which a person may achieve. For example, a technique for a tennis serve is built upon a series of beliefs, such as a a belief that you enjoy playing tennis and want to improve your game. If your foundation was a belief that you could never master tennis and your serve would always be weak then your learning process, and therefore your learning outcome, would be subtly different. Maybe not different enough to affect a friendly game in the back garden, but certainly different enough to make the difference between picking up a medal at Wimbledon and picking up litter on Wimbledon Common.

'Traditional' schools of thought see something like a phobia as being rooted in the past and therefore difficult to change, whereas alternative therapies often see a phobia as being learned in the past yet replayed in the present, making it easy to change.

We could perhaps compare it to something like a book versus a document on your computer. A book was written and printed in the past and is fixed. You can write on it, highlight text, but you cannot fundamentally edit it. If you cut some text out, a gap remains. A document on your computer can be edited any time you like and it will reformat seamlessly around the changes.

I don't know which is 'true', and I don't suppose there will ever be a universal agreement until we can talk to whoever designed us, but since there is some debate on who that is, there can be no single point of view. Make up your own mind despite what anyone else says, unless someone else is saying make up your own mind in which case just do what they tell you to.

We are models

In the article 'Mirror Neurons and the Simulation Theory of Mind Reading', Gallese and Goldman[2] evaluate evidence for our ability to infer others' internal emotional states as well as the processes behind their behaviour. They put forward the idea that we developed this ability in order to learn behaviours, and that this ability now gives us empathy and the ability to predict others' behaviour.

A map is a model. It is not the same as the place that it represents, but it helps you to condense a representation of that place onto a single sheet of paper so that you can find your way around.

Our ability to construct abstract models of the outside world means that we are ourselves models of reality. Knowing that $2+2=4$ is not the same as having 4 apples, and we understand both how to create abstract models as well as how to apply them to real life situations. As you saw from a previous chapter on brain development, young

---

2 Trends in Cognitive Sciences, December 1998

children have to count the apples as they have not yet developed the ability to count symbols which represent apples.

A thought about a thing is not the same as the thing itself. The model is not reality. The map is not the territory.

Consider this model of sensory filtering, and consider how it guides our own learning processes.

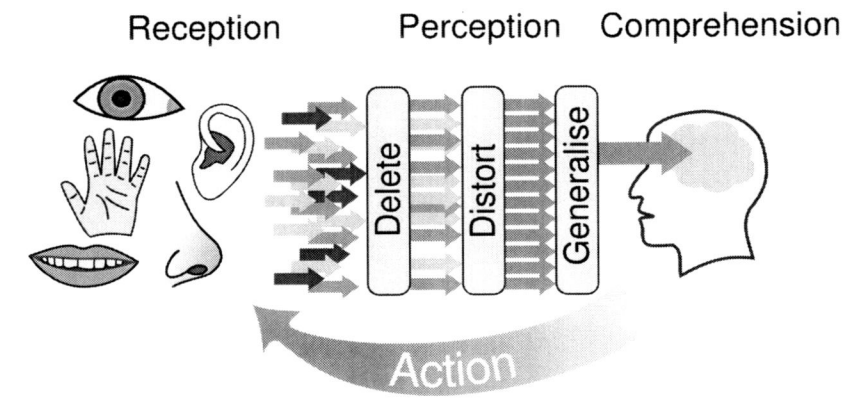

We can't prove that this model is correct, but I urge you to always bear in mind the difference between a model and a theory. A model is a generalisation of something that can be observed, whereas a theory is a generalisation which must then be tested with observations. This model of the processes of sensory reception, perception and comprehension follows a logical sequence; light must interact with your retinas before the signal can pass to your brain, which must happen before you can become aware of the image of these words, which must happen before you comprehend their meaning.

The way in which those sensory signals are filtered and generalised affects our perceptions and must surely affect what we can comprehend and therefore learn.

Recognising Models

Let's start our modelling journey with a deceptively simple exercise. It's important to begin by understanding the distinction between a thing and a model of that thing, because we generally use language interchangeably in this respect. A colleague might point at some pixels on a computer screen and say, "The report's here, but I can't find the supporting spreadsheet for it". In the Steve Martin film 'The Man with Two Brains', a journalist asks about the doctor's wife, points to a doll and asks, "Is that her?" The doctor replies, "No. That's just a statue of her."

If you look around you, you'll see models as well as models of models. You'll also see people interacting with models as if they are interacting with the real thing. Is it that they can't tell the difference? Not necessarily. It's more likely to be a demonstration of our remarkable ability to interact with abstract concepts *as if* we are interacting with real, concrete concepts, a sign of reaching the developmental stage of symbolic operations, mentioned earlier. We use a map as if it really is the territory.

Can you recognise the models that are all around you?

7.1 Every Model is a Generalisation

In order to simplify an experience into a model, we have to delete some of it and distort the rest so that it can be generalised into a simple concept or representation.

List as many types of model aeroplane as you can. I don't mean Spitfire, Lancaster, Tornado etc., they might all be 'Airfix kits'. You need to list other types of model, only in the left hand column:

Type of model
'Airfix' kits

What examples of model aeroplanes did you come up with? Here are a few suggestions for you to compare with your own list:

- A paper aeroplane
- A computer simulation of airflow over a wing
- A wind tunnel model
- A bronze statue of an aeroplane
- A Hollywood film set
- The phrase "Boeing 747"
- A flight simulator
- A derelict aircraft used for fire training
- The word "aeroplane"
- The sound of an aeroplane
- A CAD drawing used to build an aeroplane
- The image that comes to mind when you think of an aeroplane

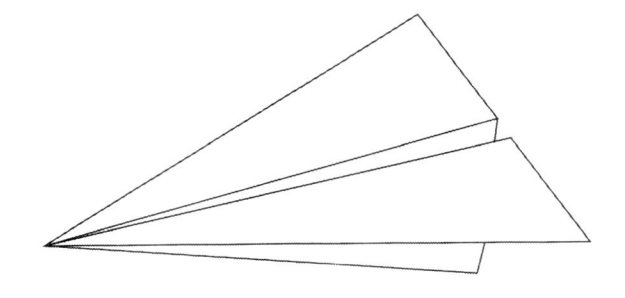

7.2 Every Model Has a Purpose

> In the right hand column of the table in exercise 5.1, write the purpose of the models that you have listed.

Every model is generalised from the original, and that process of generalisation is guided by the model's purpose. For example, the purpose of an Airfix model is to physically represent the real item but on a smaller scale and to be easy for someone to assemble themselves at home. Therefore, some of the physical details of the real aircraft are missed out because the plastic moulding process cannot reproduce them, and the model itself is made of a material which the real aircraft is not made from.

Every model has a purpose. Every model is functional.

For example, if we list some models of a television set, we might have a circuit diagram, a dolls house model and one of those fake televisions that you find in show homes.

Each has its own purpose.

The dolls house model does not have the same level of detail in its surface appearance as the original, and the circuit diagram tells you nothing about how the television looks. The show home television looks like any television, but none in particular. Its features are generalised so that it does not endorse a particular manufacturer or infringe any registered design features.

Even the word 'television' is itself a model of a television, generalised for communicating the concept and experience of a television to another human being.

The purpose of a model tells us how the original object or event has been condensed into a format suitable for human experience.

Remember that we are generalising objects and events in the outside world, so the first level of filtering is that we are unable to sense much of the information that is available and our perception imposes qualities on an object that are not inherent in it.

You are no doubt aware of the example of colour. This paper is not white. The combination of frequencies of electromagnetic radiation reflecting off the boundary between two regions of matter interfere with cells in your eyes in such a way that your visual perception creates the experience of colour which you have associated with the word 'white'. Because that's such a long winded description of the process, it's easier to say that the paper *is* white, when in fact it isn't. It's also easy to say that the spider *is* scary or the manager *is* mean or the train *is* late, when in fact they are all qualities of our experience, not inherent qualities of the object or event in question.

The word 'is' is a complex equivalence, and a complex equivalence, in meta model, is a generalisation, and in order to generalise, deletions and distortions must first take place, and distortions require internal comparisons in order to know what to distort and how. The whole sequence of events is a complex relationship between external events and internal models of previous events.

A Context for Modelling

Modelling is simple. We all do it. As a young child, it was your *only* way of learning, and for a long time you consequently learned many things which weren't of any use to you. Interestingly, neurologists don't know why the brain goes through a 'pruning' stage at adolescence, removing redundant connections. Perhaps this is why. This method of modelling simply requires you to copy everything that the subject does and see if you can get the same results. Trying to make sense of their behaviour at this stage narrows your focus and you could easily miss what turns out to be the most important thing.

In Derren Brown's[3] TV series, 'Mind Control', he gets the cashiers at a dog racing track to pay out on losing tickets. When I show this video to people and ask them to work out how he does it, they focus on language patterns, embedded commands, his hand gestures etc. They are trying to organise and code his behaviour at the same time as taking in the whole sequence, and so they inevitably miss the overall structure of the interaction between Derren Brown and the cashier.

If you model a high performing sales person, you might notice that they say, "do you know what I mean?", they drive a Ford Mondeo and they eat ham sandwiches for lunch. You might rule out these things because they obviously have nothing to do with sales performance. The modelling approach aims, where possible, to rule out nothing until you can reliably replicate their results.

---

3   Derren Brown is a British entertainer and 'mentalist' who performs psychological magic such as getting ordinary people to conduct armed robberies or confess to a murder that never happened.

I conducted a modelling project for a UK retailer where their HR team identified high performers in three roles and asked me to investigate how these people were consistently outperforming their peers, both in 'hard' measurements and in more subjective criteria.

In each case, the high performers turned out to be exhibiting different skills than those predicted by the HR team. The unique combination of their attitude, behaviour and the cultural environment of the retailer resulted in their results matching the retailer's criteria for high performance. Whilst their skills may be broadly similar to those of their peers in other retailers, there are sufficient cultural differences for this to make the difference between average and high performance.

For example, the HR team believed that coaching skills were vital for a good manager, so they had invested in a training program. The average store managers certainly spent time coaching their staff, but the high performers spent no time at all coaching staff.

Where you are modelling a very specific behaviour and you have full access to multiple role models and objective performance measurements, it can be easier to bypass this step, go directly to coding and instead select the critical elements of the model by cross referencing and comparing high performers to average performers. This is very similar to Robert Dilts' Success Factor Modelling approach. However, it can also lead you to miss vital contextual information which holds the key to excellence.

The reason for choosing average performers to compare to rather than poor performers is that it is important to keep the intended outcome consistent. It is also vital that you use external criteria as the reference point for high performance. Poor performers are too far away from the average to be a valuable comparison, and in fact what we really want to ascertain is what the high performers do differently to the average person. The lowest performers are equally different to the average, but in the wrong direction.

If you model athletes, the high performers are the ones who run the fastest. In the retailer mentioned above, the high performing store managers had the highest sales figures and the lowest wastage figures. Put them in a different retailer and their performance will be different because the cultural environment is different.

If you have already looked up 'Derren Brown dog racing' on YouTube, you might be wondering how he does it. He approaches the betting window with a losing ticket, hands it over and confidently says, "This is a winning ticket". The cashier puts the ticket into the automated reader, looks confused and says, "I'm sorry, this hasn't won" Derren bangs on the wall and says, mysteriously, "This is the dog you're looking **for**. That's why we came to this **win**dow." The cashier apologises and pays out.

"Aha!", you cry. It's obvious. The winning dog was number four, "for" is therefore an ambiguity that the cashier interprets as the winning number, and the stress on the syllable "win" is an embedded command which the cashier is unable to resist. It's a nice theory.

However, step back and look at the big picture. What is the cashier's job? Is it to determine if bets have been won or lost? No, the cashier's job is to take bets and then to pay out on winning bets. Why would anyone approach the window with a losing bet? The job is fairly monotonous, the interactions with customers minimal and the routine is check ticket, pay out, check ticket, pay out, check ticket.... and so on.

It makes more sense to pay out than not, so the cashier does what we all do when facing conflict; she overrules the one piece of information which doesn't fit the norm; the small detail that the ticket is for a loser.

Meta Model

Meta Model, literally a model of models, is a way of interpreting language as a symbolic model of the internal representation of a person's experience.

A person experiences reality and generalises it into their internal model of the world. By regarding the structure of this model as significant in itself, we can determine the means by which that person creates that model.

My father still has the A to Z road map of Birmingham and the road map of Great Britain that he had when I was a child. They don't have any of the roads that have been built in the past 40 years on them, and some entire towns are missing too!

A model being out of step with reality doesn't make it wrong, it simply represents a different reality. When that reality, or more accurately the 'reality map' no longer reflects the reality shared by the majority of other people, no amount of organised behaviour will ever bring the 'desire map' towards the 'reality map' because the reality map is so inaccurate.

Therefore, Meta Model can recover the information lost when our perceptions are encoded into our world model, enabling us to update that model and function more effectively. By effective, I mean that our chosen actions are more likely to get the results we want because the model that those actions are based on is sufficiently useful that our actions have a similar result in 'real life'.

In coaching, we talk about the importance of the 'first minute'; the time at the very beginning of a coaching session when the client is communicating their unconscious and conscious desires and experiences. You could consider the 'first minute' to be the time when the current model is being 'loaded' and represented without judgement or distortion, hence the similarity between the unconscious representation and the external communication which enables us to deduce the structure of the model (problem etc.) very quickly, if we are paying attention. In reality, a minute is far too long, and if you are trying to pay attention to all of the person's communication for this length of time, you will most likely have missed the structure, which is usually played out before they begin to speak.

For example, on a training course, I asked for someone to help me demonstrate this principle. A student volunteered, walked towards the chair at the front of the room, stopped half way, returned to his chair to have a drink of water and then came to the front. When I asked him what behaviour he'd like to use as an example, he said that he often starts projects but hesitates before he starts, goes back to make sure he's doing the right thing and ends up feeling unproductive. What he said about a generic work situation mirrored his behaviour in joining me at the front of the room.

By paying attention to what the client does *before they think you have started*, you will gather all of the information you need in order to effect change.

Personally, this never ceases to amaze me. By observing someone carefully before they 'begin', you can actually stop them mid sentence, tell them the exact nature of their 'problem' and effect a solution, without them telling you anything about it, or so they think. In fact, they had been screaming the information at you from the moment you first saw them.

Being able to model a client's reality and mental processes requires a thorough understanding of the Meta Model. When you can use the Meta Model, you can model the sequence of events that took someone from being afraid of dogs to being comfortable with them, or from being afraid of picking up the telephone to make sales calls to finding it a relatively easy part of their job.

When you understand the Meta Model, modelling really will "fall into place" and you will be able to amaze your clients and colleagues by telling them all about their "problem" when they don't think they have told you anything about it. As a coaching tool alone, it is invaluable for getting inside the client's world and I can't encourage you enough to learn it thoroughly.

Mind you, if you do now go and learn it thoroughly, then I obviously *have* encouraged you enough, thereby proving myself wrong.

Isomorphism

Literally, a similarity in shape. The structure of a person's language is the same as the structure of their experience and perceptions. Their language and their behaviour are isomorphic. The structure of one gives us the structure, and the ability to predict and influence, the other.

An oak tree and the human brain are isomorphic, in that the physical appearance and function of the tree's branches and the brain's blood vessels follow similar mathematical rules for their growth and therefore look alike.

The phrase, "Let's hit the shops" could have a structural similarity to the way in which someone approaches a shopping trip, and afterwards, they might quite literally feel, "wiped out".

Taking language literally is probably the single most valuable skill in learning and applying the meta model effectively. Treating metaphors as if they are literal descriptions of an internal experience is usually far more productive than pushing the person to abandon their metaphors and give you a detailed analysis of their experience. For example, when someone feels deflated, or pushed from pillar to post, or like a kid in a sweet shop, they are using metaphorical language to convey a very literal experience. I suppose the rule of thumb is that all language is metaphorical, in that a word is not the same as the thing it represents. Since all language is a representation, we are potentially talking about two different types of representation; a more literal one where the person is choosing their words perhaps carefully, and a more metaphorical one, where the person's unconscious mind has more of an input into the language chosen, revealing the unconscious thought processes that drive the behaviour in question.

In coaching, I find it personally useful to visualise the forces acting upon a person as indicated in their language. For example, frustration combines a force or desire acting upon an immovable barrier. When you absorb yourself in the client's language, it is easy to accept the constants of the situation; that they cannot move the barrier, that they must achieve their goal and so on. Yet, when you visualise frustration as a force acting against a barrier, it is easy to see some potential solutions:

- Move the barrier
- Go round, over or under the barrier
- Apply the force in the opposite direction
- Stop applying the force
- Have someone help you
- Stand on the other side of the barrier and pull
- Recognise the barrier as a *safety* barrier
- Notice that the barrier has gaps in it
- Send information over the barrier instead of trying to physically move past it
- Recognise that it is actually the belief in a need for force which created the barrier in the first place

A director of a public sector organisation recently told me about some organisational problems. Six years after a merger with another organisation, they two were no more integrated than they were before the merger. The executive team were highly educated and, on paper, had the right capabilities. Yet what they had actually created was a divide, a barrier between themselves and their managers. A barrier stops you getting out, but it also stops nasty things getting in, and, the executives had protected themselves against bad news.

In the space of one three minute conversation, the director twice used the phrase "go around it" as a metaphor for "solve the problem".

What does that metaphor say to you? Does it suggest that the problem is something that the executives are ready to tackle and resolve once and for all? Or do you think they're still trying to avoid it?

Until the executives stop trying to go round the problem, they won't succeed. Why? Because there is no problem to go around. The 'problem' is a metaphor for their behaviour. How can they go around their own behaviour?

As a course of action, this metaphor alone tells us that the executives need to accept responsibility for their own behaviour and results before any changes can be made. It also tells us that they are very sensitive about the issue, and we have to tread very carefully.

Just taking a moment to think about metaphors in literal terms is probably the single biggest time saver for anyone involved in problem solving of any kind.

Strategies and the TOTE Model

The ability to change the process by which we experience reality is more often valuable than changing the content of our experience of reality

A strategy is a specific sequence of steps that are necessary to perform a particular task.

Crucially, a strategy is NOT a behaviour. You cannot say that you have a strategy for cooking pasta to perfection. It's a program, at best, and if there is any conscious thought involved at all then it's not even that.

Strategies are by definition unconscious, therefore they are decision making processes that take place before you are consciously aware of an external stimulus. In fact, your moment of awareness often coincides with the output of the strategy. For example, if you are afraid of spiders then your strategy has finished long before you are aware that there is a spider in the room. The strategy is the decision making process, and when we are modelling talented people, it is their decisions that we must value most.

Pretty much any idiot can copy a behaviour. The key that marks out the difference between average and exemplary performance is the ability to make decisions that govern that behaviour.

Driving a car comprises a very simple set of behaviours. You wave your hands up and down, you do something akin to stirring a pudding and you move your feet up and down. But knowing when to do these things, and how much to do them, is the key to being able to drive and just 'going through the motions'. When you first started learning to drive, going through the motions is exactly what you did. You made no decisions about where to go, how fast to get there, when to start, when to stop, when to turn and so on. All you could manage was to operate the controls of the car. Anything else was way above your level of competency. As you began to master the mechanical movements that cause the car to respond to your commands, you could relax a little and concentrate on the outside world. Whoa! There are other cars out there! And people! And stray dogs! The roads are a dangerous place, and you had to learn how to navigate the many obstacles that appear before you. The majority of this learning process isn't mechanical, it's purely mental. However, we can't see people doing the mental stuff, so we assume that driving, or playing football, or Tai Chi are physical skills when in fact the physical movements are merely manifestations of an underlying mental process.

A strategy, then, is a habitual decision that results in a certain course of action based on a certain sensory stimulus. The input and output are both external, because the strategy is triggered by some external event, and results in an action based on that event.

For example, a skill for goal setting might comprise:

1. Visual construct of desired outcome
2. Kinaesthetic check for congruence of outcome
3. Visual recall of current situation
4. Visual construct of steps required to reach outcome
5. Kinaesthetic check for congruence of outcome

In other words, the person imagines what they would like to have, feels good about it, imagines the steps they need to take and, if it feels right, they do it.

TOTE is a concept developed in 1960 as an extension to the Stimulus Response theories of people such as Pavlov. It simply means that you have a way of knowing to start doing something, a way of knowing to keep doing it and a way to know to stop doing it, and then you can stop thinking about it.

The TOTE model adds an extra layer of formality to the basic strategy in that it adds criteria for starting the strategy and ending it. TOTE stands for Test Operate Test Exit, so to the above example it adds "how do you know when you want something?" and "how do you know when you've got it?" The 'TOTE' is essentially the start and stop for the strategy. You know to shake hands when you meet someone and see their outstretched hand, and you know to stop when you have finished the handshake. You can observe different strategies in operation when the other person wants to hold on for longer than you do, or your hands don't quite connect properly. You may even have experienced shaking hands with someone who didn't intend to shake your hand!

You will typically find that your subject has very specific criteria for the Test and Exit stages, for example someone who is scared of public speaking may know to get scared if there are more than 3 people in the audience. If there are fewer than 3, it doesn't count as a presentation so the 'get scared' strategy doesn't run (the Operate part). This in itself is a very useful change tool - shifting the criteria so that the problem strategy no longer runs. By coaching in this way, you are acknowledging the value of the behaviour, the strategy, and simply changing the situation in which it is generated.

To make it easier to write a strategy down as a person is speaking, we can use a notation for the steps, as follows:

V	Visual	I	Internal
At	Auditory Tonal	E	External
Ad	Auditory Digital i.e. Language		
K	Kinaesthetic	C	Constructed
O	Olfactory	R	Recalled
G	Gustatory		

All steps of a strategy are sensory components[4] or modalities, and they can be generated either internally or externally.

For example, Visual Internal, VI, denotes a 'mental image', which could be recalled, such as an image of a recent night out, or it could be constructed, such as an image of you on a future night out.

Clearly, external stimuli are in real time and are neither constructed nor recalled. This presents an important distinction for understanding metaprograms, specifically the idea that all metaprograms are context specific results of an internal or external focus of attention..

Here's a strategy written with the above notation:

Ve > ViR > AdiC > Ki

---

[4] The notion of 'five senses' is an anachronism. There are many, many more, possibly as many as 21. Simplifying these into just five isn't accurate, it just makes the coding process a little simpler.

To indicate a strategy where the person sees something in the outside world, then remembers seeing something, then hears some internal dialogue and finally has a feeling about that - a judgement or conclusion.

The Exit of a strategy - the conclusion - is external to the process, and often takes the form of a bodily feeling. You'll hear people describe this when they say that a decision feels right, or that they have a gut feeling about something, or that they had a feeling that something was right or wrong. Remember that a feeling results from the activation of muscles and glands.

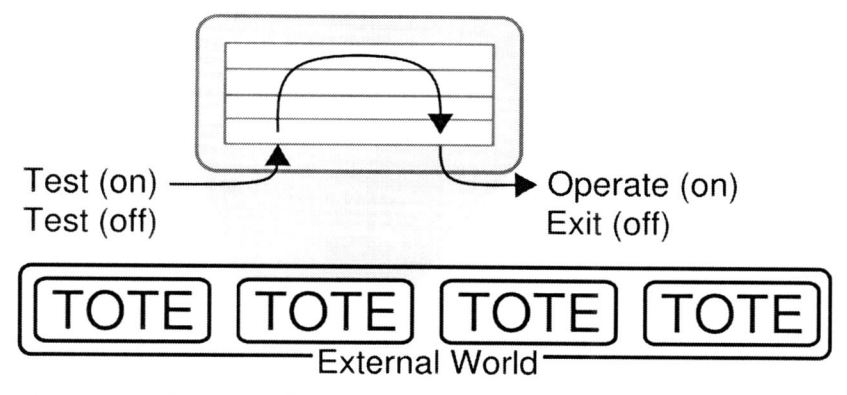

Test (on)
Test (off) ———————→ Operate (on)
Exit (off)

| TOTE | TOTE | TOTE | TOTE |
———————— External World ————————

For example, I might see something in a shop, remember one that I have at home, say to myself, "I could do with a new one of those" and then feel a desire to buy it. The same overall structure could equally apply to me seeing an apple, comparing it to an internal representation of an apple, saying to myself, "This looks like a nice apple" and feeling a desire to eat it. I could also see someone's face, compare it to a time when that person was angry, say to myself, "Here we go again" and feel a sinking feeling.

The first Test is triggered by the external stimulus, and the Operate stage switches on, which continues until the second Test confirms that the outcome has been achieved and the program can Exit.

The entire process activates motor nerves which in turn activate muscles which in turn creates feedback through sensory nerves. You act, and you feel, and see, the results of that action.

For a person, strategies tend to be consistent in multiple contexts. After all, why waste time learning new strategies? Life in general is very conservative and human beings will tend to be consistent, so eliciting a strategy in one context is often valuable in many contexts.

The test of a strategy is only consistency. If a person can get the same result without having to think about it, they are working perfectly and their behaviour is working perfectly because it is achieving what it is meant to. Remember, every behaviour has a positive intention - it is designed to achieve something. Whether that something is good or bad depends only on context.

If we represent a simple TOTE such as shaking hands as a flowchart, this is what we get:

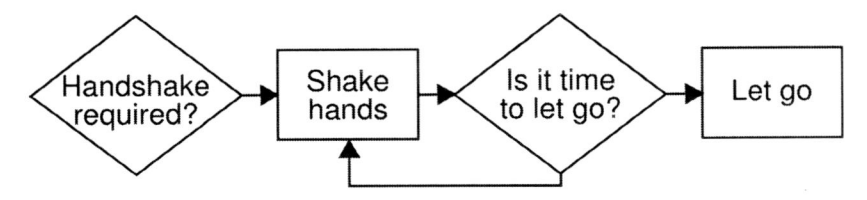

Handshake required? → Shake hands → Is it time to let go? → Let go

As you can immediately see, we have a problem when representing behavioural decisions in this way. How do you know if this is someone you should shake hands with? Have you met them before? Is it a social situation? Is anyone else shaking hands? Do you have anything sticky on your hands? Are you holding a glass? Are they holding a glass? Do they want to meet you? Once you're shaking hands, how many times do you shake? How long do you hold on for? When do you let go? How do you let go?

Even a very simple behaviour breaks down into so many decision points that to represent it using TOTE flowcharts would be very complicated. In order to make sense of the behaviour, we have to assume so much that the model is generalised beyond comprehension to anyone except someone who already knows how to shake hands.

Whilst some trainers use TOTE as a modelling concept, or as a word to describe a skill or behaviour, I would suggest that it complicates things somewhat, because it is too simple.

Let's start with something easier, and which introduces the essential approach to modelling.

7.1 Sequences

Work in pairs for this exercise.

One person describes, for two minutes, a recent experience such as a holiday, night out, party, work situation etc. The other person notes any sensory specific clues that indicate which part of the memory the speaker is recalling at that moment, for example if they are describing an image or playing back someone else's words, or describing feelings or sensations. Just make a note of the sensory system and the clues that give this away, e.g. language, posture, content etc.

	VAKOG	Clues
1		
2		
3		
4		
5		
6		

7		
8		
9		
10		
11		
12		
13		
14		
15		
16		

What did you notice in this exercise?

Are there any patterns in the clues that you picked up?

7.2 Eye Accessing Part 1

Work in pairs for this exercise.

Memorise the question then look your partner right in the eye as you ask it. If you read the question from the notes you will miss the eye accessing which occurs as soon as your partner understands the question - usually about half way through! Make a note of what you observe in the right hand column. You can record in whatever way is easiest for you; arrows, V, A, K etc.

Do not enter into a discussion with your partner at this stage, just ask the questions and record the results.

Where is your bed in relation to the window?

What's your least favourite colour?

How does confusion feel?

Who did you last talk to on the phone?

How would an anteater sound if it could talk?

What letter is next to P on a computer keyboard?

How hard do you have to close your car door?

When was the last time that you were cosy?

Is your bathroom hot tap on the right or left?

How does it sound to walk in snow?

What do your bedroom curtains look like?

What is their texture like?

What noise do they make as you open them?

Is your wardrobe door easy or hard to open?

When did you last hear your name?

When were you last in trouble?

What's the 5th word of your favourite song?

What colour clothes were you wearing yesterday?

What colour clothes will you wear tomorrow?

What did your first school smell like?

Which cupboard in your kitchen is the tea in?

In your car, how do you turn the radio on?

What was your first taste of alcohol like?

On a telephone keypad, where is the number 7?

Where was the warmest place you've ever been?

How would you write your name backwards?

What was the last telephone number you dialled?

How does it feel to wade through water?

Which mobile phone ring tone is most irritating?

What time do you think it is? (Without looking!!)

Name one item that is in your fridge

What is your favourite kind of tree?

Genius at Work

Eye accessing is a contentious issue. It's said that, in general, movement to the left infers the recall of an existing memory whilst movement to the right infers the construction of a new experience. This doesn't apply to everyone, and it certainly doesn't mean that someone is lying, just because they're making new pictures in their head. With some people, the left to right accessing is exactly reversed so, once again, it's important to pay attention to the person in front of you, not the generalisation.

If I ask you to recall some visual detail of a memory, such as the colour of a colleague's shirt, you may not remember it right away. You might recall the overall scene, then 'try out' a number of different colours until you feel you've got the right one. This would, for many people, involve a lot of eye accessing up to the right - but you wouldn't be lying.

You will often see a sequence, for example, to recall the sound of walking in snow, you may see your partner look up first, which may indicate they're picturing snow before they can hear it.

Don't be concerned if what you saw your partner doing differs from what you'll find in other books; that's quite normal. It is far more important that you observe what actually happens than try to work out what it means.

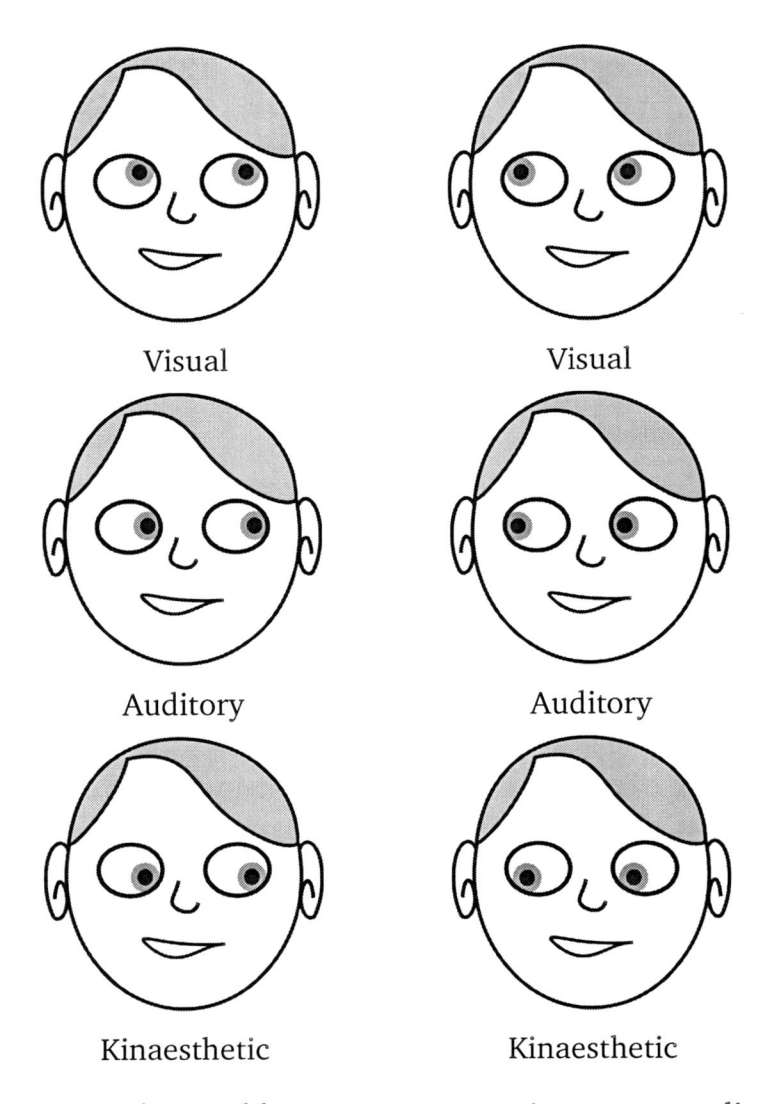

Visual	Visual
Auditory	Auditory
Kinaesthetic	Kinaesthetic

It is certainly possible to use eye accessing cues as a direct means to elicit a strategy, and certainly you will see sequences using this method. On one hand, eye accessing sequences are typically very fast, on the other hand, you may see a disagreement between a person's eye accessing and the steps that they verbalise. This is often when a step is so fast that they are not consciously aware of it. Eye accessing will therefore give you enough clues that you will be able to make a start on eliciting a strategy verbally, and will give you a means to check the strategy as you go.

The downside of using eye accessing to elicit a strategy is that many people do not exhibit the 'traditional' eye accessing patterns. You will always need to calibrate first if you plan to incorporate eye accessing cues. Regard eye accessing as a guide to help guide your questioning.

It's not necessarily important to analyse eye accessing cues in detail, and for a number of reasons, I tell students to simplify things:

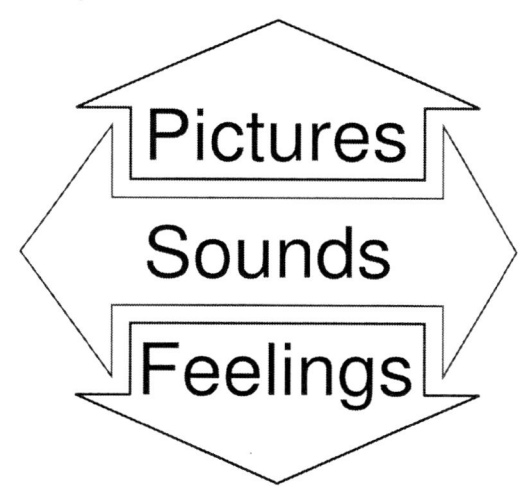

```
   Pictures
   Sounds
   Feelings
```

My reasons for simplifying the traditional eye accessing model include:

- The traditional model is fiercely disputed[5]

- Not everyone fits the traditional model, therefore it's not sufficiently generalised to be useful

---
5   Visit goo.gl/ggLls7 for recent research which disproves eye accessing

- No recognised research has yet to show any link between eye movements and sensory thoughts

- Perception and cognition are whole brain functions, not localised to a particular area, therefore the traditional neurological model is wildly out of date

- In many people, the left-right orientation of the traditional model is reversed

- The left-right orientation might hold for visual and auditory information, but the model breaks down for kinaesthetic and therefore doesn't fit what we can observe

- Eye accessing may still be useful, even though it can't be said to be 'true'

Eye accessing is valuable as part of your modelling toolkit because by observing eye accessing cues, you can make inferences about how someone is thinking and then use that to guide your questioning of them. We may not know why eye accessing cues exist or what they mean, but there is no doubt that they can be consistently observed, and you may find them useful in modelling because they can give clues that reveal underlying processes that your subject finds difficult to articulate.

In this regard, eye accessing cues are no different to any other gesture; they are one more piece of observable evidence that will add consistency to your model.

7.3 Eye Accessing Part 2

Work in pairs for this exercise.

Go back to your notes from the previous exercise. Where you saw more than a simple, single access, find out from your partner what they did in order to answer the question. For example, if you saw, in response to, "How does confusion feel?", a down, up, side, up, down sequence, you might guess that they first tried to access a feeling of confusion, then recalled an image, then heard sounds, then found an appropriate image, then ended back on the feeling.

Work through three examples where you saw more eye movement and discover why you saw a more complex response to the question.

1. Question:

2. Question:

3. Question:

Strategy elicitation

The fundamental technique in modelling is strategy elicitation. If we reduce any behaviour down to a sequence of sensory inputs and motor outputs then that unique sequence is what we call a strategy. Whilst some people refer to this as a meta strategy or a TOTE, we can simply regard a person's vast library of behavioural choices as a nested hierarchy of strategies.

Here's an example of what I mean:

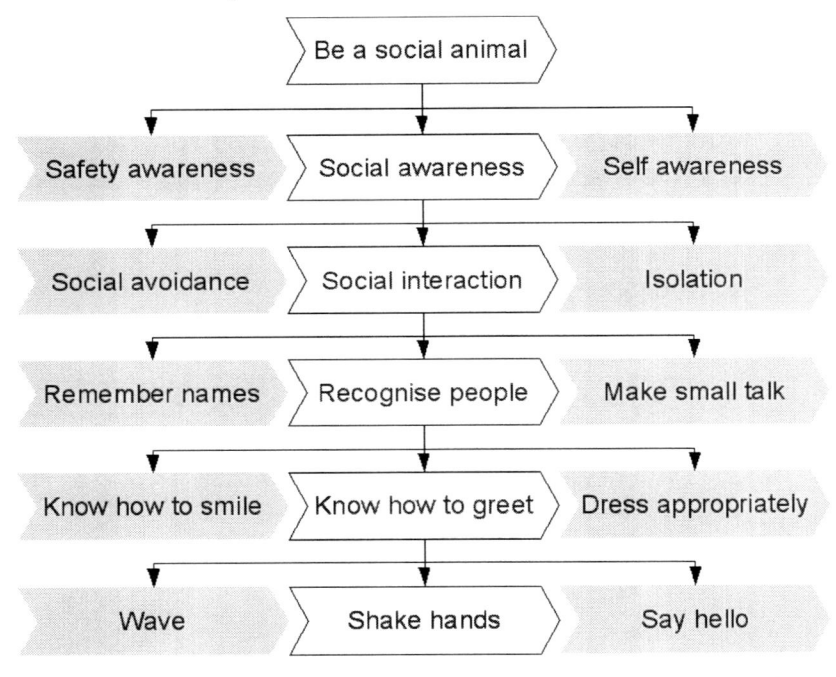

```
                    Be a social animal
                           |
    ┌──────────────────────┼──────────────────────┐
    ▼                      ▼                      ▼
Safety awareness    Social awareness       Self awareness
    ▼                      ▼                      ▼
Social avoidance    Social interaction         Isolation
    ▼                      ▼                      ▼
Remember names      Recognise people       Make small talk
    ▼                      ▼                      ▼
Know how to smile   Know how to greet    Dress appropriately
    ▼                      ▼                      ▼
    Wave                Shake hands            Say hello
```

As you can see, in order to execute a strategy, a previous strategy must have executed. We run from one thought to the next, each moment triggering multiple possibilities for our next choice. You have no doubt experienced starting one task, only to be reminded about something else that you need to do and you end up being distracted completely. Every moment leads to the next and builds on what has happened before. The decision to shake someone's hand at a party happens in the blink of an eye, or you could say that the decision happened long ago when you learned to recognise such situations and learned appropriate behaviour.

The lifelong process of learning is feedback based, so you learned that shaking hands resulted in a more enjoyable conversation than punching the other person in the face. If your outcome is to alienate people then your choices and learning experiences will reflect that too.

When you set out to learn something, you might not necessarily have an end in mind. What we do know is that learning is one of the ways in which we bridge that gap between desired state and present state, so that we can bridge that gap more efficiently next time.

Therefore, when we begin to model a strategy, we have to know the context of outcomes in which it exists. If an outcome is achieved then it is by definition well formed. Many coaches and therapists assume that if a person isn't getting what they want then their outcomes cannot be well formed. Instead, assume that whatever the person achieves is as a result of a well formed outcome, even if it is different to what they say they want. A difference between desire and reality is more often the result of conflicting outcomes rather than a single, ill formed outcome. You will typically observe sequential or simultaneous incongruence in this situation.

We'll come back to incongruence shortly, for now let's work on some strategy elicitation exercises.

7.4 Model a Decision Strategy

Work in pairs for this exercise. Ask your partner to recall something that they bought recently, which involved a decision.

First, you have to identify the very first point where their decision started; perhaps seeing something in an advert, or feeling that something needed replacing, or hearing someone talk about something, or whatever the first step was for them.

A strategy that serves a specific purpose will be consistent over time, so a decision strategy will likely be the same for any decision. You can probably see how valuable this is in a sales context.

Pin the strategy down to something very specific, otherwise there are too many variables. Focus on the specific decision point, not the whole buying process, and remember that the decision may have been made long before the purchase took place.

Often, you will find that a person has a very fast decision process followed by a longer justification process, so make sure that you focus on the moment the person knew what they wanted.

Test the strategy by playing it back to the subject.

Decision being modelled:

Strategy:

7.5 Model a Skill or Talent

Work in pairs for this exercise. Ask your partner to identify something that they would call a skill or talent and apply the strategy modelling process as before.

Be very specific about what you are modelling. If they say they are good at time management, that's far too big a set of behaviours for this exercise. You might narrow that down to their ability to choose which of two tasks is the higher priority.

Begin by asking them to tell you about something that they are good at doing and enjoy, and as soon as you hear sequences of representational systems or words such as first or next, you're hearing a strategy. Before that, you will probably hear criteria, and when you do, you can ask, "how do you know...." and that will typically lead you into a strategy.

Test the strategy by playing it back to the subject and trying it out for yourself.

Skill being modelled:

Strategy:

7.6 Model a Problem

Work in pairs for this exercise. Ask your partner to identify something that they would call a current problem and apply the strategy modelling process as before.

The key here is to remember that what they describe as a problem is in fact a talent taken out of context, so treat it with the same respect and wonder as for the decision and the talent.

Problem being modelled:

Strategy:

What did you discover from modelling a problem?

What does this mean?

8 The Meta Model

As promised, I'm going to summarise the Meta Model because it is vitally important to modelling. Hearing the structures in someone's language will save you a huge amount of time, because their linguistic structures will mirror their behavioural choices. If you want to learn about the Meta Model in depth, I've taken the Meta Model section out of one of my earlier books and set it up as a free download for you, which you can find at:

www.cgwpublishing.com/genius

Rather than start with a list of the components of the Meta Model, I'm going to start with three worked examples to show you what is possible. You might then have a useful frame of reference for the summary which follows.[6]

"I've got this situation at work that I just don't know how to handle"

This client is unhappy with a colleague. They would like to slap them in the face or push them off a cliff, but they are keen to find a more socially acceptable solution.

"I get so frustrated that I'm afraid that…"

This father wants to lash out at his child who doesn't behave as the father would like him to, but he knows that's not the best way to solve the problem because he feels angry and afraid about his own father lashing out at him.

---

6 Think back to Kolb's learning styles theory. Which style prefers to start with an example?

"I would like to be better at time management"

Either the client's colleague is more productive and the client is trying to live up to that, or the client has lost motivation and is worried it will affect their career prospects. Either way, they don't really want to be more productive, but they don't want to get into trouble for poor performance either.

How can we deduce these meanings from such brief opening sentences?

Let's work through them using the Meta Model.

"I've got this situation at work that I just don't know how to handle"

In order of priority, I would always suggest tackling nominalisations first. Nominalisations are verbs turned into pseudo-nouns, and they indicate stuck mental processes and will always get in the way of the client's progress. Can you spot the nominalisation in this sentence? It's the word 'situation', which is derived from the verb 'to situate'.

A nominalisation is worth tackling first because in doing so, we achieve two outcomes at once. Firstly, we get the process moving again. Imagine yourself at a meeting. Now imagine yourself meeting someone. What's different? I would guess that the first mental image you made was still, the second moving.

The importance of a still image isn't so much that it is a static moment in time, it is more to do with the future. A still image is a representation "through time", which means that it is *always* true. People who say they are "always in meetings" are speaking correctly, from their distorted point of view. A nominalisation and its associated still image are a prediction of the future, based on a snapshot of the past. In a photograph, the time is always *now*.

The second useful outcome is that a nominalisation, as well as being a generalisation, is a *deletion*, in that the object of the verb is missing.

Subject	Verb		Object
I	was at a	**meeting**	
I		**met** with	Fred

With the object deleted, we only have half of the story. So the word 'situation' is deleting the object; who or what the client situates themselves relative to. A lucky guess makes that a colleague, or perhaps a manager.

The second word to tackle in this statement is 'how'. When you want to go somewhere, is the mode of travel or the route the first thing that you think about? I would guess not; the first thing you think about is the destination and your reason for going there. Therefore, logically, the first thing that you think about is not a 'how' but a 'what'. For this client to be primarily concerned with the 'how' means that they *already know* what they want the outcome to be, they just can't figure out how to achieve it within the rules of the workplace.

Finally, the word 'handle' is a *kinaesthetic* word. It tells us that the barrier to action in a feeling, and a bad one. We know it's bad because it's causing a nominalisation to appear earlier on in the statement. The feeling acts as a barrier to any further thought on the matter. Good feelings tend not to get nominalised because it's in the person's interest to 'relive' that feeling and enjoy it again.

When people constrain their own thinking, a good way forward is often to have them verbalise their dark aspirations. That will not make them any more likely to act upon them, assuming that you are not dealing with someone who is mentally ill or has a track record of violence. I'm really talking about ordinary people like you and I, people who would love to give that smart-arse in the office their come-uppance if it weren't for the small matter of business etiquette. And of course the legal definition of 'actual body harm'.

I've worked with many managers who had "tried everything" to motivate a failing employee. Everything apart from the one thing that they really wanted, of course, which was to fire the under-performer. But they ruled out that possibility and immediately constrained their thinking. It was that self imposed constraint which caused the problem, not the performance, because the constraint ultimately led to an implied rule which says that no matter what this person does, you can't fire them. From that rule comes a feeling of powerlessness and frustration which adds further strain and ultimately more damage to the working relationship.

In summary, what this client has done is to deal with a problem or conflict at work by thinking the unthinkable which has created a mental loop which leads, inevitably to a 'stuck' feeling and an inability to deal with the problem effectively.

The way forward is to free them from this ever decreasing loop so that they can discover more effective ways to resolve conflict than by internalising and reinforcing their own frustration.

"I get so frustrated that I'm afraid that..."

Any parent knows the feeling of frustration when a child screams "no!" and throws a bowl of pasta across the room or flatly refuses to cooperate with an everyday request.

Effective parents are able to deal with this normal testing of boundaries by predicting and side-stepping the child's behaviour. With tactics such as distraction and patience, some parents seem to cope effortlessly, whilst others get more and more distraught. In some cases, parents are afraid that they might hurt their child, their frustration becoming unbearable.

This client is describing their reaction to the loss of control. When a child is born, it does things pretty much when its parents say so. It goes to bed where they say and when they say (although it might not go to sleep on cue). It eats what they say and it wears what they say. And one day, that child gets old enough to repeat the word that it has heard from its parents from the day that it was born; "no". It is at this point that the parent realises that the child is not a puppet but a free thinking, independent person. Some 'permissive' parents celebrate the child's independence and allow it free reign, which is actually very, very dangerous. A child does not know what is good for it, and thinks only of short term gains. If a parent asks a child if it would like ice cream for breakfast every day, most children up to a certain age will of course say yes. Children, left to their own devices, want to eat sweets, play and have their parents' undivided attention, all day, every day. But that's not feasible. When Daddy goes to work or when Mummy talks to a friend on the phone, the child reacts quite naturally to the withdrawal of attention and demands it back using any means possible; pulling on the parent's hand, screaming, singing, drawing on the wall or 'spilling' paint onto Daddy's suit jacket.

In our client's opening statement, there are three words that we need to examine; 'get', 'so' and 'afraid'. Not 'frustrated'? No, that's the feeling that *results* from the interaction of these other three elements. Frustration is the outcome, it doesn't play a part in the process.

The sentence "I get so frustrated that I'm afraid that..." is grammatically equivalent to "I get frustrated so that I'm afraid that..." and this second version makes the importance of 'so' stand out. 'So' is a sequence word. It tells us about the order in which things happen, and most importantly, it tells us that something has reached a threshold.

"It was so heavy that I needed help to lift it"

"I finished my report so I went home"

"I was so late that I decided to cancel the meeting"

The word 'get' tells us that this process is moving, building. The client isn't just frustrated from the outset, they have to *get* frustrated. That tells us that there is resistance to a course of action, otherwise that thought would rampage through to its conclusion; a behaviour.

When I'm thirsty and I imagine a nice cool drink, nothing but my own lethargy stops me from getting a drink. But when that course of action is something that I might reasonably want to avoid, such as completing my tax return, it can take a much longer time for the thought to become action.

When does that thought crystallise into action? When it reaches the threshold indicated by 'so'.

The final piece of the puzzle is 'afraid'. Another kinaesthetic word, it tells us that the barrier to action is a feeling; fear. But fear of what? In the first example, the 'of what' or 'of whom' was hidden by a nominalisation. Here it's hidden by a simple deletion; the client simply stops speaking rather than complete the sentence and speak the unspeakable. The original statement is grammatically incorrect, and the missing grammar tells us that there is a missing half of the statement; thought, but not spoken.

But how would the parent know that the subject of their fear is a viable course of action for controlling a child's behaviour? And how would they know that it's frightening? Because they have experienced it themselves.

Therefore, we have the final piece of the puzzle. Remember that I said that frustration is a result, an outcome. It isn't actually the client's primary emotion; that being *anger*.

Let's put it all together. Parent experiences loss of control, seeks to regain control through violence, feels the fear that he felt as a child and puts a stop to the thought process. The cycle continues, and reinforces itself every time. The client has probably learned some coping strategies for dissipating the feeling of frustration, which may include walking away to take a deep breath, passing the child to its mother to deal with, going off to play golf or even drinking to numb the anger and pain.

It's a sad predicament. The client simply needs a little help coming up with some more effective ways of gaining cooperation from his child. But while he's stuck in this anger/fear cycle, that is very unlikely to happen. In his mind, he has tried everything. In fact, he has tried 'everything' to deal with his frustration, believing that his child's resistance to control is immutable.

The parent would never, ever verbalise his darkest fears because what parent would ever admit to harbouring thoughts of harming their child? This desire to obscure the unthinkable is revealed in the silent second half of the statement.

"I get so frustrated that I'm afraid that... I might hit my child so much that I hurt him, or worse, but it's the only way that I can get him to listen to me."

If you are a parent, you will absolutely understand this heartbreaking contradiction; that the person you love most in the world is, at the same time, the most difficult person to learn to deal with.

Introducing effective parenting strategies is a job for a specialist. What I have illustrated here is how the parent's thought patterns create a prison which can only ever spiral inwards until, one day, the client can contain their frustration no longer. By revealing the cycle, they can question some of the fundamental preconceptions that it is based upon, such as:

- I am in control of other people
- My child is challenging my authority
- My child won't listen to me
- My child will starve if he doesn't eat this meal
- My child will never stop crying
- I will turn out like my father before me

When we question our preconceptions, we open our minds for growth.

"I would like to be better at time management"

Again, there are three important elements in this statement, 'would like', 'better' and 'management'.

'would like' presupposes a following 'but...'. The statement sounds like a grammatically complete sentence, but it isn't; it's a sentence fragment.

'better' is a *comparative deletion*, where the object of the comparison is missing

'management' is another nominalisation, and in any case, you can't manage time, you can only manage what you *do* in the time you have available.

The client is comparing their productivity to something, someone or sometime else. They feel that they *should* be more productive, but they're not. The 'but' is the barrier in this statement, creating the loop which is expressed as the nominalisation.

You might respond to this statement in a number of ways:

- "Who or what is more productive than you, or when were you more productive?"
- "What do you want to do with your time?"
- "But.... what? You can't be bothered? You don't want to set yourself up to be given more work?"

The comparative deletion possibly implies an exclusion, such as, "I would like to as productive as Fred, but I'm not Fred so I can't be", although we can't guess at this until we've recovered the object of the comparison.

The Meta Model

The Meta Model deals with Deletions, Distortions and Generalisations, as follows:

Deletions

Something has been removed and must be recovered.

Distortions

Something has been changed and must be changed back to its original form.

Generalisations

Something has been simplified and must be specified. Some generalisations also generalise time, so that a single event becomes projected into the future.

Unspecified Nouns

An unspecified noun deletes either the subject or the object of a verb, forcing the listener to insert their own expectation. The noun might be missing altogether, or it might be replaced with a word like "it" or "thing".

Unspecified Verbs

Either the verb is deleted or its adverb is unspecified, putting the speaker's focus on the end result rather than the way in which it was achieved.

Nominalisation

A nominalisation is a verb that has been turned into a noun, indicating a "stopped" mental process. The object of the verb is also hidden.

Lost Referential Index

This deletion misses out the person or thing that the statement is attributed to, so we cannot test the validity of the statement.

Distorted Referential Index

A common distortion is to say "you" when I mean "I", which implies a dissociation where the speaker sees themselves as if they are looking at a film or in a mirror. The speaker's sense of self becomes detached from the visual representation of themselves.

Simple Deletion

A simple deletion is also known as a "sentence fragment", which may or may not be grammatically correct.

Comparative Deletions

A hidden comparison is implied by words such as 'better' or 'faster'. The deletion hides both the reference point and the criteria for making the comparison.

Complex Equivalence

The speaker takes two unrelated concepts and holds them as equivalent and therefore both true at the same time.

Lost Performative

A performative verb is a statement which is itself an action, such as "I'm telling you to tidy your room". The action in the statement is the telling, not the tidying. A child's response might be, "I'm doing it now", when it would be more accurate to say, "I'm telling you that I'm doing it now". The response is a distortion because the child isn't doing it now, they're only saying so because what they really mean is, "I know you've told me to do it, and I'll do it later", with 'later' meaning 'never'.

Selectional Restriction Violation

The class that something belongs to defines the qualities that it may have; a room may be cold but not sad. A person may be sad but not blue. We might resolve these incongruences by transferring the qualities to ourselves.

Mind Reading

With a mind read, we act as if we know what someone else is thinking or more likely project our own thoughts and attribute them to someone else.

Cause and Effect

The cause and effect implies a relationship in time, so that when one event takes place, a second event will automatically follow.

Presuppositions

Presuppositions are the implied 'facts' which must be held true in order for the sentence to be grammatically correct.

Universal Quantifiers

A type of generalisation, the universal quantifier takes a single example and makes it apply to all cases or at all times, e.g. always, everyone, all, never, nowhere, nothing.

Modal Operator of Necessity

Modal operators modify the verb and are often an indication that the speaker is basing their behaviour on rules, e.g. must, need, should, ought.

Model Operator of Possibility

This modal operator implies choice and options e.g. can, might, may, could.

9 Beyond Simple Strategies

Imagine for a moment that you are a computer. What is it that defines you as a computer? Is it some physical hardware? A computer with no software would then be the same as one with software, so there must be an element of function or purpose contained within the definition.

What is a computer designed to do?

We might say "Browse the Internet and write letters" or we might say "extend the capabilities of a human being"

One does not preclude the other - they are both true, at different levels of detail.

We could imagine a hierarchy of functions, of purpose:

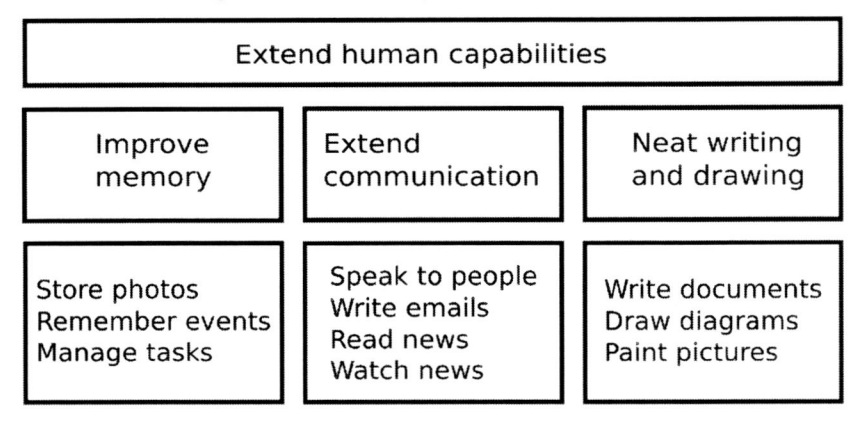

Extend human capabilities		
Improve memory	Extend communication	Neat writing and drawing
Store photos Remember events Manage tasks	Speak to people Write emails Read news Watch news	Write documents Draw diagrams Paint pictures

Now consider that each of the functions in the bottom row is performed by a software program, and each program has millions of instructions or rules for what to do when the user moves the mouse, presses a key etc.

Each of those basic rules is analogous to a strategy.

A typical computer has 1,000,000,000 connections or transistors.

A typical human brain has 1,000,000,000,000,000 connections or synapses.

This means that a million computers would be required to provide the same connective power as a single human brain. And those million computers would have all have to be connected to each other.

The challenge for us is to understand what makes a role model by mapping out these simple strategies, and so we need to understand how they all fit together into a hierarchy of perception, behaviour, beliefs and a sense of identity and self awareness.

A strategy must serve a function otherwise it would not have been created. That function, or purpose, or outcome, may be outdated, nevertheless it still defines the strategy. The context or environment within which that strategy was learned is also necessary in order for that strategy to fulfil its function.

Changing Context

A belief, behaviour or strategy creates a reality around it, and that reality has a whole set of dependencies which have to be maintained in order for the belief to be true.

The effectiveness of a strategy within a context, such as the avoidance of flying within the context of not needing to fly, creates a unique relationship between the strategy, the outcome and the context.

For example:

> I'm afraid of flying. I don't go on holiday anywhere that requires flying, so it isn't a problem. Today, I received an invitation to my best friend's wedding, in Spain. It's really impractical to get there any other way than by flying.
> I want to go but I'm afraid of flying.
> I'm so afraid of flying that I have never been on an aeroplane.
> What can I do?

Do you see what is happening here? The person is behaving as if their model of reality IS reality. Because I think flying is scary I don't fly, in fact I have never flown. It's like a person who says they don't like prawns, having never eaten one. I don't like lobster. I never ate it until I tried it on holiday. I was glad I tried it, but I probably won't have it again. This is very different to 'I never eat lobster'.

When we generalise, we don't just generalise within a category e.g. all sales people are the same, we also generalise through time. All sales people are the same because they always have been and always will be.

Because I imagined flying being dangerous in the past, I choose not to fly now, and now has no end point and therefore represents the future.

The person has equated a thought about flying with the experience of flying itself, generalising their inner model outwards onto the world.

Another way to think about generalising through time is that it is always now, therefore past, present and future are all happening at the same time, so we can create causal connections between events that are in reality unrelated, hence our reliance on lucky charms and rituals.

When the context around a belief changes, it can break these connections and the generalisations collapse.

Coaches and counsellors often say:

There is a positive intention motivating every behaviour and a context in which it has value

Perhaps if we think in terms of strategies, we could rephrase that belief as:

There is an outcome directing every strategy and a context in which it aligns with higher outcomes

In other words, every strategy is useful in that it is directed by and leads to an outcome, when it is in an appropriate context. When that context changes, either the outcome or the strategy need to change.

Alternatively, we can change the context in order to change the strategy. This is the essence of reframing as a change approach.

In order to effect a change in a person's situation, we can change either the strategy, the outcome or the context, and various techniques exist to do this.

For example, if you don't get on with someone at work, your friends might suggest that you either try a different approach with them (change strategy), just focus on getting on with your job (change outcome) or change jobs (change context).

By the way, no-one is afraid of flying, or heights, or spiders. These things are all very safe. What people are actually afraid of is falling from the sky in a ball of burning wreckage, hitting the ground with a loud 'splat' and giant spiders crawling over their faces and eating their brains. And let's face it, you'd be crazy for *not* being afraid of such horrors. Fear of such things is normal. The unusual thing is that people are afraid, not of what is actually happening, but of what they *imagine* will happen.

Well Formed Outcomes

You're probably familiar with SMART objectives, so here's another goal setting method - Well Formed Outcomes. You would use this to align a desired result with your ability to achieve it, your underlying beliefs, the system you're operating in and the available resources.

While the four criteria may seem obvious, they were in fact created using the modelling process that we're working with in this book. If you haven't come across them in coaching books then the reason that they might seem obvious is because they are really an innate part of our natural ability to set and achieve goals. Think about the neurological 'desire map' that we talked about earlier;

Well Formed Outcomes could be said to be the way that we naturally program that map when we get what we want, but sometimes we get caught up in conflicting priorities and we forget how to do it. That's when a goal setting tool comes in handy.

My simple acronym for remembering the Well Formed Outcomes criteria is PURE:

Positive:	What you do want?
Under your control:	You don't need anybody else; achieving the goal is solely down to you
Real:	You can see, hear, feel and perhaps taste or smell the outcome
Ecological:	You don't lose anything, or gain anything undesirable, as a result of the outcome

Therefore, we can set an outcome and work through cycles of action and feedback until the result is achieved:

PURE Outcome → Take action → Result → Gather feedback → (cycle)

Here's another belief from the world of coaching which describes this cycle:

"All results and behaviours are achievements, whether they are desired outcomes for a given task/context, or not"

9.1 Set an Outcome

Set a Well Formed Outcome for something that you can achieve today.

Outcome:

Positive:

Under your control:

Real:

Ecological:

9.2 Work Back From an Outcome

Ask your partner to list 3 things they have achieved this week. Work back from the result to what the outcome must have been. Choose the 3 results as listed below.

For each of these examples, work back to determine what their outcome may have been, even if it seems contrary to what they say they wanted to achieve.

1. One result which was exactly what they wanted

2. One result which was different from what they wanted

3. One result which was not what they wanted

What can you deduce about outcomes from a person's current situation, and how is this important when you are modelling an intuitive skill?

It's Broken

All too often, you will hear people talk about things that are broken. The TV is broken, the washing machine is broken, the car has broken down and so on. Perhaps we have become so dependent on the labour saving devices that we have created that we just expect everything to work as it is supposed to, and we expect people to do what we expect them to do too.

I want you to get used to asking a new question.

Instead of asking, "What is wrong with it?", ask

"What is it doing?"

Your washing machine is doing something, even if it is not washing your clothes. By asking what is IS doing rather than what it is not doing, you can then compare what it IS doing to what it SHOULD be doing. This is very useful indeed, and is certainly more useful than complaining about the fact that it isn't working.

9.3 What Is It Supposed To Do?

Ask your partner to tell you about something that they own that is currently not working.

Ask them:

What is it doing?

Is that what it is supposed to do?

What is it supposed to do?

From this, deduce what might be preventing the item from doing what it is supposed to do, assuming that they have a clear idea of what it is supposed to be doing!

Let's apply the same principle approach to coaching.

9.4 What Is Supposed To Happen?

Ask your partner to tell you about something in their life which is not how they would like it to be.

Ask them:

What is happening?

Is that what is supposed to happen?

What is supposed to happen?

From this, deduce what might be preventing what is supposed to be happening, assuming that they have a clear idea of that!

This is the essential difference between remedial and generative change, and it is fundamental to understanding how and why coaching techniques are used, not to fix problems, but to generate choice.

Incongruence

Earlier, I mentioned sequential and simultaneous incongruence and promised to return to the subject.

Sequential incongruence is where someone gives you contradictory information in a sequence, for example saying that they're not hungry and then picking up a cake.

Simultaneous incongruence is where someone gives you contradictory information at the same time, for example saying yes while shaking their head.

Both of these cases of incongruence reveal conflicting underlying processes which find different channels through which to be expressed. I'm sure that you have dilemmas and difficult choices every day. Some of these you resolve logically, others intuitively. Often, other people are aware of these dilemmas before you are, because they notice your unconscious communication.

You:	I must get this report finished
Colleague:	Then why aren't you working on it?
You:	Erm… I need to do something else first
Colleague:	So do you need to finish it or not?
You:	Yes, of course, that's what I said
Colleague:	It looks to me like you're putting it off
You:	Well, I suppose I am in a way…
Colleague:	In a way? You're totally procrastinating!

It's far too simplistic to regard incongruence as lying; it is more useful in some situations to regard it as an attempt by your mind to express multiple conflicting intentions or messages at the same time.

"I need to go to the shops but I don't want to go out in the cold"

"I need to go to the doctor but I'm afraid of what he'll say"

"I need to call my friend but I don't really want to go out with her tonight"

Superficially, these examples of incongruence present two conflicting needs; a need to go to the shops and a need to stay warm, for example.

These needs cannot coexist, and one must eventually outweigh the other if action is to be taken. However, on closer inspection, we often find something far more interesting. Look at the three examples above; what do you notice is structurally different about the needs expressed in each pair?

I need to go to the shops	but	I don't want to go out in the cold
I need to go to the doctor	but	I'm afraid of what he'll say
I need to call my friend	but	I don't really want to go out with her tonight

↑ ↑

These needs are quite practical and physical and are expressed as 'towards' statements

These needs are 'away from' statements, relating to the avoidance of an imaginary outcome

Let's reword these a little:

I need to go to the shops	but	I imagine being cold and not liking it
I need to go to the doctor	but	I imagine what the doctor will say and I don't like it
I need to call my friend	but	I imagine going out and not liking it

If you said any of these conflicting statements to any man in the street, you'd expect him to say, "Well, you don't know that for certain, so there's only one way to find out. Stop whining and get off your backside!"

Maybe at some level, we know that our conflicts are about avoidance or laziness, so we hide them in statements that we hope sound defensible. Most people then take these statements at face value, or perhaps they hear the conflict but can't be bothered to challenge you on it. Ultimately, you already know that the only person you really fool is yourself.

One remedy is to reverse the statement at the 'but':

I want to stay in the warm	but	I need to go to the shops
I'm afraid it will be bad news	but	I need to go to the doctor
I prefer to stay in tonight	but	I need to call my friend

Now, most people, when expressing these statements would then follow them up with a natural conclusion:

I really want to stay in the warm but I need to go to the shops **so** I'll get it over with and then I can stay in the warm all night.

I'm afraid it will be bad news but I need to go to the doctor **because** then at least I'll know for sure.

I really prefer to stay in tonight but I need to call my friend **and** maybe she'd like to stay in too.

We'll explore these chaining statements in more detail when we talk about modelling belief systems. For now, notice that re-ordering the sequence of beliefs often leads to a spontaneous reorganisation of the person's perceptions and behaviour.

9.5 But...

Ask someone to come up with a conflicting belief statement that has a 'but' in the middle. For example, you might ask them to tell you about something that they've been meaning to do but haven't. They might say, "I need to decorate the spare room but I'd have to move all the furniture out".

Recover the imaginary construction from the second half of the statement:

"When you think about moving all the furniture out, what comes to mind?"

"Oh, it will take ages and it will be dusty"

Now reverse the two halves of the original statement:

"So moving the furniture will take ages and it will be dusty but you need to decorate the spare room?"

Ask the person to comment on their thoughts and feelings about this final, reversed statement.

Strategies, Programs and Simulations

If a strategy is analogous to a program in a computer, or at least to a subroutine or module in a program, then we could think of the organisation of these programs as an 'object oriented' model. Object oriented programming categories functions and then provides interfaces between those functions. Your word processing software doesn't need to know how to communicate with the printer, it only needs to know how to correctly format a document before sending it to the printing module.

We've already talked about simulations, and you probably already realise that you're carrying simulations around all the time which influence your behaviour. For example, you might be reluctant to take a risk, your mother's words echoing in your ears, "Don't push yourself, you know you'll fail..."

On the other hand, hearing these words might spur you into action. Simulations aren't good or bad, however we must always remember that they are not real. When we are not even aware of their existence, they influence our behaviour as if they are real, and that's a problem because we're then taking mental short cuts rather than weighing up the facts of a situation.

I recently worked with someone who experienced anxiety around public speaking. As she sat down opposite me, she turned her chair to her left slightly, she faced to the left, most of the time she looked to her left rather than at me, and whenever she talked about certain aspects of the problem, she made a gesture as if she was blocking out or hiding from something that was on her right. I had no idea what this meant, but the consistency of her behaviour was not accidental, so I asked what was on her right that she was avoiding. She simply turned to her right and looked. "Oh my God!", she exclaimed in genuine surprise, "It's my siblings!"

She was genuinely astonished by this realisation. Of course, her siblings weren't really there in the room with her, but the simulation of them represented her self doubt, her need for personal perfection and her need to excel in whatever she does, her need to be outstanding.

Her siblings were not really in the room with us, yet they influenced her behaviour just as if they were, and this is exactly the objective of a simulation. If you walk out of your cave at night and your behaviour is influenced by a simulation of a hungry lion waiting just outside, then the simulation serves a useful purpose – to keep you safe.

Let's then assume that the evolutionary benefit of this ability to simulate reality is to increase safety and therefore our chances of staying alive. This is a very useful thing. We want our children to simulate dangerous roads, dangerous strangers and dangerous risks. However, those simulations ultimately become a limitation in themselves. The woman's siblings posed no threat to her professional career in reality, but in her mind, she made the threat very real. As a result, she avoided high profile presentations and therefore missed out on career opportunities. Ironically, the very opportunities which gave her what she most wanted – to excel, to stand out – also represented what she most feared. However ironic this may be, it is common. In fact, I don't think I've ever met anyone who isn't motivated towards and away from something at the same time. It isn't a question of the direction of their motivation, it's a question of which motivation wins at a particular time.

The woman I mentioned also carried a simulation of her mother, someone who was simultaneously an inspiring teacher and a ruthless critic. For the woman, to be strong meant to be unpleasant, so her choice in conflict situations was to back down. Of course, when you step back and think about it logically, there's no reason why you can't be resolute *and* gentle. Some of the strongest people speak the most kindly. The simulation of the woman's mother precluded this possibility, and as soon as we explored the 'rules' of the simulation, these new possibilities were exposed and new behavioural responses opened up. No need for months of counselling or a dream quest, all that was needed was for the simulation to be updated to the latest software.

A simulation of siblings, parents, teachers, bosses, role models, mentors or heroes is not some spiritual, esoteric, new-age, airy-fairy weird thing. These simulations are not ghosts, or angels, or extra-terrestials. It is the natural result of your brain organising your experiences into a set of representations which keep you safe.

However, what was necessary to keep you safe as a child is no longer necessary now that you're all grown up.

10 Metaprograms

Metaprograms have been the subject of work by a number of people including Robert Dilts, Rodger Bailey and Shelle Rose Charvet.

You can think of metaprograms as organising patterns, e.g. if you imaging looking at the pieces of a jigsaw puzzle, you might start by sorting them into sky, trees, edges etc. At the highest level, the shape of a piece is an organising pattern, at the next level down, the colour of the piece is an organising pattern. By organising our perceptions, we can handle more information, sort it and make sense of it more easily.

Therefore, metaprograms tell us how a person organises their perceptions and therefore how that person might interpret and act upon those perceptions. Think of them as patterns of deletions, distortions and generalisations.

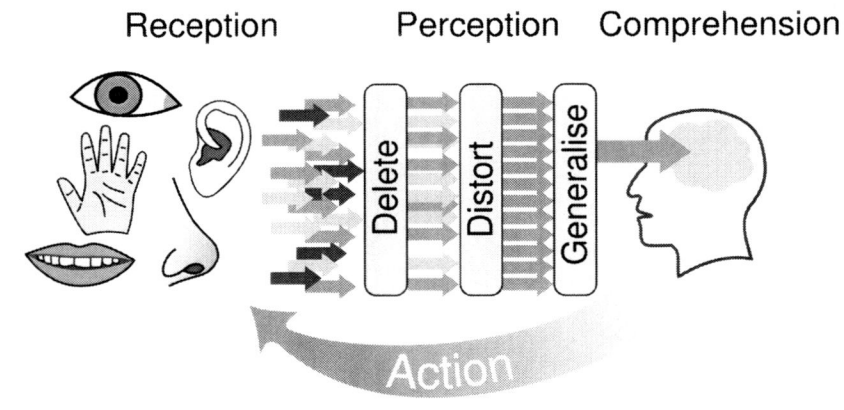

From a purely behavioural point of view, if an individual automated behaviour is known as a 'program' then a 'metaprogram' could be a program for selecting programs. For example, on your computer, Microsoft Word could be a program, Windows could be a metaprogram. If we understand the metaprograms, we can work at a higher level than the individual behaviours. In coaching, we can organise seemingly different behaviours into generalised patterns and introduce choice at a higher level, thereby increasing flexibility and the effectiveness of change.

For example, eating snacks, fidgeting, chewing pens, being irritable and becoming addicted to Nicotine patches seem like different behaviours at one level, yet at another level they are all responses to a person's attempts to give up smoking. Getting a person to stop chewing pens will only result in the driver for the behaviour generating a different outcome, such as gaining weight from eating snacks. I'm sure that you already know that, if you want to make a change in your life, you have to identify and work on what causes the behaviour that you want to change, rather than just targeting the 'symptoms'. However, at other times, the underlying reasons are not so important because it is the symptom which is itself the problem. We have yet to cure the common cold, but we collectively spend billions of Pounds each year alleviating its symptoms.

You can see the similarity between this and (Neuro) Logical Levels, in that both are hierarchical patterns of organisation. To make a change at the level of Metaprogram is analogous to making a change at the Belief or Identity level in that a reorganisation of perceptions at all lower levels takes place at the same time. If we redefine war as protecting our national security then suddenly it becomes acceptable to imprison civilians without trial. Fortunately, not everyone is taken in when politicians try to use this as a justification for human rights violations. Having said that, the author Walter Pitkin proposes that 80% of the population are stupid, although the 20% of us who aren't greatly underestimate the threat posed by the stupid majority.

You may have heard of the phrase 'secondary gain', meaning a beneficial side effect to an undesired behaviour. For example, relaxing is a secondary gain of smoking, as is lung cancer.

I would like you to consider this: secondary gain does not exist. It is an idea created by therapists or coaches to explain why someone does something that is 'bad' for them. Smoking, in itself, is not a bad thing. It leads to some undesirable consequences in the long term, whilst in the short term it has some highly desirable consequences. These short term consequences are a primary gain - they are the primary driver for the behaviour. When the person tries to give up smoking, that driver does not go away. The person does not cease to need to look cool or to be able to relax just because they are now thinking of how to avoid the long term undesirable consequences of their behaviour.

The behavioural view of metaprograms is most apparent in the 'LAB profile' (Language And Behaviour) which proposes to predict behaviour based on a person's language structures.

Metaprograms and Modelling

You may choose to model a person's metaprograms in their language as part of your approach to generalising their behaviour. For example, you may discover that a particular corporate culture favours sales people with a particular set of behavioural traits which can be represented as metaprograms.

One way of thinking about metaprograms is to regard them as patterns which organise perceptions, making someone more likely to perceive the outside world in a certain way and therefore respond accordingly. Another way of thinking about metaprograms is to regard them as strategies for selecting strategies. Faced with a need to respond, someone will select an appropriate strategy based on an overall metaprogram or meta-strategy.

The buyers in the retailer had this metaprogram profile:

Procedures	Procedures and reports determine activity
Towards	Goal oriented, works toward a result
People	Focuses on relationships over tasks
Individual	Prefers to take responsibility and make decisions without relying on a team
Internal	Self guided, makes decisions against own internal references
Active	Will not sit and wait to be told what to do

The store managers' profile was slightly different:

Procedures	Creates procedures where non exist to increase the autonomy of store staff
Towards	Goal and result oriented
People	Achieves tasks through relationships
Team	Regards store management as a team effort, but does not lose self in the team, maintains individual responsibilities
External	Feedback and information driven, sees results in staff and store performance
Active	Takes action early, especially to turn interruptions into tasks which can be systemised and delegated

10.1 Understanding Profiles

As you read through those two profiles, imagine yourself in those two roles.

A buyer meets suppliers, chooses new products, solves supply problems, negotiates discounts and arranges the layout of the store to optimise sales.

A store manager maintains the efficient operating of the store, managing staff and targets such as revenue and waste.

Imagine yourself in the daily activities of these people, making decision based on the relevant metaprogram elements. For example, in a conflict situation, how would an Internal reference differ from an External one?

What happens if you try out these two profiles on the opposite roles? How would a store manager perform with the buyer's profile, and vice versa?

And how dependent are these profiles on the organisation's culture?

Sensory Preference

Does everyone see images of memories inside their heads? Does everyone feel an emotion in the same way, with the same intensity? Does everyone hear a voice inside their head, reading out loud, giving instructions and feedback?

As you might expect, everyone is different. Not only that, but everyone uses all of their senses to differing degrees.

You might think that it's impossible to know if someone is seeing a picture or hearing a voice inside their head but it's actually the easiest of all of the metaprograms to determine.

Listen carefully to what someone says - there will be words in their sentences which aren't part of the content which are called predicates. These predicates are biased toward the person's sensory preference.

For example, if we're talking about having a conversation with someone:

We saw eye to eye	Visual
We clicked	Kinaesthetic
We spoke the same language	Auditory

In order to make sense of information, visual people will construct imagines in their heads, auditory people will check sounds and voice tone and kinaesthetic people will check their feelings to make sure an idea 'feels right'.

We tend to put the two auditory senses together for convenience. The difference is that Auditory Tonal relates to sounds and Auditory Digital relates specifically to language.

In reality, this metaprogram is far less important than many people imply, and it certainly doesn't indicate a person's learning style. It is simply the source of information that the person attaches the highest priority to, but of course all other sources are evaluated too.

Here are some more examples of words to watch and listen out for:

See	Vision	Sharp
Picture	Outlook	Background
Look	Bright	Shine
Watch	Clear	Reflect
Magnify	Near	Far
Perspective	Focus	Eye catching
Notice	Dark	
		Distant

Listen	Quiet	Whistle
Hear	Amplify	Whine
Sound	Tell	Roar
Noise	Resonate	Silent
Replay	Whisper	Rattle
Loud	Hum	Tone
Click	Harsh	Clear

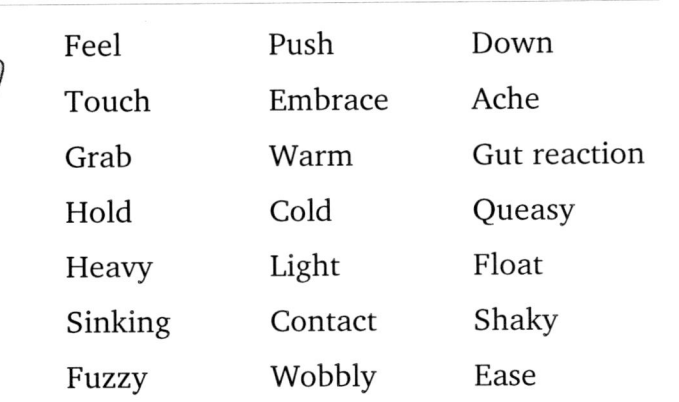

	Feel	Push	Down
	Touch	Embrace	Ache
	Grab	Warm	Gut reaction
	Hold	Cold	Queasy
	Heavy	Light	Float
	Sinking	Contact	Shaky
	Fuzzy	Wobbly	Ease

In some circles, the senses are called **representational systems** because that's what they do - they represent the outside world like a projector in a cinema represents an external reality. Philosophers call this the 'Cartesian Theatre'. We can never truly know what is going on around us, we can only ever know the projections that we create within our own minds. Not all philosophers agree with this way of thinking.

Your conscious awareness includes components both from the outside world and from within your memory, and when we remember something, we use our preferred sensory system to bring the information into that awareness. What do you remember about your first car, or a childhood pet? The sensory system chosen is apparent externally in things like language and also in body posture and eye movements.

Some researchers believe that much of the environment we experience is actually made up of memories so that we can reduce the amount of information we need to process. They propose that most of what we think we see is constructed of memories and expectations, not of 'reality'.

Motivation Direction

Are you motivated by goals or by avoiding problems? Do you avoid unpleasant situations or do you know what you want and go for it? Are you good at identifying all of the potential drawbacks of a plan or do you dive in and find out about the problems later?

The direction of motivation is simply this: do you move towards desirable things or away from undesirable things?

To find our whether a person is motivated by moving towards things they want or by getting away from things they don't want, first ask:

"What do you want in (some area of their life or a decision)?"

Then ask the following question 3 times to get a majority answer (ask each question of the previous answer)

"And what is important for you in (previous response)?"

The answer may include something similar to:

Towards	Away from
To get	To avoid
To have	So I don't have to
To become	To get away from
I want	I don't want

This is useful when motivating a person to perform a task or for changing behaviour. It's pointless telling a 'towards' person that by doing something, he can avoid problems later. It's just as pointless telling an 'away from' person that by doing something she will achieve great things.

It is important to bear in mind that an 'away from' motivation is not bad or negative. Tidying the house because you don't want to see the mess feels just as good as tidying the house so that you can see it nice and tidy. The important thing to determine and remember is the direction of the motivation. Even an away from motivation will have an outcome, and if that outcome was achieved then it was well formed which means that it is positive, which means that an away from motivation still moves towards a goal.

Consider driving from London to Birmingham. At any point, do you notice how many miles it is to Birmingham or how many miles you have travelled from London?

An alternative view (i.e. my opinion) is that an 'away from' motivation, characterised by avoidance behaviour, is in fact a 'towards' motivation where there is some fear or undesirable outcome attached to the goal. We are goal directed, therefore a goal or outcome is always in our focus of attention. We may want to achieve that outcome, in which case our behaviour is congruently aligned with it, or there may be aspects of the outcome that we don't want, in which case our incongruence or avoidance manifests itself as the behaviour traditionally described for an 'away from' motivational direction.

Reference Source

Have you noticed how some people just know what it is they want whereas other people are always asking if what they're doing is OK? Some people just don't seem to take any notice of the world around them whilst others are always checking that everyone else is OK. Do you instinctively know when something is right, or do you like to keep 'to do' lists so that you can be sure that everything's finished off?

The source of motivation is: do you use your own internal judgements and benchmarks or do you use other people's?

To find out whether a person is motivated and judged by their own internal ideals and concepts or whether they need external feedback and benchmarking you can ask this question:

"How do you know that what you're doing is right?"

Internal	External
I just know	My boss tells me
	My colleagues tell me
	I tick everything off my to do list
	I have a pile of certificates

This is useful when giving reasons as to why someone should perform a task or change behaviour. If you tell an internal person that they should agree to something because everyone else in the team does, they will say "so what?". If you tell an external person that if they think something's right then that's good enough, they may get quite frustrated.

A very Internal person might not even understand the question, the thought of asking someone else's opinion being so alien to them. Internal people tend to hear instructions as comments - External people tend to hear comments as instructions.

Remember again that this is context specific. When a wife wonders how the bedroom would look with new wallpaper and comes home from work to find her husband redecorating, they may have demonstrated an internal/external relationship which can be reversed in other situations.

A coaching client was recently telling me about how he knows when he does a good job - a question that his manager had asked him. I asked him what they answer was and he said "It's just a feeling of satisfaction", a clearly Internal answer. He then went on to say that the feeling comes from feedback from other people, from seeing the results of what he has achieved. - a clearly External source.

The source of new information always has to come from outside, and a feeling is always generated inside. The decision to act on that information, though, can be biased either internally or externally.

A coaching client recently told us that he knows he is doing a good job when he gets a satisfied feeling..... which he gets when he sees his financial data balancing.

It sounds like his reference criteria is internal, but what you're actually hearing is the end point of his strategy. The start point, as he goes on to say, is external.

Choice

Some people never seem to do things the same way twice. Others seem unable to innovate or create and will continue to do something the same way until external events force them to change. Options thinkers are good at being creative and thinking up new ideas and ways to do things. Procedures thinkers are good at finishing things and following routines. You wouldn't want procedures people in creative jobs and you wouldn't want options people in jobs that were heavily regulated. To find out if a person likes to have many options available at each decision point or if that person needs to follow a set procedure, ask:

"Why did you choose this job/car/house/etc."

Options	Procedures
Modal operators of possibility	Modal operators of necessity
Answers **why**, very quickly with well defined reasons like mental bullet points	Answers **how** the choice came to be
	Tells a story

Useful in understanding how a person will react to rules and work structures. Useful in predicting how a person will react to obstacles. Determines how a person will set objectives and what path will be taken to reach those objectives. An options person would need to always have choices and would be frustrated by set procedures and agenda. A procedures person would find choice and indecision frustrating and would seek out procedures and rules.

Generating possibilities can also be a way of avoiding taking action, relating to an 'away from' motivation direction. A procedural bias can indicate a high degree of motivation or commitment to achieving a goal - the same single minded commitment that can lead to either success in the face of obstacles or complete failure when the person fails to take a changing environment into account.

If you watch TV programs such as Dragons' Den, you will see entrepreneurs presenting their business ideas. Sometimes, an entrepreneur has persevered with their idea despite many setbacks and obstacles, and sometimes, those ideas are innovative and worthy of investment. Other times, the idea is just plain daft and the entrepreneur is told to give it up and do something more useful. When people have invested years of their lives into their ideas, it seems unfair, yet this can be a consequence of their unrelenting drive; procedures, internal, towards oriented.

Sorting and Comparison

This simply relates to whether people first notice the differences or similarities between two different concepts or situations. If you're good at 'spot the difference' puzzles, you have a difference bias. If you're good at making connections, metaphors and analogies, that indicates a similarity bias.

Remember that you have the ability to notice both, it's simply where your attention naturally focuses first, and it's important to us because it enables us to make connections to past and future events that ease the change process.

"What is the relationship between this job and your last job/car/house/etc?"

Difference (Mismatch)	Similarity (Match)	Similarity with exceptions
Different to	Same as	Same as… except for
Compared to	Compared with	
One was…	They were both…	They were both… except…

This is useful in learning and decision making, e.g. a differences person would base a choice on the differences between options.

In order to make a comparison, you have to have at least one internal reference. Even comparing two things 'side by side' means that you have to have a comparison criteria, which involves deletions, distortions and generalisations, as well as an internal reference.

Let's say you're buying apples. You hold two up and work out which one is most ripe. You have a criteria, let's say colour, which lets you know that an apple is ripe. This means that you already know the 'right' colour, and you compare the apples in your hand to that. If you compare the two apples to see which is closest to your desired colour, you have to remember one while you look at the other.

Therefore, you might consider this metaprogram to be about the comparison criteria rather than the method of comparison itself. Noticing similarities is primarily a process of generalisation because in order to group items or experiences, they must be generalised into categories. In order to generalise, you first have to delete what is not relevant and then distort the remainder so that it fits into a higher category.

Sorting for similarities is about matching, and sorting for differences is about mismatching. Either process requires an internal reference point and a set of criteria.

Scope Level

Do you like to see the big picture, or is the devil in the detail? Can you easily work out complex relationships or do you like things to be presented bit by bit?

Do you talk about overviews, missing out all of the detail, or do you assemble the picture starting from the detail and working up?

'General' people will start at the top and work down. They'll give you short, generalised answers and when giving directions will start at the destination and fill in major landmarks. 'General' people are better at identifying the relationships between points of information.

'Specific' people start at the first point of detail and work forwards, so in a complex situation they can get lost. 'Specific' people are good for making sure the details of a plan don't get lost in the overview.

As you can see, the scope metaprogram is about generalisation, and the extent to which someone generalises their experiences. You know what a key looks like, even if you haven't seen every key in the world. You know what a door looks like, and you know how to use one, even if you haven't seen a specific door before. When you first used a hotel room key that looked like a credit card, you had to redefine your category of what keys looked like.

If a person thinks at a low level of detail than this tells you that they have more categories into which to sort their experiences, which means that they are deleting more and distorting and generalising less.

If a person thinks at a high level of detail then this tells you that they are working with fewer categories, which means that they are mostly distorting in order to generalise their experiences.

At a high level of detail i.e. with more generalisations, a person would see these items as 'all keys':

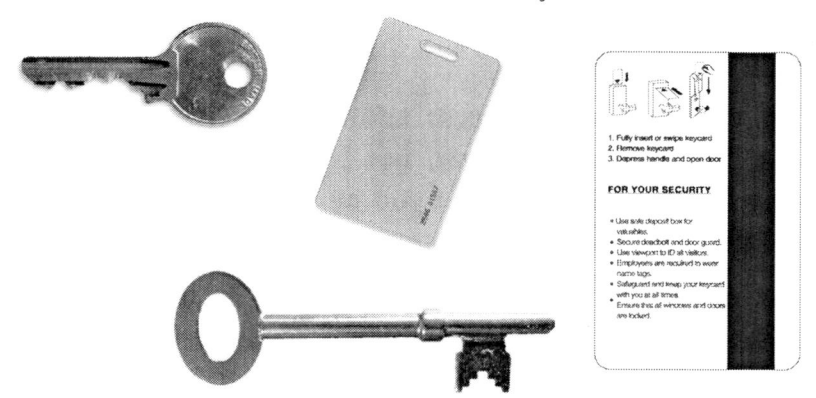

whereas a person operating at a low level of detail would see them as being different.

However, this doesn't tell you anything about the person, only about their current frame of reference. Adding an item which sits outside of that frame will lead to a reorganisation of the available data:

If you imagine what 'key' means to you, you may picture something that is similar to one of the keys above, or it may be different to all of them, yet you can still recognise those items as keys. Someone operating at a low level of detail might not classify the above objects as keys because they were different to their internal model. However, the broader we make our definition of 'key', the broader the category has to become for someone to even regard something as a key. They become more 'open minded', simply because we have used a wider set of examples for them to draw upon.

You will hear this process taking place when someone says, "Well, it's *like* a key, but it's not really a key, it's more like a credit card, but you put it in a slot in the door and the door unlocks, so I suppose it's a key really".

The difference seems subtle, but it is an important indicator that the person is creating separate categories for the different keys rather than distorting them and placing them in the same category.

When you hear phrases such as, "They're the same thing", you're hearing the process of distortion in order to generalise. Here's a typical office conversation:

"Anyone want anything from the shop?"

"Could you get me an egg sandwich please?"

Later…

"This is ham and egg salad!"

"Yeah, same thing, isn't it? It's got egg in. Just take the ham out if you don't like it."

"But I'm a vegetarian…"

A student on a training course recently told me about an incident in a bank, many decades ago. The office junior was sent out to fetch morning snacks for everyone and asked the chief clerk what he wanted.

"Get me some (specific brand) tobacco, and if they don't have that, get me anything."

The office junior returned with a pork pie.

10.1 Metaprogram Profiling

Interview some colleagues and pick out their metaprogram preferences for a particular context, remembering that if you change context, the profile may change.

Remember that these are preferences, not traits, so these aren't an either/or categorisation but a spectrum of possibilities within a given situation.

Name:		Context:	
Sensory preference	V	A	K
Motivation	Towards		Away from
Reference	Internal		External
Choice	Options		Procedures
Sorting	Same	Except	Difference
Scope	General		Specific

Name:		Context:	
Sensory preference	V	A	K
Motivation	Towards		Away from
Reference	Internal		External
Choice	Options		Procedures
Sorting	Same	Except	Difference
Scope	General		Specific

Name:		Context:	
Sensory preference	V	A	K
Motivation	Towards		Away from
Reference	Internal		External
Choice	Options		Procedures
Sorting	Same	Except	Difference
Scope	General		Specific

Name:		Context:	
Sensory preference	V	A	K
Motivation	Towards		Away from
Reference	Internal		External
Choice	Options		Procedures
Sorting	Same	Except	Difference
Scope	General		Specific

Name:		Context:	
Sensory preference	V	A	K
Motivation	Towards		Away from
Reference	Internal		External
Choice	Options		Procedures
Sorting	Same	Except	Difference
Scope	General		Specific

Metaprograms

Metaprograms - an Alternative View

Having explored Metaprograms, I would now like to present you with a new controversial, opinion on the subject.

There is only one metaprogram. All of the others can be explained within the context of a single principle of operation.

Your attention can be outwardly focused, on real time outside events, or it can be inwardly focused, on internal memories and simulations. All of the metaprograms can be described as aspects or consequences of this shift in focus.

Real time events are always outside, always unknown, full of possibilities and uncertainty. We aim to control the unpredictable world through our fears, rituals, dreams, self help training programs, rules, laws, gurus, religions, horoscopes, lucky charms, incantations and corporate visualisation workshops.

Unfortunately, despite the best efforts of the people selling you these predictions, the outside world still doesn't quite behave as you would like it to. Specifically, the people in the outside world don't behave how you would like them to.

Therefore, options and choices always lie in the outside, external, real time world. Whether to go this way or that way, climb this tree or cross that river, eat this fruit or that vegetable, the ability to analyse choices conferred significant evolutionary advantages. We could assess a number of options and incorporate multiple criteria into decisions. I know there's food by the watering hole, but there was a lion there yesterday so I think I'll head to the woods instead.

The internal world is one of certainty. I can distinctly remember the feeling of running away from the lion, and I know exactly how to do that again, should the need arise. Procedures are fixed, certain, sequences, memories, internal and in the past.

Towards and away from are about comparisons, and in order to make a comparison, only one of the criteria can be external. Compare this character ♀ with this character ♂. You can't focus on both at the same time, so you hold one in memory whilst you look at the other. Therefore, comparisons are always internal and therefore in the past. Towards and away from are behavioural responses to the result of that comparison.

Equally, sorting by similarity or difference is a result of a comparison. Whether you notice the similarity or the difference first depends on the category that you put the first item in, and the comparison is made to either an internal or external reference. This apple is the same as one I ate yesterday, or it is different. If its appearance is close enough to group with the memory of yesterday's apple then I have noticed the similarity. If it is different enough then it might be rotten, or it might not be an apple at all - another evolutionary advantage. We learn which characteristics are worth comparing, and if you go to the supermarket and watch people buying fruit and vegetables, you will see these comparisons and criteria in action.

As babies, we become accustomed to either having our needs met by a carer, in which case we feel safe relying on someone else, or we become accustomed to not having our needs met, in which case we feel safe when we rely on ourselves. Parents have a tough job; they mostly want to meet their child's needs, but they also have to ensure the child becomes self sufficient. This is a difficult balance to get right, and perhaps there is no 'right', only some kind of developmental outcome that allows the child to become a socially functional adult.

Look through the Metaprograms and ask yourself how each one can be described as an aspect of an internal or external focus of attention. Finally, consider how this fits into a perceptual process of deleting, distorting and generalising.

It's also important to understand that, in terms of our frame of reference for 'reality', an internal or external reference will affect how we evaluate new information. More importantly, these perceptual frameworks are created within the first few weeks of life, and are the foundation that all of our perceptions are based on. Whilst these foundations don't change, we do learn to adapt in order to function effectively in the world. The extent to which people adapt their thoughts and behaviours determines how effective they will be at meeting their needs in a complex, dynamic world.

Consider yourself and your immediate family and friends. Some of them will automatically reject advice, others will automatically accept it and question their own views. What's happening here? Is it simply arrogance?

There are two sources of information in every decision; the outside world, which represents the present moment, and the inner world of our memories and imaginations, which represents the past and future. We use both to arrive at balanced decisions about a course of action, however both can be equally misleading.

If my frame of reference is internal, then my constant is what I already know, and my variable is external information, so I achieve my goals by changing external data.

If my frame of reference is external, then my constant is external information, and my variable is what I already know, so I achieve my goals by changing my experiences.

In order to change the world from its present state, something has to change. In an equation, we often have a constant which cannot change, such as the speed of light or force of gravity, and we have variables which we can change, such as mass or force, in order to achieve a goal, such as velocity. So for NASA to calculate the flight path of their probe, there were constants which they have to allow for, and variables which they can alter in order to achieve the desired result – contact with the comet.

In the same way, our automatic assumption, based on our perceptual foundations, is that either the present outer world or the past inner world are the constant, and we then adapt accordingly in order to achieve a goal. Our external appearance is then judged by other people and becomes what we know as 'personality'.

Reference	Constant	Variable	Appearance
Internal	Internal	External	Assertive
External	External	Internal	Compliant

Alternatives

You probably have a favourite psychometric instrument, and if you do, you might be wondering how it fits into this modelling approach. If you can identify a correlation between a psychometric profile and your high performers then by all means, use it to determine a predisposition to high performers. For example, if you like MBTI and you find that your best customer service staff are all 'Intuitive' then that's an easy thing to check for at the selection stage for new recruits. However, not all Intuitive people are good at customer service, so don't overlook all of the other key factors in your model.

The modelling framework that we're working through in this book is agnostic when it comes to psychometrics. As with any tool, in the right hands, psychometric instruments can be a powerful and insightful way to gain both interpersonal and intrapersonal awareness, leading to more effective working relationships and a more efficient alignment between an individual's strengths and their working environment.

However, in careless hands, psychometric tools become a box to put people in.

The important point is that you have to be very confident that there is a causal link between a personality trait and an outcome. I have personally found that beliefs and motivations are a stronger factor in determining high performance than the personality dimensions typically recognised in common psychometric instruments. However, some people would equally argue that good sales people are insecure, narcissistic and influential.

Remember the importance of context, though. Those qualities make someone a good salesperson *in a given context*. In another organisation, the highest performers will be secure, mentally resilient and compliant.

The bottom line is this; use whichever tool serves a useful purpose within your model, but don't use a tool just because it's your favourite.

I have a favourite hammer, but I've found that it's best used selectively. Otherwise, everything begins to look like a nail...

11 Modelling Systems

Success Factor Modelling

Robert Dilts is one of the best known creators of models of excellence, having modelled people such as Walt Disney and Albert Einstein and produced models of generic skills such as leadership and creativity.

Dilts' Success Factor Modelling approach requires that you find a number of people who appear to share a common skill or talent. The whole modelling process is as follows:

- Interview the individual
- Interview the people they work with or relate to
- Watch them in their normal environment to confirm the model
- Check the model against their peers to benchmark their performance
- Check the model against your own peers to check current research or thinking
- Check the model against the individual or organisation's vision - their stated future direction
- Check the model against the individual or organisation's past - their legacy or habits

From all of these separate models you can then refine a model of the specific skill that can be used by anyone to achieve the same results.

The book 'Alpha Leadership' by Dilts, Deering and Russell contains a good example of Dilts' Success Factor Modelling as applied to modern leadership skills.

Modelling Belief Systems

'Expert Systems' are software programs which emulate human decision processes, and you will find them in call centres, diagnostic systems and so on. Software engineers interview humans and develop decision trees which guide a user through a decision making process.

For example, your computer might have a troubleshooter program that pops up and gives you advice when something goes wrong. It makes a suggestion, then asks if it fixed the problem. If not, it makes another suggestion. This is a very simple example of a decision making program that contains some basic diagnostic knowledge.

Jonathan Altfeld combined this approach with strategy modelling to create what he calls 'Knowledge Engineering', which he used to run training programs in. You can still buy a home study Knowledge Engineering kit from his website at www.altfeld.com

Essentially, we need to regard beliefs as specialised rules about responses and behaviour, and if we regard rules as elements of strategies then we can regard the modelling of a set of beliefs as a more complex application of strategy modelling.

For example, knowing whether to shake someone's hand is a strategy, you also have a set of rules for it and we could call those rules a set of beliefs about greeting people. For our purposes, these terms are interchangeable.

11.1 Complex Strategies

Consider again the example of shaking hands. List as many different criteria as you can that would influence your decision to shake someone's hand:

On one hand, this may seem unnecessarily detailed. On the other hand, if we want to truly understand and replicate a skill, we have to understand exactly how it works, otherwise we risk missing something important. We risk shaking hands in a situation that isn't quite right and becoming embarrassed. That's a minor risk, perhaps, and one that we can learn from, so the model is always the starting point that we have to integrate into our own experience and build on with future experiences.

It's all very well teaching someone how to shake hands, but that skill is useless without teaching them when to shake hands.

Robert Dilts proposed a 3 part structure to beliefs:

IF > THEN > MEANS

IF someone is holding out their hand to me THEN I shake their hand which MEANS that I know how to behave in social greeting situations.

Or it could mean a number of other things, in different contexts. If someone states a belief, such as 'I am socially adept' then we could ask them how they know that, how that belief manifests in their behaviour. This enables us to work backwards from the belief to the underlying programs or strategies.

We also have beliefs that influence the operation of other beliefs, for example, I get up early, except if it's a weekend.

Remember that the usefulness of any model is contained within the purpose of the model. If we are modelling in order to replicate results then the test of the model is that it allows other people to replicate the subject's results.

We're not aiming to clone a person - only to find a way to transfer and integrate a specific skill of theirs to other people. Therefore, the level of detail that you go into is determined by the results of this process.

For example, let's say you're modelling a high performing sales person. You observe him at his desk and you notice that the first thing he does is get a pen and scribble on a pad of paper which he then leaves to one side. The behaviour seems irrelevant, so you ignore it.

If you ask him why he did that, what might he say?

How about, "I want to make sure I have a working pen and some paper to hand so if a customer calls, I am always ready to make notes".

Now, that sounds interesting. Why does he do that? What does this rule mean?

"It's all part of giving a professional image"

Another rule. What does it mean?

"Well, the first impression is the most important thing"

So by investigating a seemingly irrelevant behaviour, we learn something very valuable. If you were to then ask for other ways in which he ensures he makes the best first impression possible, you will learn more rules and strategies that you can teach to other sales people.

Once again, we can start modelling at the highest level and from that work down through a hierarchy of beliefs, rules and behaviours in order to understand how the role model's experiences, goals and behaviours fit together. From this, we can see how different behaviours in different contexts are linked, and are examples of the same overall approach.

We can now regard Behaviour, Capability and Beliefs as levels within the overall hierarchy of rules, beliefs, behaviours and strategies.

```
System      Society
Identity    Values
Beliefs     Rules
Capability  Outcome
Behaviour   Strategy
Environment Context
```

How we distinguish between one and another is simply a matter of current focus, i.e. Behaviour is what the person is doing now, and that current focus is an example of a current Capability and Belief which we can use to elicit other behaviours.

With our scribbling sales person, we can ask for other examples of how they ensure they make a good first impression, using an observed behaviour to deduce a set of higher level beliefs which in turn enable us to discover other behaviours which we may not have observed directly.

Because ←

I have said many times that "Why?" is not a useful question in coaching because it elicits reasons rather than causes. In other words, when you ask why someone did something, what you get is an answer to the question, but it will probably not tell you anything about the actual causes and criteria at the time of whatever it is they did.

In modelling, the question "Why?" will, as usual, elicit an answer beginning with "Because…"

Where this is not generally useful in coaching or change work, because the reason embeds and reinforces the behaviour that we want to change, it is useful in modelling because it enables us to work backwards to the rules that determine the behaviour.

"Because" tells you that you are hearing the end of a sequence, a strategy, and what you hear after the word 'because' is the rule or belief. This doesn't give us the cause, but it does give us their reasoning, which is exactly what we want because it is their unique mindset that we are modelling.

So That →

Phrases such as 'so that', 'and then', 'which leads to' etc. tell you that you have just heard the rule or belief and what you are about to hear is the consequence or result of it. "So" oftens gets moved around in grammar, but its meaning stays the same. "It was raining so hard that…" is equivalent to "It was raining hard so that…" in that speaker is telling us two crucial pieces of information; firstly that something happened next, and secondly that there was a triggering event or threshold. "It was raining so hard that I stayed at the office for a while longer". This tells us that the speaker made a decision, and a decision is based on a rule, and that rule is based on a threshold about what to do when it's raining. If you listen carefully, you'll hear thresholds all around you:

"I miss you so much (that I could cry)"

"The system is so overloaded that it's going to fail"

"The book was so good that I couldn't put it down"

But/Except ↗

But and except tell us negative exceptions to the strategy. "I always... except if", "I usually... but when".

When a rule reaches an exception, the person doesn't stop in their tracks, they branch to another rule, for example:

"I start work on the report but then the phone rings so I answer it..."

So you can hear a 'but' as an interruption to a strategy and another strategy beginning. The interrupted strategy may well resume at a later time.

Some people say that the word 'but' negates what came before it, for example, "I want to go to the party but I'm so tired". This is not at all true. While it is logically correct to say, "I want to go to the party *and* I'm so tired", it's really not what people naturally say, because the thought process which creates the language structure is an exception, not an addition. The word 'but' indicates that a higher level rule (tired) is operating, and the lower level rule (party) is then obstructed.

Which Means ↑

Rules exist in a hierarchy, and a chain of decisions will often branch into a series of lower level decisions, just like a computer program branches into a 'subroutine' which can easily be repeated for common tasks.

When a speaker signals a shift to a higher level of belief or rule, you'll hear phrases such as "which means" and "so, obviously".

"Which means" tells you that a number of rules have been grouped together into a common process. Normally, the speaker doesn't voice this summary statement, unless we specifically ask them to.

"The door was open, and his coat wasn't on his chair, and his computer was on(which meant that it was OK for me to go and check his emails)."

"It was raining, and I had a lot of paperwork to carry, and I really had to be there on time (so obviously I had to take a taxi)."

This could either be a rule for taking a taxi versus public transport, or it could be a rule for justifying an expense claim. Either way, the speaker stacks a number of more specific rules inside another more general one.

Coaching with Beliefs

Being able to navigate through a belief system is very useful when coaching. When you want to explore the mental processes that underpin a person's behaviour, you can control the conversation using the very words that they would use to signal branches in a decision process.

When I say that you can control the conversation, I don't mean that you are leading the person to a particular conclusion, because that would not be coaching. Think of yourself as an investigator, searching through surveillance videos to find a series of key events. You need to be able to pause, move forwards and backwards and take snapshots that you can assemble into a simplified sequence. The content is the same, the events are the same. Your ability to control the conversation simply gets to that result more effectively than just letting the client talk freely and hoping that you can pick up some clues here and there.

Here's an example of how you can use this method of to determine an underlying belief structure. The reason for doing this is simple; when a pattern of behaviour repeats itself over the course of a person's lifetime, what they experience is the same underlying process playing out in different situations; relationships, career changes and so on. The scenery and the actors are different each time, but the story remains the same. In Transactional Analysis, these underlying structures are called 'scripts', which are analysed at length in order to understand their role in a person's life and present opportunities to make better informed choices. An alternative view is that the underlying structure of behaviour can be changed without analysis of the events that created that structure. I'm not saying that either of these approaches is right, I'm merely comparing them for your viewing pleasure.

In this example, the client repeats a pattern of behaviour where they enter a new relationship or job with great enthusiasm, only to later discover that they are not valued or respected, which leads them to move on to 'greener pastures'.

"I'm so unhappy about being undervalued at work."

"So unhappy that?"

"That I'm thinking of leaving."

"But?"

"But I'm worried that this is a phase I often go through."

"So?"

"So I'm starting to wonder if it's something about me, the way I'm seeing things."

"Because?"

"Because when I look at my CV, I feel that I've moved jobs too often in the last few years."

"Because?"

"I start to feel like I'm being taken for granted, that they don't value me any more."

"Because?"

"I find that people start to change their attitude towards me, stop making an effort, try to take advantage of me or they're just inconsiderate."

"Which means?"

"Well, I used to say that people make an effort at first, but then they get bored of me. But I'm starting to wonder if it might be at least partly down to something I'm doing."

In this conversation, do you see the way that the client's thinking moves forwards, backwards, up and down? "Because?" moves the client's thinking back to a preceding rule, so that we can start to understand the conditions that must be in place for the situation to progress to the point where the client wants to move on to a new employer or relationship. If you have studied Transactional Analysis, you'll recognise some scripts in there too.

I'm going to run through that conversation again, this time with some comments that might explain what's going on, and might certainly echo what you yourself thought as you read it the first time.

"I'm so unhappy about being undervalued at work."	"So" indicates a threshold. Instead of asking why they feel that way or what is happening, we want to find out about the threshold.
"So unhappy that?"	
"That I'm thinking of leaving."	"Thinking" means that something is stopping them, otherwise they would be leaving, not thinking about it. "Thinking" is the primary verb here, so don't be distracted by "leaving".
"But?"	
"But I'm worried that this is a phase I often go through."	"But" gives us the exception to what they would have done on previous occasions. "So?" moves them forwards along that branch of thinking.
"So?"	

"So I'm starting to wonder if it's something about me, the way I'm seeing things."

"Because?"

"Because when I look at my CV, I feel that I've moved jobs too often in the last few years."

"Because?"

"I start to feel like I'm being taken for granted, that they don't value me any more."

"Because?"

"I find that people start to change their attitude towards me, stop making an effort, try to take advantage of me or they're just inconsiderate."

"Which means?"

In the past, they wouldn't have been having this conversation because being undervalued would have been "reality" and therefore not up for discussion. "Because" moves back to a preceding step.

A feeling is the trigger for the self doubt that has led to this conversation. "Because" moves to a preceding step.

"Start to" means that something came before that feeling and triggered it, "because" moves back to find out more about that trigger.

The client is now mind reading, so we have arrived at a point in the process which must be under their control because they have chosen what to deduce from other people's actions.

| "Well, I used to say that people make an effort at first, but then they get bored of me. But I'm starting to wonder if it might be at least partly down to something I'm doing." | "Which means?" moves up and the client then begins to acknowledge a level of insight into their mind reading. Control is fundamental to change, so if the person is to change their world, they must focus on what they are in control of. |

As you can see, the primary input from the coach is to steer the client's thought process in order to explain the belief system which underpins their perception and behaviour. Some people say that beliefs are a filter through which we experience the world; whether today is a good or a bad day depends entirely on how you face the day, not on what 'really' happens to you.

For beliefs to function in this way, they cannot be arbitrary, intangible aspects of your psyche, they must be highly organised systems that have a deterministic structure. Whilst they may be complex, they are by no means unpredictable.

12 Logical Levels

You've already seen that beliefs exist in a matrix with each belief or rule acting as a decision point which branches on to other rules. A concept that can be useful here is that of 'Neurological Levels', usually abbreviated to 'Logical Levels'. While there is some contention about its history and validity, you can use the logical levels hierarchy to identify specific behaviours to model, starting at the level of role model, such as 'high performing sales person' or 'leader' and working down into specific behaviours that form part of that identity. By approaching it in this way, you ensure that the behaviours you model are aligned with each other and relevant. For example, you might model a leader's ability to communicate vision as well as their ability to response to setbacks, both of which may be examples of their beliefs about their relationship with other people.

Certainly, the concept of 'personal effectiveness' is very strongly linked with a sense of alignment between a person, a place and a task or activity. When I am doing something that I believe in, I am skilled in and I believe is appropriate for me and my current situation, it is fairly obvious that I will perform more effectively than when I'm doing something that I don't feel that I'm very good at, or isn't really my job. People in all walks of life and in all jobs find a way to excel, to "make it their own", and these are typically the people that you will be choosing as role models. The key isn't that a person is a "born leader", it is that they have found a way to align their self concept with their environment and goals. People are not born to be leaders or doctors; they have a set of life experiences which predispose them to succeeding in certain jobs because that is the way that those jobs work. But many people fail at those jobs too, because their concept of what the job is 'about' is different to what is required in practice. For example, a child who loves small cuddly animals dreams of being a vet, only to find that their love of cuddly animals makes the job very stressful and upsetting for them, because vets aren't usually paid to cuddle; they're paid to poke animals with needles and other implements. They care about the animal's well being, but not in the same way as they did as a child. The people who make that transition succeed as vets, the people who don't give up and take a different career path, saying, "I just wasn't cut out to be a vet". Even the phrase "cut out" implies that it is nature, not nurture, which determines your ideal career.

Logical Levels is a hierarchy of categories into which we can organise statements made about ourselves. "I am writing" and "I am a writer" are very different statements, even though they sound similar. If you are a parent, consider when you became one. Was it at the moment of your first child's birth, or was it before, or afterwards? The acceptance of an identity rarely comes at the same time as the behaviour which is the hallmark of that identity. When did you become a driver, or a manager, or a reader? Was it different to when you started driving, managing or leading?

| **System** | The system that you are part of, e.g. a culture, market, community or spiritual belief system |

| **Identity** | Your identity, how you label yourself, e.g. plumber, manager, father, king, straight, optimistic |

| **Beliefs** | What you know to be true, e.g. 'I am a good manager', 'I'm honest', 'You have to get what you can' |

| **Capability** | What you can do, e.g. 'I can drive', 'I know how to manage people' |

| **Behaviour** | What you are doing, e.g. 'I am reading', 'I am working' |

| **Environment** | Where you are, e.g. 'in the office', 'on a train', 'at home', 'it's warm' |

Therefore, you could say, "I'm in the car", "I'm driving", "I can drive", "I'm a good driver" or "I am a motorist". All essentially comment on the same experience, but they each tell us something different about your frame of reference, in that each level is a category within which other, lower level categories exist or are implied. You can see that, "I'm a parent" is a much broader statement than, "I'm helping my daughter with her homework", the latter being one behaviour which a parent would engage in.

Whilst Logical Levels is a hierarchy of categories, those categories don't exist 'out there' in the world and they are perhaps better understood as a function of our ability to categorise information. Can you name a type of farm animal? A cow? Now name a type of cow. A farm animal is a valid example, along with toy, pet or Friesian. Our mental dexterity means that we can create an arbitrary structure and then turn it on its head just as easily.

Robert Dilts defined a mentor as being a role model at the identity level, so if we set out to model a mentor we are essentially starting at the highest level and all that it encompasses, which is obviously very broad.

If you ask the role model to start at the Behaviour level, i.e. "what do you do?" then they will typically identify only the behaviours that they are consciously aware of, and these will often have very little to do with what differentiates them from average performers in their field.

Earlier, we looked at the relationship between a strategy, the outcome that directs it and the context that it exists within. We could map this onto the logical levels hierarchy as follows:

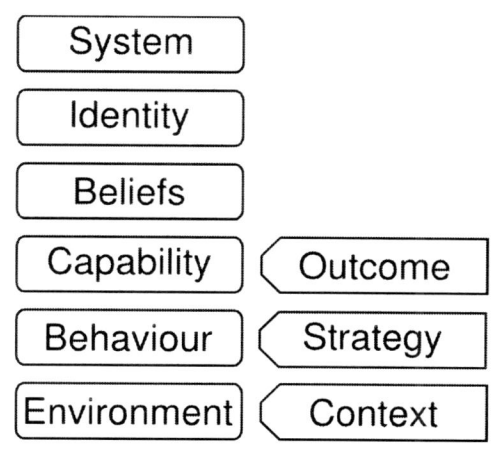

```
        System
        Identity
        Beliefs
       Capability    Outcome
       Behaviour     Strategy
      Environment    Context
```

Logical levels is useful in modelling because a role model will have different levels of awareness of what they do, and we can record those levels of awareness using the Logical Levels framework. You'll see how this works in the example modelling study towards the end of this book.

If you are interested in learning then you will no doubt have come across this theory, developed by Noel Burch of Gordon Training International in the 1970s:

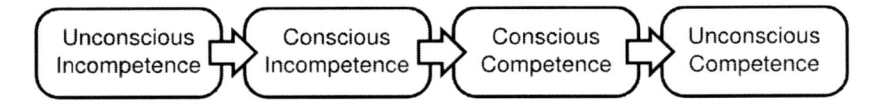

Unconscious Incompetence → Conscious Incompetence → Conscious Competence → Unconscious Competence

The idea is that when you learn a new skill, you start off not knowing that you're not very good at it. You then realise that you're not very good at it, then you learn to become good at it, but you have to think about it. Finally, you end up not having to think about it. If you can drive a car, ride a bicycle, play a musical instrument or read then you may remember how it felt to go through this process.

Whilst this theory has been disputed, as theories generally are, it is hard to deny that mastering a skill requires a stage of conscious learning where you have to think about what you're doing, followed by a realisation that you can perform the skill automatically without having to remind yourself of what to do.

We can draw some comparisons between this theory and that of Logical Levels. At the Behaviour level, someone is aware of what they are doing or not doing. At the Capability level, they are no longer thinking about the skill itself, instead their focus being on a broader set of abilities. At the Belief and Identity levels, their focus is simply on the end result that the behaviour achieves.

I think it's fair to say that learning is a fairly consistent, universal process which has been researched from many different angles, producing many different theories. Yet these theories are not mutually exclusive and are therefore facets of the same underlying principles.

As I mentioned in the section on Kolb's learning styles, the more you understand about learning from the broadest possible perspective, the more easily you will be able to replicate excellence using the modelling tools in this book.

12.1 Logical Levels Modelling

In 3s, 15 minutes each, 45 minutes total.

Use the Logical Levels hierarchy to work from a role model's Identity down to specific behaviours.

Start with some specific ability that you want to model.

Identity Who are you when you do this? How do you see yourself when you do this? What are you aiming to achieve when you do this?
Beliefs What makes a good [Identity]? What is important for a good [Identity]? What do you believe about yourself when you do this? How do you know that you're good at this?
Capabilities What skills do you have that enable you to do this? How did you learn how to do this? Do you set specific outcomes when you do this? How do you know you've achieved what you want?
Behaviours What specifically do you do? How could you teach me to do this?
Environment Where and when do you do this?

13 Neurologic

London taxi drivers were placed in a brain scanner and the blood flow in their brains was monitored while they calculated routes[7]. From this, the experimenters discovered that a part of a taxi driver's brain is more active than those of other people. The learning process that they go through - 'The Knowledge' - increases the number of connections in a part of their brain that we all have, but which for them contains details of the 25,000 streets of London plus countless landmarks, offices, bars, congestion points etc. So the scientists know which part of a taxi driver's brain is used to calculate a route, but this does not constitute knowing how they do it.

Make sure you read the article 'Mirror Neurons and the Simulation Theory of Mind Reading' by Gallese and Goldman[8]. They evaluate evidence for our ability to infer others' internal emotional states as well as the mental processes behind their behaviour. This is proposed as the basis of our unconscious modelling ability, the ability to emulate others, as you will see very young children doing naturally in order to learn to walk, talk etc.

One thing that we do know is that the human brain is an incredibly complex structure. Traditional thinking is that nervous system cells are never replaced once they die or are damaged, yet even this thinking is changing. Certainly, where brain cells themselves may not regenerate readily, the connections between them are highly adaptable.

In the past, neurologists thought that regionalised brain function meant that specific cells were responsible for

---

[7] Recalling Routes around London: Activation of the Right Hippocampus in Taxi Drivers, Maguire, Frackowiak & Frith, The Journal of Neuroscience, 15 Sept. 1997
[8] Trends in Cognitive Sciences, 1998

specific tasks and functions. Over many years, scientists mapped areas of the brain; sensory areas, motor areas, areas for emotions, language, short and long term memory and so on. Yet there are many cases where people recovered from severe head injuries, not because their brain cells regenerated but because areas of their brain changed function as connections were reorganised.

Look up the following names on the Internet to see two remarkable stories:

Phineas Gage

In 1848, a 25 year old construction foreman named Phineas Gage became famous for having a hole in his head. While working on a [industry]road project in Vermont, he experienced a severe brain injury when a metre long tamping iron was shot through his skull by a stick of dynamite. He lived to tell the tale - with a very different personality.

Dr. Lionel Feuillet

A 44 year old French man's brain had been reduced to little more than a thin sheet of actual brain tissue, due to the buildup of fluid in his skull ["He was a married father of two children, and worked as a civil servant"]. In July 2007, Fox News quoted Dr. Lionel Feuillet of Hôpital de la Timone in Marseille as saying: "The images were most unusual... the brain was virtually absent."

To return to the relevance of this to modelling, we know that there are connections between brain cells, and that these connections can cause other cells to activate or inhibit their activation. We also know that computer circuits operate in a similar way. Computer circuits, based on elements known as transistors have tended to work in a strict on/off way, whereas brain connections seem to be much more flexible, behaving in a way that we might describe as on/off/maybe. Recent developments in the application of quantum physics to computing have created potentially powerful quantum computers that have very similar logic states.

Since the number of these connections between brain cells appear to be limitless, this implies that there are limitless possibilities for rules and therefore beliefs, experiences, learning etc.

In a computer, there are essentially two types of logical connections; AND and OR. These can also be negated to NAND and NOR. We also have the concept of eXclusivity.

AND - if **all** of the inputs are active, activate the output

OR - if **any** of the inputs are active, activate the output

NAND - if **all** of the inputs are active, deactivate the output (Not AND)

NOR - if **any** of the inputs are active, activate the output (Not OR)

XOR - if **any** but **not all** of the inputs are active, activate the output (eXclusive OR)

Using these connections, we can create interconnected rules which support or inhibit other rules and in doing so create a behavioural output from a set of complex criteria.

We can draw circuit diagrams for logic circuits such as those in your computer or mobile phone. Here's a very simple one from a computer that was built over 30 years ago:

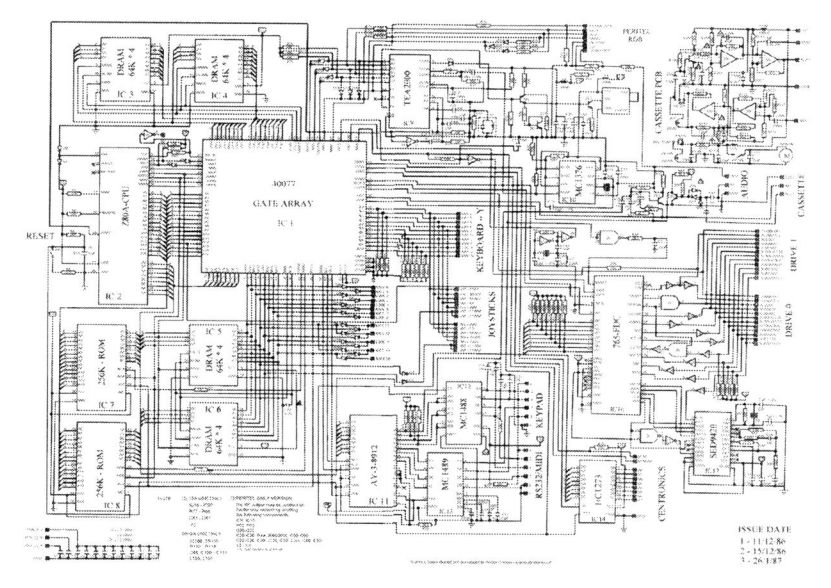

This is essentially what researchers have done recently in transferring the 'connectome' of a worm's brain into a robot's software, with the result that the robot produced the same emergent behaviours as those observed in the worm. The worm only had around 300 connections, your brain has something like one hundred billion.

But don't worry, we are not going to draw a circuit diagram for your brain. We'll start with something a little simpler.

In circuit diagrams like the one above, there are specific symbols for the different logic gates. We won't bother using those, we just need to think about the basic principle of how we can represent the connections which form the basis of a strategy, decision or behaviour.

Here's an example for telling the time, where the black dot negates the input:

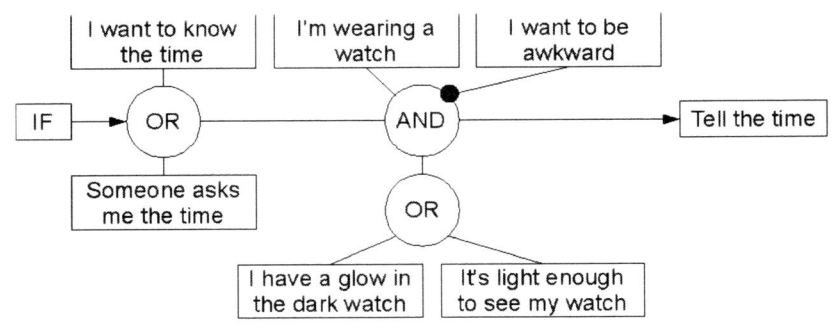

In other words, if either I want to know the time, or if someone asks me the time, and I'm wearing a watch, and I can see it, and I'm not being awkward, then I'll tell the time. Being awkward would mean that when the person asks, "Can you tell me the time?", I answer, "Yes".

Here is a different way of representing a belief system; this one is a decision strategy for having some chocolate:

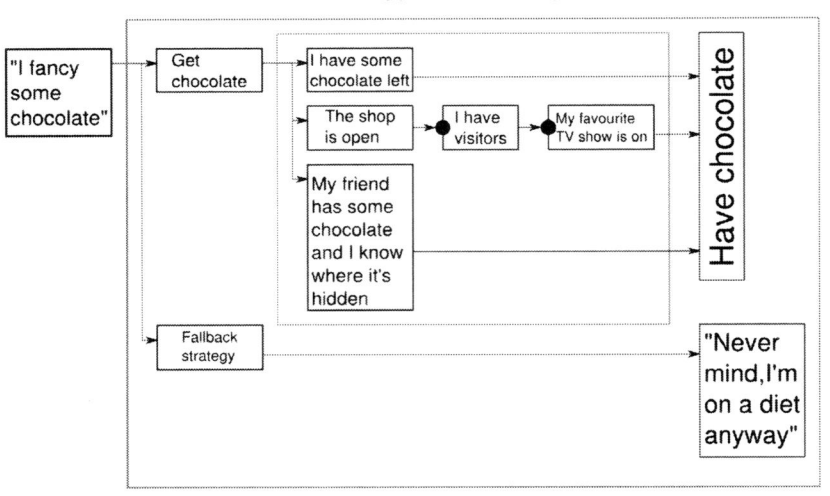

This is a decision strategy, so the entry and exit points are external. Feeling hungry, taking action to get chocolate

217   Genius at Work

and saying that you didn't want any anyway are all external to the thought process or strategy.

The final OR is an exception to the whole strategy. In computer programming, there are If... THEN statements such as IF this condition THEN do this action. The ELSE statement provides a way out for if an unforeseen IF condition exists. So in the above example, if I can't easily get some chocolate then the ELSE or 'otherwise' outcome is to justify why I didn't want or need chocolate anyway. This is a common control strategy; if you can't get what you want, maintain control by not wanting it anyway.

Overall, that makes this a strategy about getting chocolate embedded within a strategy for self gratification, which therefore implies that there is some guilt attached to having chocolate in the first place, and therefore some merit in not having it.

Incidentally, having read through this decision strategy in 'slow motion', are you now thinking that you would quite like some chocolate? Well you can't have any, I've eaten it all.

As you can see, every strategy is nested within another. This is why it is so important to be very specific about what you are modelling.

The rule of thumb is that if you reach an external step, you're no longer dealing with a strategy. A strategy is a purely mental decision process; a way of selecting one course of action from a range of possibilities.

13.2 Designing Logic 1

Using these simple logical connections, design a logic circuit that produces a cup of tea.

13.3 Designing Logic 2

Now design a logic circuit to perform the decision strategy that you modelled from someone earlier.

14 Creativity

One of the most coveted skills in business is that of 'creativity', and a great deal of academic research has been done in this area, which I won't repeat here. Instead, I want to discuss a very specific type of creativity, which I have found is what most people are really talking about in business when they say that they want people to be more creative. My experience over the past 27 years in business is that when managers say they want people to be more creative, what they really mean is that they want people to solve problems more quickly and not be constrained by obstacles or cultural limitations.

Of course, any strength, when applied to excess, can become a weakness. Coming up with exciting new ideas is fine, but sooner or later, someone needs to turn them into operational activities. Determination is a good quality until it becomes stubbornness.

It turns out that the techniques that we can use for modelling talents can also be applied to increasing creativity, particularly in the area of problem solving.

The most common obstacle to creativity is when people get stuck down a particular line of thinking, having assumed that one aspect of a situation is fixed. Creative insights come when someone turns the situation on its head and questions what had previously been held to be an immutable fact. Much research has been done in this area, producing such theories and models as 'groupthink'[9] and SCAMPER[10]. The 'Five Whys'[11] technique aims to get problem solvers to work backwards in a cause and effect chain, asking "Why?" five times. This technique works

---

9   Irving Janis
10 Bob Eberle
11 Sakichi Toyoda

very well in mechanical systems that have deterministic operating rules, but very badly in human systems where people make up the rules as they go along.

Asking "Why did the machine fail" can generate a variety of responses, from, "Because the planned maintenance was not carried out so the driveshaft seized up" to "Because you're always demanding that we work longer shifts and I've told you a thousand times that something's got to give and those idiots in finance are always stopping us from making the right investments and in any case we can either stand around here talking about it or you can let me get on with my job." The latter reason can loosely be translated as, "I didn't do the planned maintenance properly because I'm lazy".

When applying systemic problem solving tools to human systems, the results can be unreliable because human beings may not be straight with you. Defensiveness, avoidance and misdirection will plague you if you try to apply a simplistic approach. By looking at belief systems, it doesn't really matter whether someone gives you straight answers or not, as both are equally meaningful.

When you want to foster creativity or solve a complex problem, you can use the basic modelling techniques listed here to understand the system within which the creative approach is required. Any behaviour which leads to a consistent result is a skill, whether or not we like that result in a particular context or not, and you can model 'failure' as easily as 'success', and often with more interesting results. By mapping out the intuitive processes of a system, you can easily uncover the hidden assumptions that would otherwise stifle creativity.

15 Installation

And now we reach the important bit. Having created a model, how do we turn it into something useful? Perhaps a new business process or an activity on a training course?

The process of modelling has turned a complex behaviour into a strategy, a series of decisions, by abstracting a behaviour from the context within which it was modelled. You will have achieved this by comparing counter examples, external perspectives and by testing your theories. What you will end up with is a strategy which can then be taught to someone else, or 'installed', as we might say.

Let's say that you modelled someone's skill for being afraid of spiders? Why would anyone want to learn that skill? Remember that the talent is totally independent of the context or result. A talent for being afraid of spiders is actually a talent for distorting sensory data in order to produce a heightened emotional response. Imagine you're in a sales meeting, hoping that your customer will buy something from you. Would a talent for producing a heightened emotional response be useful?

Essentially, when you want to install a strategy, you need to turn it into a series of steps that a person can practice explicitly. You can also expect them to modify it so that it fits into their existing skills and experience. You also need to ensure they are clear on the outcome and purpose, and the success criteria for the strategy.

Rituals and Incantations

I recently enquired about holidays in a High Street travel agent's office, and at the end of the conversation, she asked if she could call me in a few days time to follow up. As I always do with sales calls, I said, "Yes, of course". After all, if you want to find out what the best sales people do, you have to spend time with sales people.

As promised, a couple of days later, the assistant called and asked if I had made a decision about my holiday. I said that I hadn't and she said that if I needed anything, don't hesitate to call, or something equally vague.

Just a few weeks later, exactly the same thing happened in a mobile phone shop. The sales assistant was decidedly disinterested throughout the conversation and only perked up to tell me I was wrong about a mobile phone that I used to own because he'd had three of them. Bowing to his superior knowledge, I was happy for him to call back in a few days time to see if I had made my mind up. Once again, the box on his sales sheet was ticked and I received my call. His disinterest was much the same as the experience in the shop just a few days earlier.

What's going on? Is this a coincidence?

A few years ago, I visited a car dealership to look at a particular model. The salesman told me, through the gift of non-verbal communication, that I really wasn't worth five minutes of his valuable time. Tabloid newspapers don't read themselves, you know. As I looked over the car, he seemed to be doing his best to make me feel like an unwelcome visitor, and when I handed back the keys, he summoned up all of his enthusiasm and muttered, "So, can you see yourself sitting in a new Peugubishi?"

I said, "No", and left the dealership.

Here's what happens. A company's sales trainers go out and spend time with the staff in the branches. When they see someone performing well, they watch what they do. When they think they've figured out a particular phrase or behaviour, they build it into the sales process and teach it to new sales recruits. By the time the behaviour gets to the corporate classroom, it has lost any glimmer of a talent that it once held and has been reduced to a line in a script, a letter in an acronym, a step in a sales process.

Once upon a time, there was a salesperson who made follow up calls and, as a direct result, they sold more of their product or service.

Another salesperson discovered that certain language patterns, used in hypnosis and 'corporate visioning' led the listener to imagine themselves using the product or service, and that imagined experience would create emotional engagement which would make the listener more likely to become a buyer.

Whatever the 'technique' is, there are fundamentally two reasons why these approaches work:

1. The salesperson genuinely cares about the sale
2. No-one else is doing it

If you take the behaviour and reduce it to a script that is then beaten into a classroom of sales recruits, what you will end up with is something that the sales people only do *because they have been told to*. And that is a recipe for failure.

Of course, when a company has tens of thousands of sales people, most of whom only stay in the job for a short time, it's just not cost effective to drag them all up to the corporate training centre to explain the finer points of the psychology of sales. It's much easier just to turn the high performing behaviour into an instruction which is then monitored by mystery shoppers who are given a specific list of words and actions to watch out for when posing as a real customer.

If you've passed your driving test then a familiar incantation will be "Mirror, Signal, Manoeuvre". However, your driving instructor probably also said something like, "But keep checking your mirrors", to make up for a shortfall in the incantation.

The incantation suggests this:

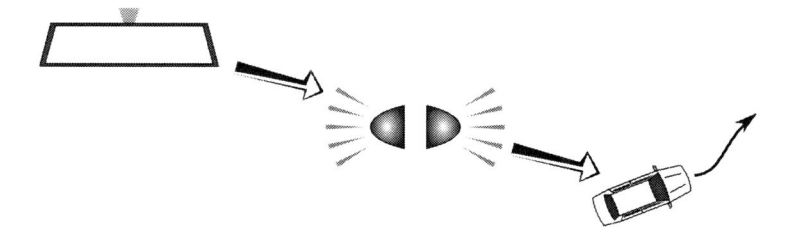

But 'real life' requires this:

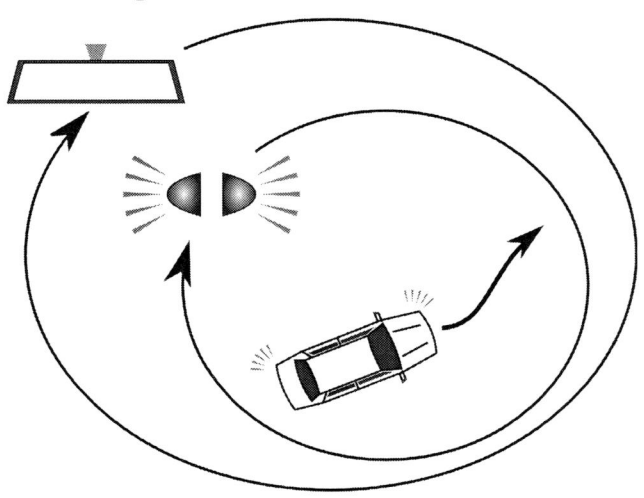

The mobile phone company instructs its sales people to do something else too, which is very interesting. When you ask about a particular model of phone, they don't give you a demo model, they ask you which colour you would want if you bought it, and they then fetch a brand new phone. They sit down, cut the security tape from the box, open it, assemble the phone and then hand it to you. But they don't just throw it across the desk, no. They hand it to you using *both hands*, like a Chinese businessman would hand his business card to you.

A number of very peculiar things are happening in this transaction, including:

- You choose your colour at the start of the transaction, rather than at the end which would be more usual

- You are led to think that the sales person has gone to a lot of trouble to open a brand new phone for you

- You are made to feel guilty that they can't now sell this 'used' phone to someone else because it has been taken out of its packaging

- The 'two handed pass' implies that the phone is of great value, something precious and special

How do I know all this? Because I was that mystery shopper, and all of these cues were in the instructions for the visit. Rather than teach the sales people the underlying principles, it's easier just to send each store manager a set of instructions and then monitor the sales people to make sure they're following them.

This method keeps the costs to a minimum, but the results will be unreliable. The company perhaps sees it as a 'numbers game', where their high profile TV and press advertising creates a steady flow of people through the shop doors, and if the clumsy techniques work with 1% more people, that means increased turnover. It doesn't matter if the majority of customers stare in disbelief at the sales person handing over the phone, thinking, "What are you doing? It's a phone not the crown jewels!"

You can create mnemonics and checklists for the talents that you model, but you cannot use those mnemonics as the foundation for installing the model into other people. The checklist must emerge from the installation process rather than defining it.

The two handed phone pass is a ritual, a prescribed action which is believed to lead to a desired result.

A scripted statement such as, "So, can you see yourself sitting in…" is an incantation, a magic spell which will command the customer to part with their hard earned cash.

But rituals and incantations do not belong in a 21st century, buyer-aware, sophisticated sales process. They belong in a cargo cult.

Wikipedia defines a Cargo Cult as "… a religious practice that has appeared in many traditional pre-industrial tribal societies in the wake of interaction with technologically advanced cultures. The cults focus on obtaining the material wealth (the "cargo") of the advanced culture through magic and religious rituals and practices.

Cargo cult activity in the Pacific region increased significantly during and immediately after World War II, when the residents of these regions observed the Japanese and American combatants bringing in large amounts of matériel. When the war ended, the military bases closed and the flow of goods and materials ceased. In an attempt to attract further deliveries of goods, followers of the cults engaged in ritualistic practices such as building crude imitation landing strips, aircraft and radio equipment, and mimicking the behavior that they had observed of the military personnel operating them."

Behaviours such as making follow up calls and encouraging customers to picture themselves driving a new car are not talents; they are the observable results of an organised sequence of thought patterns. They are the signs or symptoms of a talent, but they are not, in themselves, the thing to be modelled. When you teach your sales people to make a follow up call, you are creating a cargo cult where your staff are led to believe that, with the right incantations, success will surely follow.

The distinction is that the highest performers don't *always* hand over a phone like that, or ask that question, or make a follow up call. Follow up calls are targeted, just like everything else that a good sales person does. Not every customer gets a follow up call because a good sales person knows that it is not the call that works, it is the management of the customer's decision process. A follow up call is made to customers whose decisions can be influenced, otherwise it's intrusive and actually puts off someone who may have come back and bought at a later date. As a potential customer, I just feel like I've been processed through a sales technique.

"But, oh wise one", you say, "If I can't teach a simple sales trick that my staff can use with every customer then how do I tell them which customers to use it with?"

And that is absolutely the key to understanding modelling. Anyone can make telephone calls. Anyone can manage a staff rota in a supermarket. Anyone can polish a turbine blade. Knowing how to do these things is not what sets a high performer apart from their average or poor performing colleagues. The star player is not defined by what they do; they are defined by their skill in knowing precisely *when to do it*.

We need to replicate the underlying beliefs and attitudes, not just the tip of the iceberg behaviours. That's why the modelling process looks at the behaviour within the person within the culture to produce a rich, multi-dimensional blueprint for success.

The alternative, to use this modelling process to produce rituals and incantations is fine, nothing wrong with that at all, just as long as you understand that the more you strip down the model, the fewer customers it will work with. Whether you model excellence in sales, leadership, complaint handling, technical design or customer service, the more complete the model, the more widely applicable it is because you are installing both the working talent and the skill which created it in the first place and which will allow it to evolve; flexibility.

One of the most important ways to install a strategy is to generalise it in multiple contexts. Remember my example of teaching children to type more confidently, at home, at school, with friends, with family. In Logical Levels terms, if you only install the strategy at the level of behaviour, it will often be wedded to a particular environment and will not transfer to other situations. A manager might learn to prioritise tasks at work, but not at home. A parent might learn to manage difficult behaviour at home but not imagine that they could take a similar approach at work.

As a person generalises a new behaviour, you will hear changes in language which reflect the way that the behaviour becomes part of their capabilities and even their identity.

15.1 Modelling Solutions

Work in a group of three for this exercise.

Model someone who used to have a problem and now doesn't. For example, they used to find it difficult to get up early for work and now they don't, or they used to always overcook boiled eggs and now they get them right every time, or a person at work used to irritate them and now they don't.

Two of you will model how they made that change, all three of you will then turn that model into a technique to be used with anyone with a similar problem.

Remember to test your technique within your group.

For you to deliver elegant and effective coaching or change work, here are some simple steps to follow. While they are simple, they are not trivial. Don't be seduced by complexity. Appreciate elegance.

15.2 Custom Technique Design

Model

Many people just want to rush into a technique because they feel like they're really doing something. You must model, model, model and test, test, test. 90% of your time spent modelling and testing is time well spent.

Only when you really understand the structure of the behaviour to be changed, its purpose in the system and you can test and reproduce the behaviour consistently can you even begin to think about changing it.

Get the Structure

Form a representation in your own mind of the structure of the behaviour to be changed - see it, feel it, try it on. Put yourself in there. Visualise it as a machine with real moving parts. Imagine it as a flow of energy, as a road map, as a traffic jam. Find what works for you and stick with it. In essence, you need to make the client's problem real for you. It becomes a shared journey, rather than you just yelling instructions at them from a distance.

Find the Weak Link

A process is always a sequence, and like any connected series of components, there is a weak link - a connection that is easier to get at, easier to influence or simply easier to interact with.

How do you find the weak link? You test.

Create a 'Technique'

Finally, a technique. Imagine the problem as a physical thing, and then think outside of the constraints that define it as a problem. If you see a jigsaw puzzle, where are the missing pieces? If it's a machine, where does the oil go? If it's a traffic jam, where is the short cut? Create a physical metaphor of the solution that complements the metaphor of the problem. Don't think about this, metaphors are unconscious processes. Just go with it.

Do not, ever, under any circumstances, ever, never, ever, try the technique. Either do it or don't do it. Never try it. If you know you're trying, the client won't expect it to work. So either the technique is ready to go, or it isn't. There is nothing in between. The technique doesn't need to be complete or perfect; it only needs to move you a step closer to the client's desired outcome. Often, it's enough to get the client moving, they'll do the rest for themselves.

Test

Now you need to be able to reproduce the solution, the desired response, at will.

Generalise your test through a number of different contexts and future pace in each and overall.

A Worked Example

It might be useful to work through an example in some detail, so I'm going to share a case study of a recent coaching session where a colleague and I worked with a client to create a new method of dealing with customer complaints. The client, let's call him Jack, had endured a couple of particularly difficult complaint calls which had left him feeling shaken and lacking in confidence.

The first thing that we did was to figure out the essence of Jack's problem. We knew that Jack had all of the components parts necessary for effective complaint handling. He could answer the phone, hold a conversation and write things down. No other equipment was necessary for excellence in this task. The essence of the problem was very easy to identify. I simply emulated the behaviour of one of the difficult customers and Jack immediately reacted in a very specific way, raising his hand to his mouth, flushing bright red and experiencing a sudden knot of tension in the centre of his chest.

I find it useful to see such behaviours as purely mechanical responses, as if you're observing a machine and working back through a chain of events. A hand to mouth gesture might indicate that someone is trying to stop words from coming out, words that they want to say but feel that they must not. The knot of tension is a common result of the suppression of an instinct or desire, as if muscles are working against each other, one set trying to act, the other trying to prevent that action, with the result being a tangle of muscle tension.

When I asked Jack about his reaction, he said that it was how his father had made him feel. When I asked Jack what he had wanted to say to his father when he felt like this, he said, "I hate you".

I don't want to look at this in any kind of existential, psychological or spiritual way, just a logical sequence of events, a machine trying to execute its function in unfamiliar circumstances. As a child or teenager, Jack was so practised at reacting to his father in this way that the behaviour, a defensive posture, became second nature. Whenever Jack experiences aggression, he reacts in the same way. Even when driving, Jack reacts to other drivers trying to push into a line of traffic in the same way.

The first part of teaching Jack a more effective complaint handling method is therefore to remove Jack's tendency to shut down and withdraw when faced with conflict or aggression. Getting Jack to verbalise his feelings and say the things that he would never normally say expands his choices and that restores Jack's sense of control. Instead of Jack keeping quite because he can't say what he really thinks of someone, he keeps quiet because he knows it's a more useful choice for him. He could call anyone anything that he wants, any time, anywhere. But as a professional and ethical adult, he chooses not to. Being 'not allowed' to use bad language is something a child would think, not a responsible adult.

With the conflict reaction now dealt with, we started to build a complaint handling process that could be used in any situation. The process was created entirely within the session and was custom designed just for Jack, although as with most models, you'll probably find it will be effective for almost anyone in any situation.

The entire model is also multi-dimensional. Its core purpose is to put Jack in control of the interaction and it does this on a number of levels. At the most obvious, yet most often overlooked level, *any* process would achieve this because the simple act of having a process to follow gives Jack a sense of being in control, of knowing that he would be caught off guard again.

Within the process, each step leads Jack through a kind of 'story' which flows naturally and enables Jack to adjust the pace to the needs of the caller, again putting Jack in control. Then, each step within the process is also designed to put Jack in control. For example, taking notes is just good practice and is something that Jack already did. However, the purpose of taking notes has changed, from recording information to controlling the flow of the conversation. Recording the details of the complaint is the *result* of taking notes, it is no longer the purpose.

As we worked through the process, step by step, we aligned it with Jack's existing skills and experiences. We used Jack's examples and scenarios to create mental rehearsals of each step.

But did it 'work'? Here are Jack's words:

"Well …… I have had to speak to one or two marginally irate parents (although not as difficult as some I could mention!). I applied some of the bullet-point notes that I learnt on the course, and the system worked really well! I must say that having that little list to hand is comforting at the best of times."

A very interesting phenomenon often arises from this kind of work; the client, in this case Jack, goes back to work, armed with their new skill, hoping that a difficult complainer or awkward colleague will give them the opportunity to try out their new approach and see if it works. Often, they're almost disappointed to discover that people seem generally more agreeable than they had before.

Is it a coincidence that their colleagues or customers seem more agreeable? Or has something changed?

Remember that a metaprogram is an organised set of perceptions, and for a behaviour to permanently change at an unconscious level, the perceptions that drive it must also change. Changing experiences and beliefs changes perceptions, and when those perceptions change, the world seems to change too.

Finally, please remember context. In the mobile phone shop, the assistant treats the phone as a thing of great value, but the environment is still a shop full of mobile phones and "Sale!" signs, and the assistant is wearing a cheap suit, with food stains down his tie and looking like he has been dragged through a hedge backwards, forwards and then backwards again. He sneers and scoffs at my current phone. He belittles another store assistant.

He shows none of the respect that I am expected to feel for the precious treasure that he passes to me. And so the entire sales process is an utter waste of time and money, and worse still, it confuses customers.

The culture of mobile phone sales is that I want the best package and the newest phone for the least money. Retailers try to attract new customers with offers, free games consoles and so on. But really, the business model of a retailer is defined by its suppliers and its customers. It was brave of them to try something new, but ultimately futile.

About two years after I wrote about the mobile phone shop, I spoke at a sales conference in Kiev, Ukraine. At the end of my presentation, a lady approached me and told me that she was the head of marketing for Ukraine's largest mobile phone retailer, and they had just bought the entire sales model from the UK retailer.

I asked, "And what effect did it have on sales?"

She replied, "They went *down*."

Another year later, and the original retailer, a dominant player in the UK market for almost 20 years, went into administration and disappeared from the High Streets and shopping centres for ever. Did anyone even notice?

16 Instructional Design

The design of a 'training course' is an important part of many installation processes. A number of different instructional design methods exist, ranging from the strict, script based approach through to a more flexible, outcome based approach.

For our purposes, it doesn't really matter which method you prefer to use because there are some useful principles to bear in mind which will make the installation process more effective.

I'm only going to discuss the principles here because a detailed exploration of instructional design to incorporate models of high performance is big enough to take up another book – and as it happens, I'm working on exactly that, a companion installation guide to this book. I haven't decided on a title yet, so keep an eye on my social media or websites.

Nesting the Model

A model will usually be a sequence of steps, and it is important that your training design follows the same sequence.

Let's say that you're teaching travel agents how to sell cruise holidays. Using this modelling approach, a well known holiday company modelled its highest performing agent and found that he did something very different to the average agents. Rather than checking availability at the end of the call after talking about the itinerary and so on, he checked it at the beginning. He didn't sell the caller a holiday, he sold them *their* holiday, in *their* cabin on *their* cruise.

So let's design a training course for travel agents which incorporates the model.

We start with a re-enactment of an 'ideal' conversation. It might be done by the trainer, or the trainer might play a recording of such a conversation with a real customer which had previously been recorded 'for training purposes'. Don't explain anything about the call for now, just play it and allow the learners to take in whatever they can. What you're aiming to achieve is to give them an overall sense of the call; the tone, the attitude, the pace and so on.

Now we break the call down, step by step. Take the learners through the procedure for taking a call and operating the telephone system at the point in the process when they would answer the call. Get them to practice answering a call – just the introduction.

Next, get them to take some details from the caller. Their name. Their phone number, so you can call back if they get cut off. And to save them time in case what they want is fully booked, ask which cruise they're calling about. And which dates. And what kind of cabin would they like? Ah, a balcony. Beautiful. Well, cabin 401 is available so now I can answer all of your questions.

It's time to give the learners their product knowledge. The features of the cruise, what facilities are on the boat, the itinerary etc. Have them practice the introduction, then move into the questioning.

What's next? Payment details perhaps? This will no doubt require some more procedural training around the payments system, so now's the time. And how do they practice using the payment system? That's right – they practice the introduction, leading into the questioning, and then into the payment process.

Each time they practice, they rerun the whole model up to that point. Everything that they do follows the same sequence, and everything that they learn comes at the same point as it would in the live call.

If there are connecting flights, which airports? Luggage allowances? Door to door pick-ups? Insurance? Dietary requirements? All of these are now closing details, the necessary points to cover off to complete the booking.

Note that there have been no clumsy trial closes, no, "So if you are happy with the holiday that we discuss, will you be going ahead today?", nothing that seems out of place. No peculiar handing over of mobile phones. No, "So can you see yourself enjoying one of our cruises?"

The high performer placed the customer in *their* cabin on *their* cruise at the start of the call, and that created the frame of reference for the entire conversation.

The training design reinforces the model by nesting it as many times as possible within the training session.

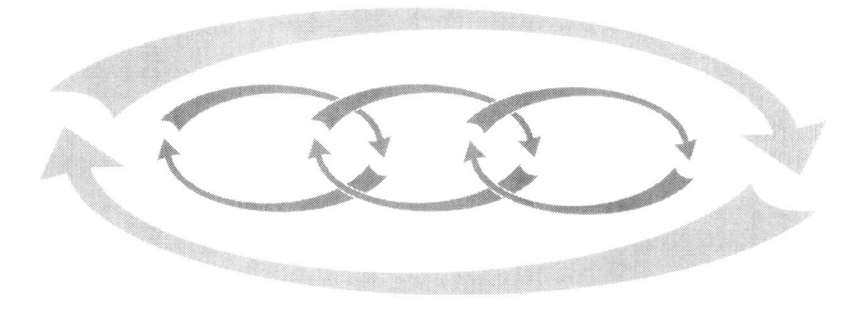

Naming

Use course and exercise descriptions that complement the model and presuppose success. For example, in sales training, the term 'cold calling' is often synonymous with an undesirable and difficult activity. Instead, choose a title which implies that the learners will be calling someone they haven't spoken to before and asking for something; a task that most of us perform every day.

Mnemonics

This next point is really just good training practice, but I feel it's worth mentioning.

Instead of telling the learners what the mnemonic is, have them create it. But like any good magician, use forcing techniques to ensure they end up with the mnemonic or acronym that you had printed on the hand-out cards.

"OK, so what's the first step"

"Find out which cabin they want"

(Write that on the flipchart, but leave space above it)

"That's important, does anything come before it?"

"Answer the phone!"

"Yes, good. Obvious but important! What's next?"

"Introduce yourself and take their contact details in case they get cut off"

(Write those three steps above the cabin selection step)

"Great, what next?"

And so on. Once you have the steps mapped out, and you've paraphrased the group's answers so that the words just happen to spell out the mnemonic, you can do the 'reveal' of the flipchart that you prepared earlier.

This approach is important because by getting the group to create the mnemonic, you are actually forcing them to rerun the model in their minds, over and over as they break it down and search for each step. Their recall of the mnemonic and the steps of the process will be far higher when they understand what's going on behind the process, and you avoid creating an incantation, which is what tends to happen if you impose your own mnemonic.

Remember, also, that the high performer's real talent doesn't show itself where you think it will. An outstanding sales person does not wait until he or she is sitting in front of the customer, it's too late by then, whereas a poor to average sales person will focus only on the customer interaction and forget the planning and preparation. Therefore, by getting the learners to realise that they forgot 'answer the phone' as a step, you reveal a key difference between an average and high performer.

I'd have to add that poor trainers only focus on the customer interaction, because then it looks like they're teaching some cool, rare techniques for influencing the customer. The best sales people know that influence doesn't happen in the sales meeting, it happens long before. What makes a trainer look good is not what enables your learners to deliver outstanding results. Neither is right, you just have to decide what you're paying for – results or entertainment.

Most importantly, the mnemonic comes at the end, an output of the learning process, not at the beginning, where it would create a frame of reference which constrains everything that happens afterwards.

Multiple Methods

You are unlikely to install a model effectively by using one method alone. As with any other learning experience, the more ways that you can engage the learners the better. Here are some ways in which you can do that:

- Have the learners physically walk the model
- Have high performers talk about what they do
- Have the learners read case studies
- Take the learners on a site visit for a live case study
- Have the learners 'role play' through the model
- Create games and exercises which are themselves models of the model (isomorphic exercises)
- Have the learners create the model for themselves
- Observe practice and give real time feedback
- Use guided visualisations
- Show film scenes which convey the attitude of the high performers
- Have high performers mentor the learners
- Coach the learners using a coaching framework based on the high performance model
- Have the learners create metaphors for the model

Many of these ideas will be familiar to you, so I'll just expand on a few which may not be.

Walk Through

Write the steps of the model on pieces of paper and arrange them on the floor in a line or circle, whichever is appropriate. Have the learners physically step through the model, at each stage explaining what they are doing, what they are thinking, what might happen, how they might respond and so on.

When you use a physical exercise in this way, you will see people embodying their internal experiences. They will play out their comfort zones and fears, regardless of what they say. For example, if the model is a sales process, you'll see someone stop at the cold calling step as if they're standing at a cliff edge. They literally play out what they are creating in their minds. You might also see them linger in the needs gathering stage because that involves talking at length with the customer; the part they enjoy most. By reflecting back such reactions, you can increase the learners' acceptance of the model, coach them through any personal barriers and give them a multi-sensory experience of 'stepping through' it.

Isomorphic Exercises

An isomorphic exercise is one where a seemingly unrelated activity bears a structural resemblance to the model, thereby encouraging the learner to generalise their experience which embeds it more effectively and makes the learning accessible in a wider range of situations.

When you deliver an isomorphic exercise correctly, you'll hear your learners say, "Ah! This is just like..."

For example, let's say that you want to install Jack's model of complaint handling. One of the key steps in the model is the taking of notes, because it serves as a 'flow control' mechanism whilst also signalling to the complainant that you take their complaint very seriously.

Let's say that you want your learners to practice writing notes verbatim, because in complaint handling, it's very important to be factually correct and not change the complainant's words.

Make an audio recording of an angry complainant, speaking too quickly for the learners to write down their words. Put the recording on a computer or a tape so that the learners can control the conversation with the pause, rewind and play buttons. Focus their attention on the overt purpose of the exercise by having them check each other's transcripts and awarding points or prizes for the most accurate.

When you set the exercise up, position it only as a note taking activity, but when you later move onto a face to face interaction exercise, point out that taking notes, and the interpersonal skills required to do so, are the equivalent of the pause, rewind and play buttons. By practising first on the recording, you take away the stigma attached to interrupting the complainant and not wanting to appear rude or inflame the situation, and by then reintroducing the concept later on, the learners have already practised the mechanism. The learners will learn to take notes more effectively, because there was no interpersonal barrier of having to interrupt another person, as there would be in a pairs or group exercise. The learners are completely free to hone their note taking skills, and we'll add in the interpersonal skills later on.

This achieves the following outcomes which are each characteristics of the high performer's approach:

- Separate the flow control mechanism from the emotional stigma of interrupting the complainant
- Record the complainant's words verbatim
- Take notes to signal the complainant's importance
- Take notes to control the conversation, stick to the facts and prevent emotion from taking over

Now, you might wonder what makes an isomorphic exercise so special. After all, separating out the note taking from the interpersonal skills is logical, isn't it?

Firstly, how many trainers do you honestly think would separate the two? Isn't it more likely that most trainers would have the learners practice note taking with each other, because that's just easier?

Secondly, there are lots of ways that you could have your learners practice note taking. What is special is that you have chosen a practice exercise which uses a number of metaphors for the approach that you want them to take in handling a complainant. The metaphor works both ways; controlling the recording is 'like' controlling the complainant, and treating the complainant factually and objectively is 'like' pressing play, pause and rewind without worrying about how the tape recorder feels about it. When you install the complete model effectively, you don't have to install any incantations for reassuring the customer, such as "Your complaint is important to us", because the complaint handler demonstrates that the complaint is important. They don't need to signal to the complainant that they care, because their whole attitude to the interaction is one of concern and care. If you teach a disengaged, disinterested car salesperson to say, "So, can you see yourself..." then the harm caused by the incongruence far outweighs any statistical benefit of the incantation. A disinterested and sarcastic complaint handler will damage your business far more than the product or service issue that the complainant is contacting you about. Good complaint handlers have an attitude which clearly signals:

- We're not perfect but we want to get better
- I'm grateful that customers make the effort to give me feedback rather going to our competitors
- We won't get it right every time
- My job is to listen, not to judge
- Without customers, we wouldn't have a business
- I will concentrate on the facts, hear all sides of the issue and put right what we've done wrong
- Some problems are outside of our control
- The customer is always right, but that doesn't mean they automatically get their own way
- One unhappy customer impacts our business more than a hundred happy customers

Remember, of course, that a high performing complaint handler does not use their notes as a barrier, because that will frustrate the complainant further. The high performer uses their notes as an *enabler*. How do they achieve this subtle but vital difference? Because it's important that you understand that the tiny difference between the two means the difference between installing an effective model and creating a cargo cult with its rituals and incantations. The difference is that the high performer doesn't shut the complainant out while they take notes; they keep looking at them or talking to them. Their focus is on the complainant, not the notebook.

Guided Visualisation

The touch typing exercise with the children used a guided visualisation to create a mental context for model installation. Guided visualisations don't have to involve darkened rooms and whale song, they are simply a hybrid of reality and imagination, structured by an external guide. High performers in a company providing home improvements would take the customer into their dark, dirty garage and have them visualise how it would look as a home cinema. The overt purpose was to have the customer select power points, windows, roof style and so on, but the side effect was an amplification of the customer's desire to go ahead with the project, created by the customer's return to the harsh reality that their garage isn't a home cinema, it really is just a dusty garage.

A travel agent might talk a customer through the layout of the holiday complex, using strong visual language to elicit an imagined experience within the customer's mind, which will automatically fill in the gaps to create a more complete experience.

"So your room is here (marks it on a map of the complex) and as you come out of your door and into the garden, it's really bright and sunny as you look across the bay, so you can imagine seeing all the boats with their white sails, honestly it's such a beautiful scene to enjoy over breakfast, and if you turn to your left you'll follow this path to the health club, and here's where you can…"

Is sunshine cold? Is a sparkling blue bay with white-sailed boats a depressing sight?

High performing finance managers in the retailer visualised the operation of a store, using spreadsheets as their guides. High performing project managers and engineers create a visual journey through a technical project, checking for anything they've missed, step by step. You might do the same thing when you're going on holiday, imagining your journey; "Passport, tickets, book for the flight, rental car paperwork, driving license, directions to the villa…"

Whenever you describe a series of physical actions to your learners, you are essentially guiding a visualisation because they are unlikely to be able to make sense of your description without visualising themselves performing those actions in relevant surroundings.

For example, if I 'walk through' the following steps with you, pay attention to whatever thoughts you have. Do take a minute or two on each step to make sure you think about it carefully and pay attention to whatever thoughts or images come into your mind.

1. Finish reading this book
2. Think of someone who has a skill that you admire
3. Model it at a very simplistic level
4. Pick out the most useful steps
5. Find a situation where you can try out those steps
6. Use exercise 9.2 to reflect on what happens

What did you notice?

Your learners will visualise anyway, so help them by guiding the process.

Metaphors

When you create a metaphor, you create new mental pathways to the same underlying information. Metaphors enrich the original experience and make it more vivid and accessible, which makes it easier for the learners to apply the model in different situations. Throughout your installation process, you can have your learners create metaphors, which might be:

- Synonyms for the objectives of the model
- Acronyms and mnemonics
- Examples of the model in action
- Icons, pictograms or 'mind maps' to help remember the stages of the model
- A modelling clay sculpture of a successful outcome
- A painting or other artistic representation of the steps of the model

- A 'thought wall', where learners can pin notes, slogans, poems, pictures, sketches, cartoons, logos, musical notes, colour codes, diagrams, flowcharts or anything else which they want to share
- A song, play or comedy sketch enacting the steps of the model

If you're thinking, "I already do all that", just remember that while you may already use exercises, the key is to make them isomorphic, otherwise they're just distractions, a bit of fun. The concept of 'Brain Friendly Learning' advocates using such multi-sensory learning tools and activities, though this is focused on retention, not the installation of a behavioural program, and it is also based on a model of brain function which is now very much out of date.

Kolb's Experiential Learning

Here are some suggested activities and questions to use at each stage of Kolb's learning cycle.

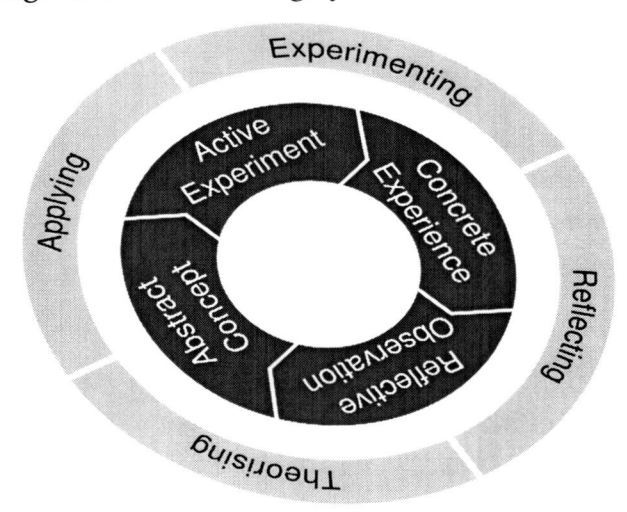

Applying

Work through case studies.

Have guest speakers talk about their experiences.

Conduct site visits.

"What examples do you have of…?"

"Can you think of these issues in your own workplace?"

"When has this happened to you?"

"How could you see this working?"

"Can you think of anyone else who does this?"

Reflecting

"What happened?"

"What would have happened if...?"

"What did you notice"

"What did you say?"

"How did the customer react?"

"How did you feel?"

"How do you think they felt?"

Theorising

"What do you think is happening here?"

"What were the steps that you followed?"

"Why do you think that happens?"

"How do you think it works?"

"How do you think you could change the result?"

Experimenting

"Have a go!"

Keep your instructions simple and direct.

Tell your learners what to pay attention to.

Create learning activities which force certain experiences or common mistakes.

Create learning activities with only 3 or 4 very simple rules which are easy to stick to yet which lead to complex patterns of behaviour.

Other Learning Theories

Kolb's experiential learning cycle isn't the only learning theory. There are many others, including:

- Gardner's multiple intelligences
- NLP's sensory preferences
- Honey & Mumford's learning styles
- Sensory stimulation theory
- Reinforcement theory
- Cognitive-Gestalt theory
- Facilitation theory
- Action learning
- Adult learning or 'Andragogy'

Are these theories mutually exclusive? I suggest that they cannot be. Whatever the method by which we learn, there is no doubt that something starts in the outside, physical world, and is transferred to the inside, mental world as a model. There can be no doubt that these words are not written inside your skull, yet you have learned their meaning, therefore the pattern of neural connections in your brain somehow represents the knowledge which you have gleaned throughout your lifetime, and that generalised representation is a model.

The truth is that we have absolutely no real idea how that happens. Are some people better at learning from images than others? Are some people better at learning physical movements than others? Do adults have a natural desire to learn which must only be facilitated? We may never know, because we've lost the instruction manual and, as far as we know, God doesn't offer extended warranties.

However, piecing together what we know by experiment and what we might deduce to fill in the gaps, I suggest that there can be no doubt that learning must have an element of real, sensory experience. Something must happen on the outside which excites our sensory receptors. We must then make sense of that new experience using our existing frames of reference, because what else do we have to rely on? We know that the brain requires a period of rest in order for new neural connections to form, and we know that knowledge must exit in order to apply it. I have to have *some* idea of what to do before I start pushing all the buttons on my new mobile phone or video recorder. And I propose to you that this sequence of events is neatly described by Kolb's experiential learning theory, and the other learning theories listed on the previous page nest neatly within it. How do you like your concrete experience? Visually? Logically? Physically? Musically? Medium rare?

Whichever of these is your favourite learning theory, I encourage you to always make your instructional design as complete and multi-faceted as your learners are.

17 Recruitment

We've talked about training and instructional design, because it's a good idea to develop your existing staff in line with models of excellence within your culture. However, it's inevitable that you'll also be recruiting new staff at some point in time, and it's a good idea to recruit people who have the kinds of qualities that predispose them to high performance within your culture.

If you think back to the chapters which focused on the modelling process, I mentioned the use of various psychometric instruments. It's very common for recruiters to use these tools, but I have never met any recruiter or hiring manager who based a hiring decision on their output. I once worked in a company where a manager hired someone who was known to many of the staff as having been asked to leave her previous employer as no-one would work with her. When she joined, she delighted in telling her new colleagues that her interview psychometric profile showed that she was a psychopath.

How, then, can you use your model of excellence to help attract the kind of people who are predisposed to high performance in your culture?

Everything that you do, from the way that you write a job advert to the way that you conduct your interview, will attract some people more than others. There are many good books on the subject of recruitment, so I'm not going to repeat what you can find elsewhere, or which you are already familiar with. Instead, I'll give you a tip.

Instead of learning all about the language patterns that attract certain types of people, just get your highest performer to write the Job advert. Simple! Ask them to write an advert that, if they were to read it, they would think, "Wow! That suits me down to the ground!"

They will, of course, use the subtleties of language that will attract people like them. It's important that you don't edit those subtleties out, of course.

For example, one of the ways in which people differ is their desire for new experiences over predictability. When a large group of people are generalised into 'a market', we see a pattern of early adoption, followed by mass market acceptance. For a restaurant introducing new choices, the phrase "Brand new menu every day" appeals to early adopters but will discourage people who want predictability. The phrase "Same great menu, new choices every day" is more likely to appeal to both types of customer, whilst the phrase, "Our great menu, now in its 25th year" is most definitely going to appeal most to a mass market or late adopter buyer. Or perhaps a new generation of early adopters, keen to jump on the 'retro' bandwagon.

When you don't recognise the importance of the language, it's easy to focus on the new menu and disregard how it's described. Yet the language spoken by your highest performers will naturally contain the words which attract more people of the same mindset.

Once you're at the interview stage, you can then use the model as part of your overall competency framework, and use it in your normal approach to interviewing; be that competency based or not.

18 Testing

Testing is important because it completes the cycle that you began with model extraction. If you don't test, you don't really know whether the modelling process was effective or not.

Yet of all the stages, testing is probably the simplest.

To test your model, place your learners in the live working environment. If they get the same results, or similar within an acceptable margin, as the high performers, then the modelling process was successful.

If the thought of releasing your learners 'into the wild' is too scary then there are other ways that you can test them.

One simple way to test is with simulations. I feel that it is extremely important to draw a distinction between a simulation and the perhaps more familiar 'role play'. The two may appear superficially similar, but there is an underlying difference which will absolutely guarantee the difference between success and failure. I would even say that this applies to any training, not just training designed to install high performance models.

When learners engage in a role play, they are asked to pretend that the scenario is real, but at an unconscious level, they know that it isn't. They know that the colleague playing an angry customer isn't really angry. They know that they won't lose their job. They know that achieving their sales target doesn't really rest on this meeting with the Operations Manager of ABC Exports Ltd.

With a simulation, we want the learners to believe that what they are practising is real, at least in the way that they unconsciously respond.

To achieve this, you might construct an elaborate assessment centre. You might have actors playing roles in scenarios which take place before the learner even knows they are being assessed.

Maybe you've seen films where secret agents are trained to withstand torture, the implication being that this is how special forces soldiers are actually trained. Their lives probably aren't in serious danger, but the situation is constructed to make them believe that there is a good chance that it is. Their fear is intended to be real.

Industrial flight simulators are incredible pieces of technology, blending real aircraft hardware, an advanced motion platform and software which can model aircraft dynamics and create real time, photo realistic views out of the cockpit windows. When the pilot walks into the simulator, he or she knows that it isn't a real aircraft. But after a two hour flight, when an engine fails on final approach, their sweat is very, very real. When a pilot 'stalls' a simulator, their stress levels respond just as if the danger of crashing is real. The simulation is so realistic that time in the simulator counts as time in the air for their log books.

But what if you don't have access to such resources? Well, the simplest approach is also the more effective, and it's important to do this even if you do have a realistic assessment centre in place.

I mentioned previously the importance of nesting the model within your learning design. Testing is not a separate phase to learning, it is part of it. In Kolb's terms, the test takes place in the concrete experience stage of the cycle. While the learners are practising, you're testing them, or more accurately, you are testing your own effectiveness at installing a model. Each individual skill that goes to make up the greater talent that you have modelled requires testing in its own right. Note taking needs to be tested. A customer-focused attitude needs to be tested. You can easily test your learners' memory of a sales process, but how do you test the change in attitude necessary for persistence in 'cold calling'?

You could tell the learners that they will be doing some cold calling shortly, and see how they react.

You could use the 'walk through the model' exercise again, this time covertly testing for unconscious resistance at the 'cold calling' stage.

Or, you could make probably the most important instructional design tweak of all; build your training programme in stages, instead of all at once, with periods of real world experience in between periods of learning. I didn't mention this in the Instructional Design chapter because I wanted to use it as an example of testing. Although, to be fair, you should really have worked it out for yourself by thinking about the consequences of Kolb's learning cycle.

You might think that you already do this; in my experience, that's unlikely. What I see a growing trend for is 'bite sized learning', i.e. a series of short, to-the-point training sessions of one or two hours duration. These sessions are usually disjointed packages of information which may link together as the steps in a learning sequence, but more generally they are like pieces of a puzzle with no common theme.

For example, one provider of such training lists these modules within their leadership category:

Building Great Teams	Coaching
Leadership Communication	Delegation
Managing Difficult Situations	Running Meetings
Performance Management	Leadership Styles
Recruitment Interviewing	Managing Change
Business Skills	Motivation

On the face of it, these seem like reasonable topics to cover, or you might feel that most of these have nothing to do with leadership. What you may not think about is that there is no single, unifying story which creates a simulation of effective leadership. These modules are offered on a 'pick and mix' basis, so how can there be an overarching story? And without that, the learners cannot effectively integrate new behaviours, which means that they might increase their 'leadership performance', they might not. There's no way to tell. We don't even know what leadership is, so how can we know if someone's ability to do it has increased? We kid ourselves that, "Oh well, it can't work for everyone", when in fact, if we do it properly, it can. When we install specific behavioural programs, we can directly measure behavioural change and therefore its impact on business performance. We then measure leadership performance by team results, not by retention of a leadership theory.

More importantly, the motivation for 'bite sized' learning is not to improve learning, it's to take people away from their desks for the shortest time possible. Don't invest in time consuming learning, when just telling people what to do will suffice. The focus is on sessions being short, impactful and fun, with impact being measured in terms of reaction, not behavioural change.

There's nothing wrong with short training sessions, the problem is mistaking training for learning, and thereby failing to integrate the training with the person's job. I'm sure you've got software on your computer, apps on your phone, even ebooks and music, which you've downloaded and installed, and never used. These represent redundant programs. Nothing wrong with them, they just take up space unnecessarily. In the same way, it doesn't matter whether a training session lasts an hour, a day or a week, it's the utility of the program which is in question.

Here are two approaches that we can compare:

Traditional Approach

The training session packs in as much learning as possible, with mnemonics to remember the rituals and incantations, such as AIDA for Attention, Interest, Decision, Action. The mnemonic is defined, examples are shared and applications are discussed. At the end of the session, the learners' retention might be tested, and they might take part in some role plays with scripted scenarios.

Cyclic Learning Approach

The training session packs in as much practice as possible. Theoretical models are sent out as pre-course reading, together with instructions for analysis and self reflection to encourage the learners to engage with the theory. The session is constructed as a series of cycles, with each cycle starting at a different point, just to add some variety:

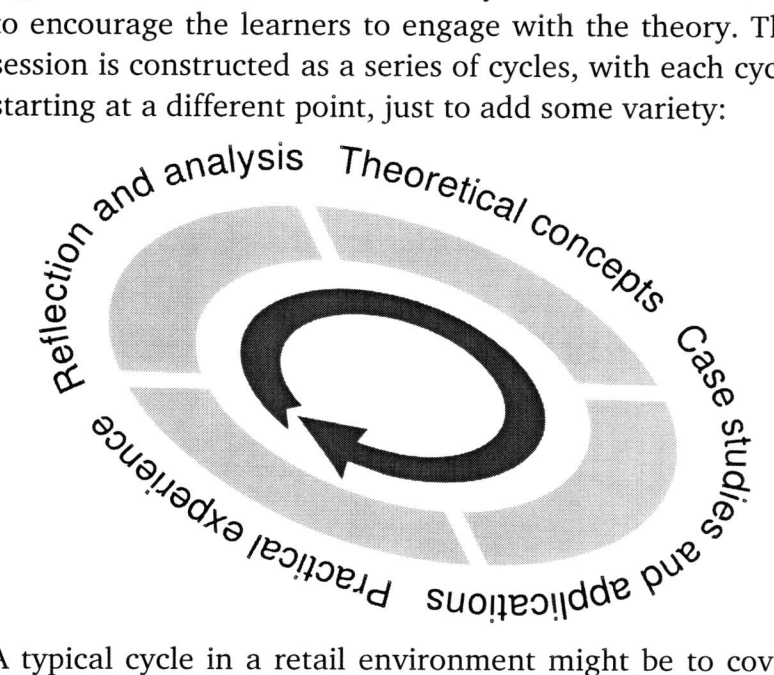

Reflection and analysis — Theoretical concepts — Case studies and applications — Practical experience

A typical cycle in a retail environment might be to cover some theory about how to approach a customer with some practical examples, followed by some time spent actually approaching live customers, followed by a session of developmental feedback on what happened, followed by some theory on establishing a customer's needs and so on. Each cycle builds on the previous ones, so in order to establish a customer's needs, the learners must approach customers again, also practising the first and second steps.

Mnemonics arise out of the learning process and represent the theory that the learners abstract their new knowledge into, rather than the theory that they have to learn to apply. If you consider the history of mankind, theorising and experimenting have always gone hand in hand, but if one has to always come first, like the proverbial chicken and egg, then I would say that it would have to be experimentation.

I find that the rule of thumb for the length of one of these cycles is one step of your model. If you try to fit two steps into one cycle then you confuse what the learners are paying attention to, which means that they merge two steps together when reflecting and theorising.

If you're wondering how you know what comprises a 'step', it's simple. It's one decision.

Unexpected Results

If your installation process doesn't quite deliver the results that you had hoped for, what should you do?

Simply use the modelling process to analyse what they are doing. Instead of thinking, "Oh no, it didn't work, what went wrong?", look at it from this point of view. The learners haven't failed, they are simply doing something different than what you intended. Rather than look for what they're not doing, look at what they are doing and compare that to your model.

We've already discussed this in chapter nine, Beyond Simple Strategies, where you learned to ask, "What is it doing?" instead of saying, "It's broken".

I have found that the most common reasons why the installation process doesn't deliver what you intended are:

1. Failure to separate skills into isomorphic exercises
2. Failure to model the beliefs which underpin the behaviour
3. Failure to cross reference the model

Failure to separate skills into discrete exercises

If you don't separate two talents and take the easy route of treating them as one, you'll find that your learner's preconceptions about one skill affects their ability to learn the other.

With the complaint handling example, the high performer exhibits two entirely separate skills, but because they work at the same time, it's easy to treat them as a single skill. The person who excels in this role is able to detach emotionally to control the conversation and yet still communicate that they care. They don't think of interrupting the complainant as being rude, they see it as necessary in order to be of greatest assistance. It's vital that you create separate exercises, otherwise the learners will only learn to control the conversation, with an unpredictable effect on how the complainant feels about the interaction.

Failure to model the beliefs which underpin the behaviour

If you don't pay sufficient attention to the underlying beliefs and attitudes, you will create rituals and incantations. It may seem like a hard line to take, but if your new recruits have beliefs which are too far away from those required to learn the model then you need to move them to something else and hire people who are predisposed to the beliefs and attitudes that you need. We'll talk about the 'talent cycle' later, and look at ways that you can attract new recruits who are already half way there.

Failure to cross reference the model

If you only model high performers then you have no way of knowing which skills are unique to them.

Extremely poor performers are in fact high performers, placed in the wrong environment, so you must disregard them too.

I recommend you always model at least three high performers and cross reference with at least three average performers, and use a full range of metrics to define 'high' and 'average' performance.

19 Evaluation

Believe it or not, I have heard it said by some trainers that Kirkpatrick's four stage evaluation model is out of date and no longer valid. I'd like to explain why it is valid, and how it aligns with the modelling and installation process that we've been exploring together.

First of all, let's hear the prosecution's opening statement.

Kirkpatrick's evaluation method[12], based on research first published in 1959, and even its 'successor', Kaufmann's five level approach[13], is focused on a 'training event', when in fact, learning takes place on an ongoing basis, both actively and passively, and these standard evaluation models do not take into account the informal and social learning which takes place.

Kirkpatrick's detractors cite these alternatives:

- Brinkerhoff's Success Case Method
- Daniel Stufflebeam's CIPP Model
- Robert Stake's Responsive Evaluation
- Kaufman's Five Levels of Evaluation
- CIRO (Context, Input, Reaction, Outcome)
- PERT (Program Evaluation and Review Technique)
- Alkins' UCLA Model
- Provus' Discrepancy Model
- Eisner's Connoisseurship Evaluation Model

So that's that. Learning in this modern age is a cool and sexy thing which no longer takes place in a stuffy old

---
12 Evaluating Training Programs, Kirkpatrick, 1975
13 Kaufman, Keller, and Watkins, 1995

classroom, so evaluation is no longer meaningful. And any theory which is more than 50 years old must be untrue.

Well, Newton's first law of motion is over 200 years old, but it still enables rocket scientists to throw a washing machine at a comet with enough accuracy to hit it head on after seven months of coasting through space.

The problem with this kind of thinking is that it leads to cargo cults. According to Samuel Arbesman[14], we can measure how knowledge changes or decays over time by calculating how many facts within a given subject area are disproven within a certain amount of time. What he describes as the 'half life' of knowledge is the time taken for half of the facts known about a subject to become untrue. When I was at junior school, the number of chemical elements was a known fact; the fixed immutable number of essential building blocks that all matter is built from. The number was 103. Today, it is 118. Similarly, back then there were nine planets in our solar system. Now there are eight. Where has Pluto gone? Has he run away to a better life orbiting another star? No, we have just redefined what we "know" about the universe that we live in.

How does this apply to evaluating learning? Well, saying that the brain is a sponge and when it's full, it's full is a fact. Saying that the brain has a fixed number of cells at birth, and as cells die off they are never replaced is a fact. Both of these facts are now known to be untrue.

However, saying that a person has to learn something before they can use it, and when they use it that action has a resulting effect in the world which can be measured

---

14 The Half Life of Facts, Arbesman, 2012

is not a fact; it is an observation. And saying that if you want that person's action to be predictable and structured then it would be sensible for the learning experience to be structured is not a fact, it is an observation of a causal relationship between learning and behaviour. And what term might we use to describe an observation of causal relationships? That's right; a model.

Critics of Kirkpatrick say that the first evaluation level, that of the learning experience, is irrelevant. 'Happy sheets' have a bad name because how much a learner enjoyed the training course has no bearing on their ability to apply their new knowledge. Well, I agree with that. I've seen learners have a whale of a time and not learn a sausage. But that has nothing to do with the importance of evaluation, it is a reflection of outcome.

I have seen literally hundreds of trainers in action over the years, and what many share in common is a need to be liked, to entertain their learners. Whatever the explicit learning outcomes are, the trainers have an innate need to create an enjoyable experience. One trainer even calls his work 'entertrainment' because he believes that the more entertaining he is, the more people enjoy his courses and therefore the more they learn. Well, like the apprentices in the workshop, they certainly do learn, they just don't learn what you were paying for them to learn.

Vocational training and even academic education has a purpose, and that purpose must surely define or at least shape the learning process. You may have seen the old photograph of girls in a Victorian school learning to swim. While sitting at their desks. Sitting at their desks, waving their arms in the air, pretending to swim. Now, this photograph may have been taken out of context. The Victorians may have taught children the basic movements of swimming before throwing them in at the deep end, which would be a very good idea indeed. I hated swimming lessons at school, mainly because the water was cold and wet, two things which I would prefer that water wasn't. So a bit of classroom preparation would have been very useful; it may have saved me from ingesting so much chlorine as a child.

Kirkpatrick's first evaluation level is not a test of enjoyment; if trainers use it that way, it tells you that they want to be liked more than they want to educate. The first level is an evaluation of *experience*. The learners may have hated the experience, and that may have been your intention. If your overall objective was "to learn that falling off an unsecured ladder is dangerous" then an unpleasant experience can be very effective. Certainly, we might say that there is no better way to learn the importance of health and safety than to have an accident at work. So the experience doesn't have to be good, it has to be appropriate to the learning objective.

Most of what I've read about Kirkpatrick's model uses the word 'reaction' to describe level one. The evaluation is how learners react to the experience. Are they thrilled? Delighted? Enthralled? Dubious? Confused? All of these are valid responses, but must be judged in the context of the desired outcome of the overall learning experience.

What about the argument that much learning today is informal, unstructured and 'social'? Well, that's true, of course. But it is not an excuse to spend less time in formal training. Informal learning is all very well, but you cannot predict what someone will learn, and when. Again, the apprentices in the workshop experienced plenty of 'social learning', and it was mostly the kinds of things that their managers would prefer they hadn't learned. If you want predictable outputs, you need predictable inputs.

But don't assume that I am only in favour of Kirkpatricks' model. I simply want to make the point that evaluation is vital at every stage of the learning process, from needs analysis through to practical implementation. Every evaluation stage forms a feedback loop which informs and shapes the entire process. Don't get hung up on which evaluation model is right, just pick one and use it, and most importantly, don't hide behind it. Evaluation doesn't prove whether your training is good or bad, right or wrong, valuable or worthless. Evaluation is an opportunity to test for unintended consequences, an opportunity to see what happened that you hadn't expected and to fine tune your approach to get the results you want.

Instead of saying, "The feedback was poor, the training was ineffective", learn to ask the right questions so that you can say, "That's interesting, the training delivered a different outcome than the one we intended. How can we refine our methods to get the results we want?"

Overall, if you don't decide how to evaluate a program before you start delivering it, you're just asking for trouble, like the reader who sent me the following email. The context for the question was training for the sales people who work on new housing developments.

Question: How can I show how effective the training we have invested in this year has been?

I am struggling - as cannot 'prove' anything e.g. if sales have increased since last year - then there are many factors that could affect that - market, prices, etc etc

How do we KNOW the Sales Execs are more effective as a result of the training? - apart from Mystery shopping?

Any ideas, thoughts please?

And here's my answer:

The important thing in any evaluation is to ask 'More effective at WHAT?'

If it's selling houses, then you have to take out external factors, so choose two areas that had very similar sales performance last year, one of which has received training, the other hasn't, and compare the two.

Otherwise, if you're saying that you can't control for those factors then sales can't be the outcome to evaluate against, it has to be the 'right steps' that lead to a sale when other factors are right.

For example, IF the location is right AND the house is right AND the buyers can afford the mortgage AND they can sell their current house THEN what sales behaviours make the difference between sale and no sale?

As you rightly say, you can evaluate whether the sales people are building rapport, for example, with mystery shopping. What you can't really do is prove a simple causal link between rapport and a decision to buy.

Speaking personally, I bought a new house last December. Our decision factors were location and price. All the sales staff had to do was stay out of the way. We looked at a few locations with different builders and observed a range of sales behaviours and processes. Again, speaking personally, the most influential behaviour of a sales person in this context isn't to shape the decision but to reinforce it. They can't make a customer buy, but they can reassure and reinforce a decision that has already been made, or at least half made.

So there is a bigger context to this discussion, which is the whole customer interaction and communication, because every 'touch point' influences the customer. Branding, advertising and signage to drive people to a development, the presentation of the show homes, the features of the house and so on. As you said, sales behaviour is one part of that sequence of events, and the question to ask for an evaluation to be meaningful must be about the role of the sales exec. Are they supposed to be selling houses? Or are they supposed to be making customers feel 'at home'? Or are they supposed to be answering questions about the house? Or are they supposed to be completing purchase paperwork?

It's easy to say that their job is to sell houses, but is it really? If that were the case then they are the major contributing factor to the sale and we can easily measure the effectiveness of the programme. But if you can quantify the other factors involved, then their role is no longer to sell houses, but to enable and manage the parts of that overall process, and that then becomes much easier to measure and quantify. Similarly, the site manager's job isn't to sell houses. Or it is, depending on how you look at it. The site managers and contractors also contribute towards the customer's feeling of reassurance.

But my guess is that you've been asked, "Is the training helping us to sell more houses?", in which case we have to go back to making like for like comparisons between developments and quantifying the ROI of the training, and it's quite likely that the answer is yes, but if the most that the sales exec contributes to a customer's

```
decision is, say, 10%, then that limits
the impact of any training. A more
valuable question might be to ask what
would happen if you didn't train sales
execs at all - you just got people off
the street and let them get on with it.
Then the question can't be whether the
training is effective or not, but WHICH
training is most effective.
```

In any open system, you can control the outcome or you can control the process, but you can't control both, because you can't predict what external factors will act upon the system.

You can either give the sales people a script, and accept that they may or may not sell houses, or you can set them the objective of selling houses, and not worry about how they achieve that, as long as they stay within the law.

But you can't tell them what to say *and* expect it to work, because no script can predict what the customers will say and do.

That would constitute a magical incantation, and if you've ever bought a house, you'll know that the only person who influences your decision is the person you're buying it with.

This is why it is so important to model the behaviour within the person within the culture, so that you can control for as many of these variables as possible.

Only then will evaluation have any meaning.

20 The Beginning

I'll bring this book to a close the same way I always do; with the beginning. When the training event, or the coaching session, or the book draws to and end, it is but one step in the learning journey. Every step is an opportunity to make a choice; either to carry on doing tomorrow what you did yesterday, or to look around you, see that the world is changing and adapt.

Our minds often fool us into only seeing what is the same from one day to the next. Why do today what you can put off until tomorrow? And why rock the boat when what you're doing works so well for you? Yet when you look back through the course of your career, or your life, or your family tree, you see that all of those tiny, almost imperceptible day to day changes created a revolution. And come the revolution, which side are you on?

We're arguably the dominant species on the planet because of our unique ability to adapt, and in adapting, we learn to shape our environment, and that changing environment holds part of our tacit knowledge, passing it to new generations. We learn the rules of the road because they are painted all over it. We learn the rules of office politics because the voices of empires past still echo through the corridors. And with the accelerating development of technology, all of the world's knowledge is just a click away.

Real time access to information, any time, anywhere, is changing the face of learning. But there will never be a substitute for watching a genius at work; a craftsman whose father before him, and his father before him, developed senses so finely tuned that he can measure more accurately than any micrometer and more quickly than any laser guided robot arm.

As we rely more and more on technology to take the mundane tasks out of our lives, we can take more time to sit, watch and listen to the craftsmen, artists and masters who are all around us in every walk of life.

Genius at Work presents a methodology to analyse and extract those innate talents, a process to refine their essence and share it with others. But, above all else, never forget what those talents represent, and never lose sight of the wonder and mystery that they hold.

Remember, wherever you are right now is no accident. You have spent a lifetime making decisions and learning from your experiences, and the path that you have followed has brought you right to this point, reading these words. Our journeys have converged on this very moment in time, and by unpicking those journeys together, we really can learn to discover Genius at Work.

21 Appendices

22 A Talent Modelling Methodology

Methodology

Typically, any organisation or team has a number of high performers who consistently outperform the average. It is becoming increasingly common that organisations have two sets of measurement criteria; explicit, task focused criteria such as sales targets and customer service metrics, and implicit, cultural criteria such as attitude, working environment and customer experience.

It is not enough to simply benchmark performance, because that benchmark is a static measurement in a changing environment. Managers often say that they have to "run to stand still" in a fast changing business environment, and part of the problem is the use of static performance benchmarks which give the illusion that the environment is changing.

In fact, it is easier to harness and direct this natural momentum for change than to create change based on an illusion of inertia.

By analysing a person's ability to get a certain result within a cultural system, we are able to discover not only the person's intuitive behaviour but also the cultural system within which that behaviour works best.

It is very common for companies to hire 'star players' such as high performing sales people and executives, only to find that they do not perform as expected. There was nothing wrong with the person, they were simply used to working within a different set of rules.

When I worked for a national telecoms operator back in the late 1990s, the company decided to make an aggressive push into the corporate market. In the past, it had made repeated, half-hearted attempts to achieve this and never succeeded, mainly for two factors which were the antithesis of the market leaders in this area – the company was slow and expensive.

In order to support this move, the company recruited 60 new sales people from companies who were known in this 'enterprise' market. Typically young, aggressive, target driven sales people with short attention spans. After a year, how many of those 60 sales people were left?

Just one.

Some people, over time, will learn the new rules and adapt to them, some will not.

Often, 'culture change' programmes are introduced at the development stage of the people cycle, by sending people on training courses to learn new organisational values. The problem with this is that it is rarely tied into the other parts of the people cycle – attraction and retention – so over time, the 'new' culture works its way out of the system, and the incumbent culture is preserved.

Culture change can be viewed as a natural process of evolution which is itself a learned adaptation to a changing environment. If your business environment is evolving, you need to evolve with it, supporting people at all stages of the people cycle at the same time. By changing the way you attract new people, those people will evolve the culture iteratively and systemically. In the long term, this creates a stable organisation, but it does require commitment and consistency of business strategy, because it will take a year or two for the new cultural rules and beliefs to become 'the way we do things around here'. Also, this is not a one off process. It is important to be constantly adapting and evolving as the market evolves. When companies only run change projects when the gap between their behaviour and the market environment is so big that profits start to fall, it is already too late.

So in modelling high performers and using that information to align the people cycle behind a vision and business plan, the result is greater alignment of the culture and the people within it. The result of this is that more of each individual's time, energy and commitment is focused on realising that vision.

The diagram to the left illustrates a poorly aligned organisation, where many people feel frustration as a result of being unable to contribute and make positive changes. Effort is wasted, re-organisations are common and, ultimately, people will disengage and do the minimum that they can.

Frustration is the feeling that forms when a person's desire to achieve a goal is blocked or hindered by a barrier which is not under their control.

This situation leads to small effects on a day to day basis, and those daily frustrations are compounded over time to lead to a real and measurable impact on business performance.

Aligning the skills of individuals with the rules and aspirations of the business as a whole encourages individuals to commit their time, energy and ideas. They feel recognised and rewarded because they feel they can make a positive impact on the business or their team.

Market
Brand
Culture
Skills
Behaviour
Workplace

Staff feel that they are making a difference to their working environment, including their colleagues and customers. As each person experiences the sense of achievement that comes from seeing their ideas and desire to achieve being put into action, they want to achieve more. This creates a strong sense that people have control over their personal effectiveness and results.

This situation also leads to small effects on a day to day basis, and those daily successes are compounded over time to lead to a real and measurable positive impact on business performance.

Benchmarking

We define a high performer simply by the results that they achieve. We don't look for who are popular, or who seems to be working hard, or who is doing things 'the right way'. Fundamentally, a high performer behaves in a way that is right for them, and because their perceptions and attitude are aligned with that of the organisational culture, high performance is the output or result. We determine the qualities which make someone a high performer and which can be replicated by comparing the perceptions, beliefs and behaviours of high performers to those of average performers.

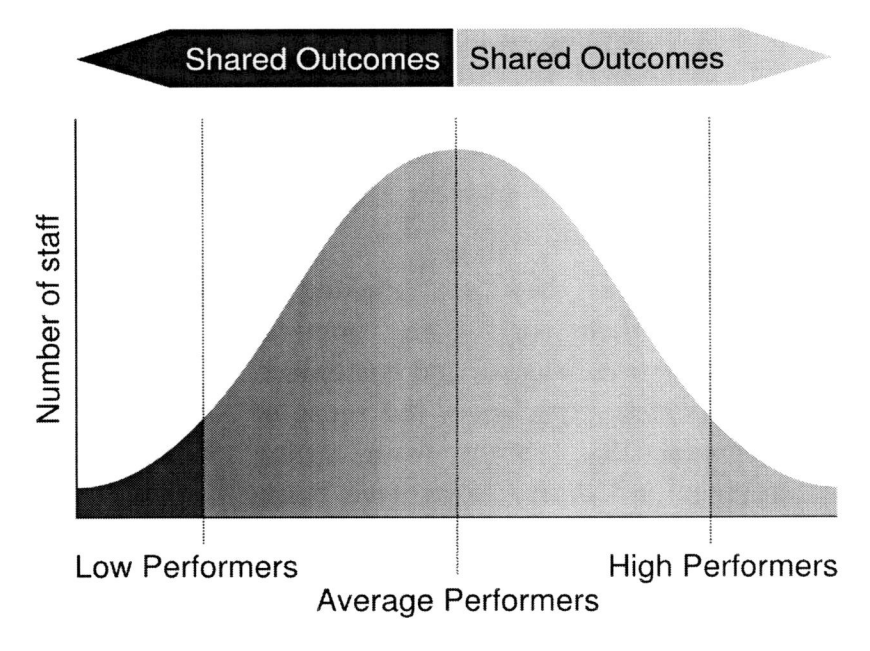

The reason for comparing high to average rather than poor performers is that the role model's behaviour is governed by a goal or outcome. High and poor performers do not share the same goals, but high and average performers typically do. What we are therefore modelling is the difference between two people who are both aiming for the same goal, one of whom has a set of skills and abilities that the other does not. Those skills are the result of typically many years of 'trial and error' learning, so their high performing behaviours have not been taught; they have naturally evolved.

Modelling

Since we are looking for the difference between a high performer and an average performer, it is not enough simply to model the high performer, because they will share many traits and behaviours with the majority of staff. What we are seeking is the small number of differences that give rise to a measurable difference in performance.

We use a hybrid approach to modelling which generates a model of individual behaviours within a cultural, systemic context and this is the key to our unique approach which preserves the cultural context for high performers.

Installation

The next stage is to install the model into people who are looking for improved performance. Ideally, we need to have contact throughout the installation process to ensure the model is being correctly installed. It is not sufficient to tell people what the steps of the process are, the installation requires an element of experiential learning which must be carefully facilitated to ensure consistent results.

Testing

We need to ensure that the model is correctly integrated into the wider system by testing the model in the live environment. Possibly the most important reason for testing is to understand how the model evolves in the live environment so that we can build that evolution back into the model.

Service integration

A logical extension of this work is to build the high performance model into areas such as recruitment, induction training, performance management and succession planning. If these systems are not integrated with each other, you're left with a number of disjointed components.

For example, if you don't learn why people leave then it's very difficult to recruit people who are more likely to stay. Very few companies conduct serious exit interviews or actively manage individuals out of the organisation, instead focusing on the 'numbers game' of recruitment and hoping that enough people stay to make it cost effective. Equally, very few companies think about how their recruitment activities attract certain personalities, and how those personalities thrive or struggle in the working culture. By seeing the people cycle as a snapshot of your culture, you can align all of the components activities to increase efficiency, engagement and productivity and reduce foreseeable attrition.

The people cycle

```
┌────Attraction────▶┌────Development────▶┌────Retention────▶
│Attract│Recruit│Select│ │Induct│Perform│Develop│ │Align│Succeed│Exit│
◀────Person────┘  ◀────Behaviour────┘  ◀────Culture────┘
```

We can apply the modelling data throughout the people cycle as follows:

Attraction — Ensure that marketing and branding are aligned with what the organisation is actually delivering.

Recruitment — Ensure that the recruitment process attracts the right people and sets their expectations correctly for the working environment and desired behaviours.

Selection — Create profiling templates and assessment centres that select in people who are most likely to perform well within the cultural environment.

Induction — Further refine expectations and align them with the reality of the organisation.

Performance — Create performance review processes that focus on high performing behaviours.

Development — Create development programmes and coaching frameworks that further enhance performance within the cultural context.

Alignment	Align individuals into teams and lead those teams in a way that enhances performance and positively reinforces the culture and environment.
Succession	Plan for the progression of individuals through the business in a way which evolves the culture against market changes and preserves high performance over time.
Exit	Use exit data to adapt the performance model, and manage individuals out of the business in a way that is aligned with the culture and which reinforces your brand as one which people would want to work for.

```
┌──── Attraction ────▶  ┌──── Development ────▶  ┌──── Retention ────▶
│ Attract  Recruit  Select │  Induct  Perform  Develop │  Align  Succeed  Exit
◀──── Person ────┘      ◀──── Behaviour ────┘      ◀──── Culture ────┘
```

The three broad phases of the people cycle work as follows:

- **Attraction** gets the right **people**
- **Development** shapes **behaviour**
- **Retention** builds a **culture**

23 Case Study: Retail Managers

This study was undertaken for a major UK retailer as part of the development of their graduate program which prepared graduates for one of three roles in the business. I studied role models identified by HR and business managers and compared them against average performers in order to create the detailed report reproduced here.

The study investigated three roles; store manager, buyer and finance analyst. The complete report was over 50 pages in length, this sample contains only the generic information and the store manager's role.

Some of the results were counter-intuitive and seemed to contradict training previously delivered, such as coaching skills for store managers. In fact, when analysing the results more deeply, what seem like contradictions make complete sense and reveal gaps in the thinking behind other development programs. Feedback like this enabled the client to refine other programs which were in place to ensure they were delivering against the needs of the business.

The result of the client incorporating this work into their graduate program was that they were able to deliver fully prepared graduates into the business after 9 months instead of the previous 12. Overall, the benefits of this were:

- Saving 25% on the cost of recruiting graduates into the business
- Protecting the unique culture of the businesses
- Ensuring more consistency in the retailer's approach to suppliers and customers

- Improving performance for other staff in the business
- Making future recruitment more precise, effective and economical

This chapter reproduces the modelling report in its entirety, except for the removal of any identifying details, so there will inevitably be overlap with some content that you've already read.

Project Overview

Client Organisation & Business Environment

[Client] is a UK based food and convenience retailer. The market environment ranges from large supermarkets to small privately owned grocery shops.

[Client]'s immediate competitors are national chains of small to medium food retailers and also the larger supermarkets in their small format stores.

Business Drivers for Replicating High Performance

In order to establish itself as the leading small format and local convenience food retailer, [Client] needs to attract and retain high performing people into key roles within the business. As part of this long term plan, the new graduate programme is recruiting and developing graduates into three parts of the business; finance, buying and retail. The future of the business depends on having the most effective people in these key roles.

Results and Behaviours Being Modelled

This project is primarily aimed at understanding the key behaviours of the three roles being modelled rather than modelling specific, identified skills. Therefore, the first step is to identify what the behaviours of high performers are so that these behaviours can be developed into graduates as part of the graduate programme.

Planned Outcomes

A model of high performance which can be used in the attraction and development of graduates joining the graduate programme as well as other HR processes such as the performance management system and also rewards systems.

Modelling Results

The following table captures key information about the client's cultural environment within which this modelling project has been conducted.

High performing organisations have a high degree of alignment between these levels.

Market & Trading Environment

Highly competitive, fast moving, often driven by price. Major supermarkets have traditionally driven lower prices from larger stores but are now moving into [Client]'s market segment with local convenience stores.

Brand Identity

Evolving from a legacy image that was closer to the old [previous retailer] brand to being the leading convenience retailer.

Cultural Rules and Beliefs

Not as good as the leading supermarkets i.e. higher prices, smaller range, lower availability.

Less negotiating strength due to smaller presence and sales volumes.

The brand is getting better.

Head office environment but not the pressure of London - geography/lifestyle important.

Sense of 'lucky to be here' following the redundancies. Empty office space serves as a daily reminder of this.

Focus on serving the customer through attractive stores and good product availability.

Skills, Ideas, Capabilities

Open communication, ad hoc meetings rather than using email internally.

Feels like you're working towards something.

People mostly allowed to contribute ideas and be creative, people able and expected to stretch between roles and cover for each other.

Behaviours and Key Activities

Highly team oriented, clear roles and hierarchy, junior roles analyse data, senior roles make decisions and communicate with the board, clear interdependency of roles, not only work related but also socially e.g. tea making rota.

Stores seem to be driven by executing plans dictated by decision makers and then reporting on the effect of those plans. Again, team oriented but communication seems to be highly variable amongst stores. Some rely on the daily 'huddle', other Store Managers communicate more openly throughout the working day. Again, clear roles and responsibilities. The high performing managers delegate clearly and pass both activities and performance targets down to the people in the store. The high performing managers also create their own clearly defined rules which creates a unique culture in their store.

Working Environment

Support Centre:

Friendly

It's OK to make mistakes

It's OK to not know something

Sense of 'lucky to be here' following the redundancies. Empty office space serves as a daily reminder of this

Stores

Focused on availability, customer experience e.g. cleanliness & organisation of store, approachable staff. Corporate procedures are followed as a routine.

Managers create their own rules around behaviour, standards, reward and recognition etc. which can make it difficult for one manager to step into another manager's store.

There seems to be a misalignment between the levels of cultural rules and brand identity. Whilst the new board is working hard to move away from the legacy brand image and market positioning in the same segment as [Competitor], [Competitor] etc., there are still many examples of this focus around the business.

Therefore, much of the business is still comparing itself to [Competitor] and this leads to a set of cultural beliefs that have a tangible influence in buying and retail, and a lesser influence in finance, possibly because of its less direct exposure to competition.

I don't know how [Client]'s customers view the brand, I can only speak as customers when I say that I view [Client] as the business it aspires to be, not the business it wants to move away from. The store renovation program certainly plays a vital role in that. Again, as customers, I can only comment that the store staff play a vital role in brand identity. In the stores run by high performing managers who I interviewed, there was a clear engagement of staff with the processes of running the store. I have visited other [Client] stores as a shopper and not seen this, and the brand that this conveyed was therefore quite different.

There also appears to be a misalignment between the image of the typical customer that drives decisions made in buying and finance and the actual customers in the stores. This is often to be expected as a side effect of generalisation, although I do have a concern that this also represents a change in customer demographic and behaviour which is not yet reflected in the buyers' assumptions.

Role 3: Retail

Results and Behaviour

This section deals with the key behavioural strategies of the role - what the person does, both internally/mentally and externally/physically, to achieve certain results.

Role

The store manager's role seems to be changing as the business evolves. Most notably, the store manager has much less autonomy and less influence over stocking decisions. The high performing store managers use this as an opportunity to devote more of their time to building high performing teams which are not reliant on the store manager for day to day decision making.

Managing the Team

The high performing store managers do not manage their stores. In fact, aside from looking for visible signs of the store running as it should do, the high performing manager does not get involved on a day to day basis in the detailed running of the store. Whilst the manager will take time to look around the store, talk to customers, operate the checkout if necessary and tidy up shelves, these activities seem to be based on observation rather than intervention.

The primary focus of the high performing store manager is the team. They manage the team to manage the store.

There are a number of specific ways in which they do this.

1. They use formally recorded data for feedback on store operation rather than looking at the activities directly, e.g. checking the log books for gap analysis rather than checking gaps personally.

2. They create routines for regular tasks which can be packaged and passed to a member of the team so that the task becomes part of that person's area of responsibility.

3. Interruptions which require their attention will be analysed to see if there is a way that they can be packaged as someone else's responsibility.

4. They delegate the task, the responsibility and the accountability for it, the result being that the person completely owns the task, there should be nothing that they need to go back to the manager for under normal circumstances.

5. When presented with a problem by a member of the team, they push the problem back onto the person presenting it. Only if necessary, they will offer guidance to work out a solution.

6. When giving feedback, they adopt a clear management style, not a coaching style. They give the person or team direct feedback about their behaviour and the consequences of their behaviour. They adopt this approach both for good news and for disciplinary feedback, so they don't ask "how do you think it went?", they tell the person how it went.

7. They spend time out of store, forcing their managers to become more autonomous.

8. They share data on store performance freely with the team and expect the team to understand how they influence that performance.

9. They use the line management structure in the store to manage performance. For example, if a checkout is untidy, they will ask the checkout operator's manager to give the feedback rather than intervene directly. This appears to preserve

the integrity of line management relationships, increasing the staff's autonomy.

Conversely, the average managers were focused on managing the staff, "People in store have the expertise to do what needs doing, I just need to make sure they are doing it"

The high performers manage the staff through feedback data, not by 'making sure they are doing it'.

The two high performing store managers interviewed both had a background in retail and a desire for power and authority. At the start of their retail career, they identified the store manager as the most powerful person and aimed for that role. Now, as store managers, they are both looking for their next promotion.

Their high delegation management style is therefore driven by a need to free up their time to take on parts of their managers' job such as organising meetings, collating report data and managing more than one store. The way in which they free up their time is by packaging their responsibilities into smaller chunks that can be delegated and wholly owned by the person taking on that piece of work. Once they have done this, they mainly rely on performance data as their feedback mechanism rather than looking over the person's shoulder which obviously would negate the time saved by delegating.

This approach extends into day to day store management, where the manager will look at recorded data such as in log books rather than overseeing the activities directly. This is dependent on the manager setting clear expectations about the completion of paperwork and regular tasks, so his or her expectation is that the recorded data is always true and up to date. If this is not the case, the manager speaks directly to the person responsible to remind them of the need to record the information.

Upon taking over a store, there is a period of time within which the staff are getting used to the new manager, so at this stage the manager is very clear and explicit about his or her ground rules and expectations - defining the store's culture. Once this has been established, it is not affected by staff turnover since the existing staff will educate new staff.

In contrast, the average store managers keep management tasks to themselves and do not delegate as much. There is a much stronger sense of the average store being an island, separate to the rest of the [Client] community, within which the staff have their tasks and the manager has his or her tasks, for example:

"There's an awful lot that they get protected from, a lot that I do that they don't have to see or experience because I don't think it's necessary for them"

It's interesting that the average manager thinks about protecting the staff from management tasks whereas the high performer thinks about challenging the staff by delegating management tasks. This results in an average store that is less able to cope with the manager's absence.

It would be interesting to compare store performance to the manager's working patterns to see if there is a connection between the store's performance and the manager's presence. Partly this may be due to a poor delegation style where staff may be more likely to do things properly only when they are being watched, and partly this may be due to a backlog of operational decisions that have to wait until the manager returns.

"The majority of my work's been done today because I was in yesterday" - the high performing manager wouldn't need to come in yesterday to finish his or her work because it would already have been delegated.

The 'island' is also reflected in the manager's awareness of what's happening outside of their store. The high performers knew exactly how their store compared to others, the average manages did not have as much awareness of this.

Feedback and Discipline

The establishment of rules and expectations is an important activity for the high performing manager, and it's worth understanding this in a little more detail.

When a member of staff breaks a hard rule such as attendance, the manager tackles the issue as quickly as possible. The manager appears to delegate tasks but to handle discipline issues directly.

The high performing manager reiterates the rules and expectations, and details the consequences of the person's behaviour in terms of its impact on others. This appears to be a very effective way of dealing with the issue.

In one case where the person in question did not change their behaviour, the manager again tackled the issue quickly and gave the person a formal warning. The manager said that he wasn't proud of doing things like that, but the person has to be responsible for their own behaviour, and they have to be made aware of the impact of their behaviour on other people.

You'll notice that this is essentially the same strategy as for delegation - the manager is detailing the task and giving the person the responsibility and accountability for it. If the person fails to achieve the task, the consequences also fall to them.

In delegation, the person who owns the task is responsible for completing it. When they fail they are responsible for the consequences, when they succeed, they get the recognition and praise.

In disciplinary matters, the same is true. The manager makes the person aware of what is expected, why and how it impacts on other people. The person then accepts the responsibility and consequences of either following those rules or not.

If the person changes their behaviour, the change is owned and motivated by them and they get the recognition that they deserve.

If the person does not change their behaviour, they bring the consequences upon themselves and the high performing manager is not slow to act.

The high performing manager therefore creates a set of rules and expectations which are external to the manager. Both praise and discipline are therefore consistent and fair, judged only against these external criteria. This serves to depersonalise disciplinary situations, which I imagine greatly reduces conflict and stress for the manager.

In contrast, the average manager personalises disciplinary situations, leaning on the person's obligation to the manager. This creates dependency and conflict and means that the store team is more reliant on the manager's judgement about the rules. This extends from rules about behaviour and attendance to rules about store operation. This is tied to the average store manager's involvement in the running the store compared to the high performer's desire to enable the store to run itself.

If I also compare the use of management and coaching styles, the average manager coaches much more than the high performer. The high performer gives feedback as a manager - telling the person or team rather than asking them for their opinion - and only coaches when a person has a question about a delegated task. The average manager seems to coach more often, perhaps as a result of their desire to develop their staff.

In one case, an average manager talked about a trading manager who had been promoted to store manager.

"It wasn't me that gave her the chance, she did all the hard work"

This is something that I frequently hear from "life coaches" who attribute change or learning to the client's hard work and say that they only guided the process. In contrast, the store manager is able to take responsibility for their part of the process because they have clearly delegated. In this example, the store manager nurtured the trading manager, so in a way the promotion was the store manager's responsibility. A high performer is happy for their staff to be promoted but sees this as a clear separation of roles with each person doing what is required of them.

Strategy Implementation

It was interesting to discover that the high performing store managers will question the timescales or resource implications for an ad hoc task, rather than directly criticising the rationale behind the task itself.

When presented with a task that the store manager doesn't understand or disagrees with the need for, he or she will question the rationale in order to understand it.

Here's what one high performing manager said:

"When you deliver something it's about owning it yourself so if I didn't agree with it initially I would have found out the reasons for it, looked at the benefit then go and deliver it and if I deliver it to my people then I own it"

A very useful and important process arises from this. Faced with an unpleasant or seemingly irrational task, the high performing manager will question it in order to form their own rationale, at which point it shifts from a 'head office' task to a task owned by the manager. This seems to fit with their approach to delegation where they want people to own tasks in their entirety.

For example, redundancy is not pleasant. One manager said, "If these people leave the company then it's safeguarding the company for a lot more people", thereby creating a self-owned rationalisation for the task.

I suspect that an average manager would regard an unpleasant task as being something that "they" want done and questions the task in order to delay or divert it, whereas the high performer questions the task in order to take ownership of it so that it becomes something that he or she believes in and, importantly, may be able to delegate.

Reporting

The high performing store managers appreciate the importance of reporting and they understand the meaning of the data itself. Since the manager is not looking over people's shoulders, he or she uses the formally reported data as the measure of store performance as much as people in the support centre do. In a way, this gives the store manager the same understanding of store behaviour as you might expect the people in the support centre to have.

Preparation and Planning

The high performing store managers plan for everything, even for the unexpected. They do this by accepting that there will be interruptions and emergencies, and by analysing every unplanned to event to see if they can turn it into a process or task and give it to someone else.

This is a fundamentally different approach to someone who feels that, as store manager, they are too important to get involved in low level tasks.

The high performing store manager will, if necessary, tackle anything that needs doing in store whilst recognising that fire fighting is ultimately an inefficient use of their time. Therefore they are valuing their own time and seeking ways to achieve more in the time they have available.

In short, by turning reactive tasks into procedures which can be delegated, the high performing manager frees up time to be reactive.

Attention to Detail

The high performing store manager has good attention to detail upon noticing an exception but does not get lost in the detail. Starting with a high level of detail, the high performer will notice exceptions such as gaps in availability and will then shift to a lower level of detail, asking questions to understand why something has happened and what is being done to resolve it.

For example, he or she will notice an untidy shelf and will ask the member of staff responsible (or their manager/supervisor) to take care of it. He or she will personally handle anything that is a quick task such as picking up some litter or discarded packaging, but for anything that takes longer than a few seconds he or she will delegate it, which also reinforces the manager's expectations about the task.

For example, if the manager tidies the shelves, how will the staff ever know that it needs doing, and that the manager expects them to do it? The high performing managers are therefore good at reinforcing desired behaviours and giving feedback on performance, which is dependent on their ability to notice what needs doing to a high enough level of detail.

Conversely, the average manager will tend to look more superficially at, for example, the condition of the store. The average manager will accept more inconsistency in store appearance.

Store Image

All of the store managers interviewed saw the relationship between the store's image and their own image. The difference was that the high performing managers focused on improving the store and team which reflected on them, whist the average managers focused on improving their own image which reflected on the store.

The average manager wants to be seen to be doing a good job, the high performing manager had a much lower profile and wants his or her store to be seen to be performing well.

The fundamental difference here is that when someone is concerned with their image, they automatically imply an observer. An image is not useful in itself; someone must be looking at it.

Therefore, the average store manager will adopt the ideal behaviour of a store manager when they are being observed, whilst the high performing store manager will adopt that behaviour all of the time, partly because they are the observer of the store and partly because they feel the store is always being observed by the customers and staff.

Let me summarise this important point.

The average manager is concerned with his or her own image and therefore acts as an ideal manager when being observed by someone who they want to convey that image to.

The high performing manager is concerned with his or her store's image and therefore acts as an ideal manager when they are observing the store - which is all of the time.

I suspect that the difference is most apparent in store performance data rather than in direct observation of the managers.

For example, when interviewing one of the average managers, we walked around the store several times. We passed the bread aisle where a loaf of bread had fallen off the shelf and was wedged behind a cardboard promotional display where it was plainly visible. We walked past it three times in total, twice with the manager and once with the manager and trading manager to observe their daily tour of the store to check gaps and store appearance. I didn't mention it because I wanted to see if either of them would - they did not.

Another example: in one of the average stores, there had been some damage to the store's roof and during a period of heavy rain, water had leaked in extensively, damaging stock and leaving a pool of water on the floor. The store staff had piled paper towels around the base of the shelves to absorb the water. The manager said that neither the landlord of the building nor [Client]'s facilities department would take responsibility to fix it, therefore they had to manage as best they could.

I imagine that a high performing manager would not be so accepting of the situation. I can easily imagine either of the managers interviewed clearing their diaries, driving to [Head Office], physically removing the estate manager, taking him or her to the store and doing the same thing with the landlord so that all three of them could meet in person, in the store to see the impact of the damage and negotiate a solution.

The difference? The high performing manager has achieved the position of authority that he or she has sought, therefore nothing that happens in their store is outside of their control.

Conversely, the average manager says, "If you can't influence it you can't change it so there's no point getting upset"

Staff Development

It appears that the average store managers believe that staff are inherently limited and unaware of their own potential. Therefore they break down tasks and training opportunities into what they believe the staff can manage:

"It's about giving them chunks that they can digest rather than giving it all at once"

They certainly enjoy developing the staff, the difference being that they appear to single out staff who perceive have high potential and low self belief, and the enjoy nurturing those people. The high performing manager seems to not focus on developing the staff directly but on maximum delegation which challenges the staff and they either step up to that challenge or they don't.

The high performing manager therefore sets the bar high for his or her staff, giving them all a potential opportunity to grow and learn. The average manager singles out staff for development and sets the bar at a level just above the person's own self belief:

"I've got two people who I've earmarked to be trading managers and it's really secretly training them without them knowing it"

The manager in this case believes that if these staff find out they are being earmarked for promotion they will be afraid to take the opportunity.

The high performing manager doesn't single people out in this way, and therefore is not concerned about staff not taking opportunities. The high performer will, however, observe staff performance in respect of delegated challenges and will have a promotion and succession plan in mind. This is different to developing specific people against a predetermined plan.

The average manager tends to identify people who he or she thinks needs a chance to prove themselves or a chance to shine. Certainly with the managers interviewed, a mentor had done the same for them in a key stage of their careers and they now seek out that feeling of nurturing someone else.

In comparison, the high performer's approach would tend not to develop staff who had potential but lacked self belief, so in a high performer's store, some staff may be 'left behind' who would otherwise flourish if nurtured.

Beliefs, Rules and Perceptions

The operating principles and behavioural rules that form the foundation of high performing behaviour.

These are unconscious processes which shape the resulting behaviours and as such are not normally available at the level of conscious awareness.

Behavioural Rules

Procedures	Creates procedures where non exist to increase the autonomy of store staff
Towards	Goal and result oriented
People	Achieves tasks through relationships
Team	Regards store management as a team effort, but does not lose self in the team, maintains individual responsibilities
External	Feedback and information driven, sees results in staff and store performance

Difference	Notices exceptions that may impact on the smooth running of the store
Active	Takes action early, especially to turn interruptions into tasks which can be delegated
General	Seeks out high level information then drops down to the details for exceptions such as gaps or missed KPIs

Beliefs

The store staff can step up to any challenge or task

Routines and processes are key to consistent performance

People don't need watching but they do need direct feedback

"Retail is about fighting for the customer"

"Some people have got the capability but not the confidence, some have the confidence but not the capability" (i.e. self confidence is the key to career progression)

"When you deliver something it's about owning it yourself"

The high performing store managers had followed a similar career path to that of the buyers; working in a supermarket whilst at school or university, and seeking greater power and authority. The difference was that this group identified the store manager as the most influential person in the business rather than the buyer.

It seems that many people, at the start of their careers, develop a great deal of respect for a particular person who you might regard as a mentor. The high performing store managers identified their first store manager as someone they could respect, and they identified that manager as having authority and control.

In contrast, the average store managers identified someone else as their early mentor, and I found an interesting correlation between that mentor and the manager's career aspirations and the way in which they manage their store.

The average managers did not have a background in retail but were identified by a store management development program as having the potential to be good managers. I think that they are good managers, but they are doing the job of managing, they did not spend their lives in pursuit of the position of store manager. Therefore they do what is required of them, not what they personally believe in.

At an early age, the high performing managers formed a future self image of themselves as store managers. As their careers have progressed, they have shaped themselves into that idealised image. Their drive for greater authority and responsibility has caused them to move that self image on so that it is now of themselves as regional managers.

Conversely, the average managers formed a future self image of themselves in a different role than retail store manager. They too shaped themselves towards that role but found themselves working in other roles. Whilst there was enough overlap between the two to ensure their performance in the role was good enough, it was rarely aligned with their personal identity. You can hear this in people's language in phrases such as, "It's not really how I see myself".

The average store managers can therefore perform well if there is sufficient overlap or if they can mould the store manager's role to the key aspects of the self image. For example, if their self image is of a trainer, educating and sharing knowledge, then they will focus on that aspect of the job. They will want to nurture and develop staff but the store's operational standards may slip.

Another way to look at this is that they are good managers, they are not necessarily retail managers. I believe they can learn to be, but they have framed the requirements of the job through the belief that they were hired for their good management skills and the non-retail experience that they can bring to the role. Combine this with their low exposure to other managers on a day to day basis and they have neither the incentive nor the information to make the shift from being good generic managers to being good retail managers.

"By coming across to retail I was keeping all of my management skills I was just using them with a different product"

"Retail is retail"

Does this mean you can only hire store managers who have worked in retail forever and who have always aspired to be store managers? No, it means that you have to get retail into the blood by creating the desired self image. Graduates need to be inspired by retail, not just programmed to serve. I believe that the high performing store managers would be ideal people to inspire the graduates.

Conversely, hiring only store managers who have a desire for promotion and authority then creates a future problem of too many store managers applying for too few regional manager jobs.

One store manager thought that not all store managers were interested in promotion and wanted to stay as store managers, I wonder if this is instead a lack of self belief on their part.

In any hierarchical organisation, a desire for greater responsibility will always drive the person 'up' the hierarchy in search of more of what they desire. This can create a number of effects, for example that you accept a natural turnover of store managers who become frustrated at the lack of promotion opportunities. At the other end of the scale, if you have only just enough high performing store managers for the available promotions then the result is a significant number of stores with average managers.

In the retail business, there is a budget for waste, as if it is accepted that in order to maintain availability there must be over supply. Perhaps the same approach works within the HR operation too.

Culture

The cultural rules that provide the foundation for the individual high performing behaviours.

These cultural elements describe the environment around the role being modelled and are in addition to the corporate cultural elements described elsewhere.

Each store appears to have its own unique flavour of the [Client] culture. If we regard culture as 'language plus rules' then we have a combination of the [Client] language with the unique behavioural rules of the store.

This seems to cause some problems when a store manager steps in to manager another store. The conflict of rules and expectations can cause store performance to fall, even though both the store and the temporary manager normally perform well.

Retail - the Difference

The difference between high performing and average store managers which stands out most clearly is their desire to create a self sufficient store.

(Note to readers of this book: Don't assume that all retailers want self sufficient stores, this is a cultural quirk where a more 'hands off' head office approach creates a void that some store managers step into, creating an environment which just happens to deliver against key business metrics. This would not work in a more centralised culture, and is a good example of a complex set of behaviours arising from an attitude within an environment.)

For years, management development training has taught delegation skills, but that is not what is happening here. The high performing manager does not focus on delegation - he or she focuses on creating a self sufficient store and delegation is simply one means to achieving that.

The high performing manager is focused on results, leaving staff to make judgements on what activities best achieve those results.

The high performing manager delegates in order to free up time, whereas the average manager delegates for other reasons such as staff development. The average manager is selective about what he or she delegates, based on their perception of the staff member's ability. In order to delegate for the purpose of staff development, the manager has to monitor a person's performance and give feedback, which takes time and negates the benefits of delegation.

The high performing manager sets a challenge and expects everyone to rise to it. The average manager focused on developing individuals who they perceive will benefit from development.

It's almost as if the high performers believe that their staff are inherently capable, whereas the average manager believes their staff must be developed in order to become capable.

The average manager is concerned with their self image and since an image presupposes an observer, observation is the driver for their behaviour. At one end of the scale this means they only perform as a manager when being observed or measured. At the other end of the scale this means they perform as a manager all the time in case someone visits the store to observe them.

In order to create a self image you have to put yourself, mentally, in the position of an observer and look back at yourself. This means that the self image will always be an idealised past or future representation - a snapshot of yourself as you were, or as you imagine you will be.

Since the average managers interviewed did not always aspire to be retail managers, they have created a future self image of themselves as a competent manager which presupposes they do not see themselves in that role now.

The high performing managers created the future self image at the start of their retail careers. As they have become store managers, they have recreated the self image of themselves as regional managers, echoing their continuing desire for career progression and greater authority.

The high performing managers are also aware of the connection between the store's reputation and their own, and for them this works in reverse. They are concerned with the image of the store rather than their own image, so in this case they are themselves the observer. They see their performance reflected in the store's performance. As the observer, they are always watching and are therefore always looking for ways to systemise and delegate tasks so that the store can become ever more self sufficient.

This frees up the manager's time in two important ways; it allows them time for reactive tasks and emergencies, and it frees up time for them to seek delegation from their managers, preparing them for their next promotion.

Since the average managers do not focus on creating autonomy, they tend to hold on to decision making and only selectively and partly delegate tasks, creating greater dependency. This means that reactive tasks and emergencies are an interruption and create time conflict.

The focus on staff development meant that the average managers spent more time coaching staff whereas the high performers would manage when appropriate and coach when appropriate, and there were clear distinctions between the two.

One of the high performers said, "Some people have got the capability but not the confidence, some have the confidence but not the capability". So all of the managers understood that self confidence or self belief is important in career progression. The average managers saw this is a cue to intervene in someone's career development, the high performers saw it as a way of selecting out people who don't have the confidence to seek promotion.

In summary, the average manager's role is to manage the store. The high performing manager's role is to drive the store to manage itself.

Overall Observations

Culture

Focus around the business on comparing [Client] with the big supermarkets drives a set of associated beliefs, for example:

- We're not as big as [Competitor], and therefore our suppliers don't take us as seriously

- We're not as cheap as [Competitor], therefore we have to work harder to get customers to buy from us

- Our typical customer is a retired person doing a main shop locally and are therefore not as sensitive to price and quality

Most of the people interviewed said that what drew them to [Client] is the friendly, team oriented culture. Some of the subjects had left or turned down roles in other retailers because of this cultural environment.

Data

The [Client] business generates and consumes huge volumes of data. This appears to serve the aim of presenting every customer with exactly the products they want at the time the walk into the store, and also enticing them to buy more than they had come in for, or to try new products that complement what they came in for.

Of course, the stores cannot be rearranged and stocked to suit every individual customer, so the data is generalised to create a 'typical' customer. In store, the primary focus is availability, so the stores aim to have as much stock as possible, but not too much, of the products that they are instructed to sell.

New product decisions are made on the basis of data, some of which is historical and some of which is based on trials. Therefore since data is collected from sales, decisions are primarily driven by customer behaviour.

I imagine that a consequence of this is that the data you collect from sales always confirms that you sell what you have available, so it makes it harder to change the retail strategy based on gathering sales data. The new retail strategy around the availability of core products seems to be a focusing of strategy rather than a change.

In a positive sense, this means that you always respond to the needs of your customers. On the other hand, it means that you tend to reinforce the customer profile and behaviour that you have had in the past rather than identifying the types of customers you want in the future.

There seems to be a widely accepted belief that [Client]'s typical customer is an older or retired person who shops locally because they can't or don't want to travel to a [Competitor] or [Competitor] and are therefore less sensitive to price and brand. If this is indeed the typical customer, then this potentially creates the problem that [Competitor] suffered; that the target market is shrinking.

Conversely, some of the interview subjects told me that in City Centre stores, the typical customer is a professional commuter, stopping for a top up shop on the way home. Certainly on our visits to stores, both for interviewing and for shopping, I have observed that the older typical customer makes up the minority of shoppers. Our point is that basing strategic decisions on historical data - even data from only a week ago - will tend to root the organisation in the past. This is neither good nor bad, you must simply ensure it is aligned with your strategy.

When the finance analysts provide a report on the viability of a new product range, the decision is based partly on historical data which shows that the product hasn't sold in the past. This leads to a decision based on the summary, "This won't work because...", which can lead to a risk aversion culture, which in an uncertain environment is not necessarily a bad thing. The alternative is to ask, "How do we make this work?" For example, how does [Client] attract the customers it wants in the future, rather than how does it serve the customers it has had in the past.

Overall, the culture of the business appears to be highly data driven. There is a reality of what is happening within stores which is turned into data which is sent to Bristol where it is analysed so that people can turn the data back into a mental representation of what is happening within store. Everyone interviewed in Bristol spoke about using the data from various systems to build up a mental picture of store activity; whether behind the scenes in the management of the store and the supply chain or in the behaviour of the shoppers in the store front.

In short, the decision makers in the Support Centre can't see and hear what is going on in every store, during every minute of every day. They collect data which represents what is happening and from that, attempt to recreate the reality of what is happening in a generalised way that they can apply to all stores. They then make decisions using that data and turn those decisions back into data that can be communicate to stores. The stores take action on that data and as a result, what is going on in the stores changes. And so on.

The diagrams below shows this communication cycle with the three roles that have been modelled mapped onto it.

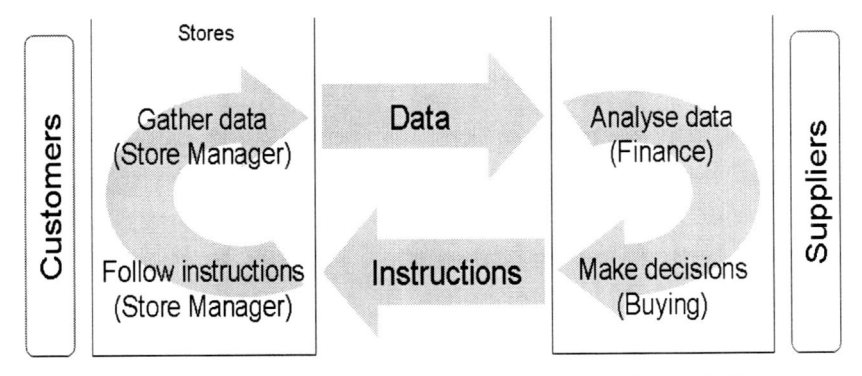

[Diagram: Customers | Stores: Gather data (Store Manager) → Data → Analyse data (Finance); Follow instructions (Store Manager) ← Instructions ← Make decisions (Buying) | Suppliers]

Since every number in every system is gathered from an activity in the business, effective decision making means turning those numbers back into a representation of the original activities.

This is essentially the same process of deletion, distortion and generalisation that is present in human sensory perception where the stores are analogous to the body and sensory organs, and the Support Centre is analogous to the brain. Internal data capture and communication systems are analogous to the nervous system.

This metaphor is important for two reasons:

1. There is always a time delay between data, decision, action and feedback. Shortening this time enables higher quality feedback, more accurate behaviour and therefore better decisions that increase the organism's chances of survival.

2. The process of deletion, distortion and generalisation means that the organism responds, not to reality, but to an approximation of reality that is only as accurate as the organism's ability to handle the amount of data generated.

If we view the organisation as a large scale organism, we can see that the same two issues of information handling exist.

1. It's not the big that eat the small, it's the fast that eat the slow. Response time is critical to survival in a changing environment.

2. Simplifying data makes it less accurate, therefore you can either hire more people to process more data, or invest in more IT systems to process more data, or base decisions on the most useful generalisation, accepting its limitations. Believing the data to be 'true' is probably the greatest risk of all.

The most notable generalisation is of the typical [Client] customer which seems to drive buying decisions and retail strategy. The question is therefore not how to gather more data on more customers to create many typical customers, but what the ideal customer will be in the future in order to achieve the business strategy. Whilst this is still a generalisation, it is one which guides organisational responses towards the future rather than into the past.

When limited IT systems were available to analyse data in the past, the key problem seems to have been generalisation, for example what products were popular in a store in Eastbourne were not the same as those for London or a petrol forecourt. Greater granularity of data addresses the problem of generalisation, but it creates another - information overload.

This was particularly evident amongst the buyers who make decisions almost entirely on the data presented.

There are too many factors to take into account, so they appear to make decisions based on immediately available data and then tweak their decisions based on subsequent findings. Clearly, the more experience a buyer has of his or her product area, the more informed these decisions are. They certainly seemed to base stocking decisions on a small number of criteria which in turn represented a broad base of product and retail knowledge.

For instance, to stock a new product means to take another product off the shelf. Apart from the sales data of the product that will go out of stock, it seems very difficult to analyse all of the consequences of the decision, so the approach taken appears to be to do it anyway and then wait for the data to show the effect of the decision when the decision may then be reversed.

Whilst this broad knowledge may seem difficult to replicate within the graduates in a short space of time, we should remember that there is sufficient data generated within the business to allow anyone to make these decisions because the cause of making, for example, a change to the ranging priority of a product is the sales data itself.

Deletion and distortion seem to be less evident in the communication chain. In particular, the honesty of the finance teams was interesting. They appeared to be happy to present good or bad news as long as the quality of the analysis was not in question. Therefore, they are not inclined to present the numbers that people want to see; they present the numbers as they are. The only issue with this is that the numbers as they are may not reflect the future direction of the business as I have mentioned previously.

The board's shift of focus from chasing [Competitor] to being the leading convenience retailer doesn't seem to have reached all parts of the organisation. Prices are compared to [Competitor]'s, mainly because it is easy to gather [Competitor]'s prices electronically. The stores compare their offers to [Competitor]'s and the buyers compare their buying power to [Competitor]'s. Clearly [Competitor] has dominated the retail landscape, both amongst its customers and with the general public through its huge media presence.

If I were advising on retail strategy, I would be suggesting that you need to focus more, right across the business, on the convenience market and leave [Competitor] to fight their own battles. You need to find your own niche and stick to it rather than confusing the issue with any mention of [Competitor]. For example, the buyers don't think they have the buying power of [Competitor], however it is not in the interests of manufacturers to increase [Competitor]'s market share. Instead of feeling second best to [Competitor], the buyers should be driving the point that, as the leading convenience retailer, [Client] is in a unique position that [Competitor] will never occupy. I still believe that the local presence and the personal relationships between staff and regular shoppers are key to [Client]'s success. As new entrants such as [Competitor] come into the market, I suggest that [Client] risks being caught in the middle market; not the cheapest, not the biggest, not the most expensive, not the smallest. Historically, companies that are caught in the middle of a market struggle to survive, unless they create a niche.[15]

In talking to the store managers and asking them what they think a typical customer is, they echoed our own observations in store - there isn't one, at least not in social demographic terms. The typical [Client] customer appears to be 'someone who lives locally' and again I would suggest that this is your key strength which you can still do more to build upon.

But since I'm not advising you on retail strategy, I won't mention it.

There is one more important point about basing decisions on current sales data - you only know what customers are buying, not what they are not buying.

One of the buyers mentioned a specific flavour of a product and said that it isn't stocked because the typical [Client] customer doesn't understand what it is. When I was in one of the stores talking to the manager, a woman of about 70 asked for that specific flavour and was told it wasn't stocked. She was exactly a typical customer, according to the generalised model, and she certainly understood the flavour. It's easy to say this is an isolated case and you can't stock every product that everyone wants. On the other hand, what are the chances of a buyer mentioning that flavour and on the day I was in store, a customer asking for it? There doesn't seem to be a system for recording this kind of data about what your customers are not buying because it isn't stocked. By basing decisions on what they are buying rather than on

---

15 About a year after this report was produced, this prediction came true. The retailer was acquired by a competitor and all of its stores were either rebranded or closed.

what they want to buy, you may be missing important opportunities to develop the brand in line with your customers' changing needs.

Decision Making

To an external observer, the organisation appears to be driven in a highly centralised way with the board driving strategic decision making and the buyers driving tactical product decision making. Particularly in the stores, the impact of these decisions was visible, along with the conflict that is sometimes created, for example around task deadlines and workload.

It appears that this highly centralised decision making function relies heavily on data, however the journey that the data takes to get to the board, as described above, may impact on the quality of that data and therefore the quality of the decision making process.

I would define the quality of a decision based only on its longevity. If you find that the decision does not meet your expectations in 'real life' and you have to change the course of action, this is often a sign that the data supporting the decision did not reflect 'real life' in the first place.

One example of this is the new store rota scheduling system. It seems that data has been collected from all store staff in order to categorise their level of flexibility around working patterns. The collection of the data itself caused some workload conflicts in larger stores. Our understanding is that the data will be used to build a software scheduling system which will deliver store rotas based on staff flexibility which takes into account seasonal retail trends.

The obvious downside to this is the time delay. By the time the data is collected, sorted and used to generate a rota, the level of flexibility of staff will have changed and store managers may have to make manual adjustments. I suspect that for a large number of staff, their flexibility is not static and changes around school terms, holidays, health etc. If staff are to be shared between stores then I can see the benefit of a centralised rota scheduling system. Otherwise, it adds delay into what I suspect is a very dynamic decision making process.

I trust that there are sound operational decisions for introducing the system, I'm just using it as an example to illustrate the point about delay in a decision making system.

I would also guess that high performing store managers experience fewer staffing problems and therefore benefit least from the new system. I would suggest that this is due to two key reasons; firstly, communication with staff and secondly an understanding of the retail business and its trends, gathered from their many years in the industry.

Communication

The aspect of culture that struck me most was communication. Many corporate cultures actively prevent communication, for example people who sit a few feet apart will email each other rather than have a direct conversation. In [Client], the opposite was true. Everyone's first thought on raising a question was to physically go and talk to the person with the answer. Of all of the businesses I have worked in and with, this is one of the most people driven.

A regulated business would typically be different to this, perhaps because of the need for audit t[industry]s on all communications and decisions. A blame culture tends to drive people and teams into silos, cutting off communication from the rest of the business and causing people to communicate via email so that they don't have to deal with the immediacy of face to face interaction.

Of course, other organisations don't actively block communication, but if you start a new job and receive emails from people who you can see sitting at their desks, you learn that this is the accepted way to communicate, and this is the way that cultural rules are passed on to new generations.

The people driven nature of the business leads to the subjectivity of decisions that I have already mentioned. Once again, this is neither good nor bad and it has both advantages and disadvantages compared to automating decision processes.

Roles, Hierarchy and Knowledge

In modelling the three people from Finance, it occurred to me that what makes a high performer in a junior finance role may not be the same characteristics that make a high performer in a senior role. Certainly the people I interviewed seemed quite content for their managers to take the responsibility for decision making, and viewed job and industry experience as a valuable asset that they did not necessarily possess. For example, the ability to use their years of experience to make a complex financial calculation mentally and for the result to be very close to the result that came from data analysis.

The downside of this is that it potentially places the decision making responsibility with senior managers, taking [Client] back to the old culture where tacit knowledge was protected instead of being systemised and widely available. The creation of bespoke analysis systems for different teams is a part of this process of knowledge protection, for example Access, Excel, SQL and all of the mainframe systems such as those for gap analysis, product ranging etc. - "We keep all our information separate to the rest of the business because it's quite important"

I believe that from a corporate point of view, it is not a good idea to be reliant on people who can use their experience to make mental calculations, because that makes the organisation highly dependent on those individuals, a situation which appears to have been changed by the redundancies but which may be creeping back in. The issue is not the risk of mistakes but the risk of losing a person with irreplaceable knowledge.

The good news about this for the graduate programme is that the right people will acquire the right experience and will therefore, over time, develop similar abilities.

Recommendations

Self Image and Identity

Spend some time during the training program getting the graduates to form a future self image which is closely aligned with the business strategy for that role and creates a compelling point of reference for them.

Use role models and mentors to help the graduates identify the qualities which they most admire and aspire to.

Getting the Picture

Time in store is highly valuable, not just for giving graduates a sense of what happens within store but to submerse them in the [Client] culture. The more time they spend in a variety of roles in store, the more accurate their mental representations of store activity are likely to be, and spending time in store is something that I suggest the graduates do throughout the program, not just at the start of it.

Recommendations for the Talent Cycle

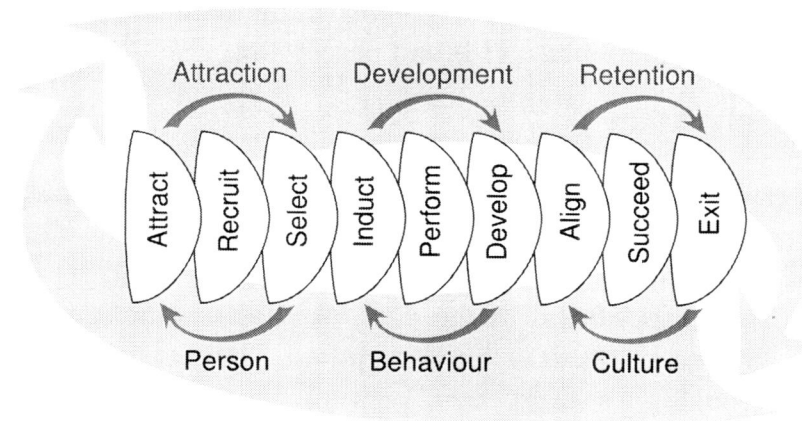

Attraction — Attract, Recruit, Select — Person
Development — Induct, Perform, Develop — Behaviour
Retention — Align, Succeed, Exit — Culture

Attraction

Many of the people in buying and retail roles had always worked in retail, starting off 'stacking shelves' and aspiring to a role with more authority, either in store as a manager or at 'head office' as a buyer. The choice seems to depend on where they perceived the power and control being. Therefore, the stores are probably a good place to look for future talent in store management and buying. In finance, it is important to attract people based on the [Client] culture as a friendly, supportive environment which enables a better quality of life than would perhaps be the case at [Competitor].

Recruitment

No data was gathered on the current recruitment process. This year, the graduate programme will recruit 29 graduates. The business as a whole will recruit around 20,000 people. It seems logical to apply the same care to the majority of people that [Client] recruits, especially since the majority of these will be customer facing staff and will therefore have a greater immediate impact on customer experience and brand perception.

Selection

Interview subjects who had previously joined as graduates regarded the assessment centres highly, commenting that they were tough, thorough and were good at selecting in the right candidates. In the past, the assessment centres for finance seemed to have recruited some people who were looking for short term, high impact development of the kind they might get at a 'big four' accountancy practice. I understand that this has now changed.

Induction

The rotation aspect of the graduate programme was again highly regarded. To enable even greater openness and communication between teams, and to protect against isolation of departments, you might consider giving graduates rotation assignments outside of the role that they are recruited into so that they can experience everything that happens in the business and clearly understand the impact of their role on it.

Performance

Other than financial reporting data and business KPIs, I did not see any personal performance data. As a general rule, individual performance goals should be closely aligned with business performance measures.

Development

Not enough data was gathered. The internal development programmes that were mentioned were the CIMA qualification and the store manager's programme which were both highly regarded.

Alignment

Teams seem to be closely aligned around roles and responsibilities. Communication within teams was generally good, awareness of other teams was generally limited to functional relationships. Some teams had regular social activities, some did not. To enable even greater openness and communication between teams, and to protect against isolation of departments, you might consider giving graduates rotation assignments outside of the role that they are recruited into so that they can experience everything that happens in the business and clearly understand the impact of their role on it. Once people are in full time positions, you might still consider even more regular exposure to other parts of the business, e.g. for a finance analyst to visit stores and see the activities that are represented in the data they analyse.

In the stores, the successful managers created their own unique culture. I would recommend building on this, adding in a stronger local element with community involvement, giving managers even more tools to build local 'tribes'.

Succession

Senior roles seemed to depend on a great deal of experience or tacit knowledge as well as a willingness to make decisions. This would therefore suggest that the people who make an effort to broaden their experience and become involved in decisions would be the preferred candidates for promotion, although this may not be fully recognised in the current interviewing process which seems to favour interview/assessment centre performance.

Exit

Since [Client], like many retailers, employs many part time and seasonal staff, care should be taken to manage the exit process so that experienced staff are attracted back into the business as their circumstances change.

24 Case Study: Facilitators

This project was delivered for a company that acts as an industry regulator in a very old industry that has been revolutionised as a result of both deregulation and fragmentation. The industry is highly competitive, highly cost conscious and responsible for the safety of millions of people in the UK every day. Balancing the needs of the different stakeholders who frequently have significantly opposing views is fundamental to this organisation's ability to introduce new operating standards, and their best facilitators achieve this with ease.

Project Overview

General features of high performers

In all of our modelling projects, we find the same general features of high performers:

1. They have a goal which is greater than that of the task which they are recognised for excelling at, so the task becomes a means to an end and not an end in itself.

2. Their intention, attitude or methods are counter-intuitive and not obvious to an observer.

3. They appear to get results easily because they actually do make it easy for themselves by implementing short-cuts or methods which are not obvious to an observer.

Our unique modelling approach therefore identifies and codes these hidden skills and behaviours so that they can be shared throughout the organisation.

Organisational environment

[Client] is a not-for-profit company owned and funded by major stakeholders in the [industry], but is independent of any one party. [Client] has around 250 staff, including experts in a wide range of technical disciplines and other professionals such as project managers, meeting facilitators and support staff.

[Client] provides support and facilitation for a wide range of cross-industry activities and is funded by levies on its members and grants for research from the Department for Transport.

[Client]'s purpose is defined as:

"In an industry with multiple stakeholders, [Client] builds consensus and facilitates the resolution of difficult cross-industry issues. [Client] provides analysis, knowledge, a substantial level of technical expertise and powerful information and risk management tools and delivers this unique mix to the industry across a whole range of subject areas.

[Client] will continue to build on this and:

Provide high quality support services to our members to help them deliver their business objectives. These services are provided particularly where there is a need for knowledge and co-operation. They will help our members and consequently the industry to:

- Where reasonably practicable, continuously improve the level of safety in the [industry].
- Drive out unnecessary cost and,
- Improve business performance"

Business drivers

[Client]'s operation depends on effective consultation with [industry] representatives, taking up a facilitative position rather than a leadership one. Reaching agreements must be achieved through consensus to ensure that new standards and operating procedures can be adopted across the [industry].

[Client]'s culture is changing as its traditional workforce of people who have worked in the [industry] for most of their lives is slowly replaced with staff with skills in specialist technical areas but who are inexperienced in the [industry]. Additionally, [Client]'s role is changing to a more consultative one, with additional revenue streams coming from outside the UK and from outside the [industry] in order to supplement the current membership funding model.

Therefore, [Client] can no longer rely on [industry] experience to ease the decision making process, and more staff must develop effective skills for chairing meetings and facilitating discussions to ensure [Client] continues to add value to the [industry] members that it supports.

Results being modelled

This project is primarily aimed at understanding the key behaviours of [Client]'s most skilled facilitators who are able to manage groups and committees in order to implement change in the [industry] through consensus amongst its member organisations.

These facilitators are able to deliver consistent results, despite meetings sometimes being challenging due to the adversarial positions taken by some industry representatives.

Definition of consensus

Consensus is achieved when there are no sustained objections to an agreement within a group.

Planned outcomes

1. A model of high performance which will be used to build a three layer development program designed to instil high performing attitudes and behaviours into a broader population of [Client] staff, enabling more staff to chair and facilitate meetings more effectively while preserving [Client]'s unique culture and position in the [industry].

2. A template which can be used to recruit new staff who are predisposed to high performance in [Client]'s culture and working environment.

Culture & Environment

The following table captures key information about the cultural environment within which this modelling project has been conducted.

High performing organisations have a high degree of alignment between these levels. For example, a company whose external brand accurately reflects its internal culture will operate more efficiently than a company which tries to present a brand image that is not backed up by its working culture. Staff will feel that leaders are 'hypocritical' and in extreme cases have used media such as social networking sites to vent their frustration.

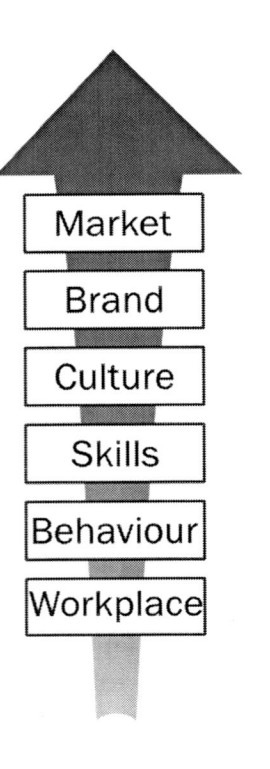

- Market
- Brand
- Culture
- Skills
- Behaviour
- Workplace

A well-aligned organisation trades in a market for which its brand is well suited. Its working culture reflects that brand, and the skills and abilities of staff closely match both the working culture and the actual duties required of them. Finally, the working environment supports those duties and behaviours and makes it possible for staff to do their jobs safely and effectively. This drives operational efficiency, productivity and a sense of fulfilment and job satisfaction for staff.

Market or operating environment

The [industry] is both regulated and competitive, creating an unusual operating environment. [Client] occupies a similar position to that of a regulator but has no regulatory powers and therefore serves in an advisory capacity, facilitating discussions between industry representatives and helping them to reach consensus over the development and adoption of operating standards.

[Client] effectively operates as a monopoly in that no other organisation provides the same service, however its not-for-profit status greatly influences its culture.

[Client] does not 'trade' in an open market, however the dependency on the members' levy may create a perceived imbalance of power and a sense that [Client] does not control its own destiny, despite publishing a business plan.

Brand identity

[Client] does not have a strong public brand as it primarily faces towards its [industry] members and serves to support them in developing operational and safety standards. Whilst these standards are for the benefit of industry members and their passengers, the standards development process can be contentious at times, which [Client] is sometimes caught in the middle of.

[Client] has no regulatory powers and the implementation of research and standards is therefore achieved by member consensus, creating an identity for [Client] as a centre of technical and research excellence. This also means that [industry] operators must take responsibility for what they agree to, as they cannot blame [Client] for imposing unpopular standards upon them. This most likely creates greater accountability in [Client]'s membership which can be forgotten by younger working generations who have no direct experience of the nationalised environment of the past.

Cultural rules & beliefs

There are lots of meetings

Decisions are made (or avoided) by consensus

People are supportive

People work collaboratively

The [industry] interface is extremely political

Powerless - because [Client] has no power to impose standards

Lifelong [industry] experience is being replaced with younger technical experts with little industry knowledge

Fairly low staff turnover, so a safe working environment

People largely manage their own work

The most notable feature of [Client]'s culture is that it is changing rapidly because of its changing workforce.

Skills, ideas, capabilities

High degree of technical expertise e.g. risk analysis, statistical analysis, human factors, research methods

High degree of [industry] experience with some staff having served over 40 years in the industry

Highly networked staff with many [industry] contacts

Behaviours & key activities

Research

Consultancy

Facilitating boards and committees

Holding meetings to facilitate cross-industry discussions and projects

Working environment

Corporate

Mostly open plan office environment

Relaxed e.g. relatively casual dress rules

Meeting rooms frequently bring stakeholders into the office environment

Many people travel a great distance to work each day because of [Client]'s unique industry position.

Analysis

Behaviour

This section deals with the key behaviours of the role, including what the high performer does, both internally (mentally) and externally (physically), to achieve their intended results.

Results are the primary means by which we identify a high performer. How they achieve those results is the purpose of the modelling project.

Role

Meeting chair or facilitator.

This is usually a secondary activity to the role model's primary role which might, for example, be that of a project manager or head of department.

Results

High performers are able to achieve the following results when compared to average performers:

- Accelerated progress of projects, standards implementation etc.
- Reduction in the number of meetings required to resolve an issue or progress a project
- Effective management of conflict leading to improved working relationships and productivity

Meeting sequence

Preparation
- Read minutes
- Read notes & papers
- Write agenda
- Send out agenda & supporting documents

Opening
- Welcome
- State Purpose
- State Outcomes
- Request AOB items
- Review previous minutes

Facilitating
- Packages

Closing
- Request AOB items
- Summary
- Next meeting
- Thank you

Chairing the Meeting

Agenda item | Topic | Goal | Decision | (Discussion) | Summary | Document

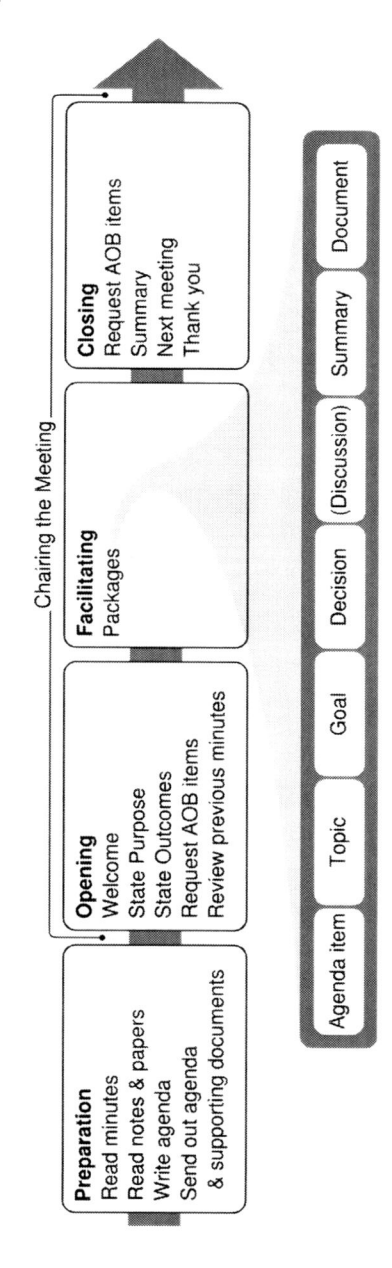

Case Study: Facilitators   370

Preparation

Preparation is a key focus for the high performer, and contains one of the most important distinctions between the high and average performers.

A poor facilitator will fail to prepare adequately, and will see the meeting as an entity in itself, with any necessary discussion taking place with the meeting boundaries. This is an extremely inefficient use of time because meetings are then used for group discussion rather than decision making. Therefore, the first difference is this:

Poor facilitators see a meeting as a discussion activity, whereas the best facilitators see a meeting as a decision making activity.

High performers therefore work hard to complete as much work as possible outside of the meeting, building relationships with members and stakeholders and carefully positioning any unpopular agenda items so that minimal discussion takes place within the meeting. A high performer will be very careful not to lobby or influence stakeholders, instead working on the wording of papers or standards proposals to lead to minimal contention within a meeting.

A typical belief from a poor to average facilitator is that any preparation is better than none, so when they are pressed for time they might send out a meeting agenda to participants the day before a meeting. This means that the facilitator is focusing only on their own preparation, and not putting themselves in the minds of the participants, as they will not have sufficient time to prepare. The consequence of this is that the poor to average performer's meetings take longer and more meetings are required to achieve a particular result, which means that the facilitator has to work harder between meetings, which means that they have less time to prepare thoroughly and give participants time to prepare.

The best facilitators will spend up to half a day preparing for a meeting, around 3 or 4 days prior to the meeting. The second difference between the average and best facilitators is the way in which they prepare:

Poor Prepare as if they are a participant

Average Prepare as if they are a chairman

Best Prepare as if they are the other participants

This distinction is not obvious from observing facilitators, as both the average and high performers prepare by reading previous minutes, papers, reports etc. The difference is entirely internal. When the average facilitator reads papers, they read them to familiarise themselves with the topics to be discussed. When the best facilitators prepare, they put themselves 'in the shoes' of the various participants in the meeting to see the issues from as many and as extreme points of view as possible which enables them to pre-empt any potentially contentious issues, giving rise to an observable output:

Average facilitators struggle with conflict for two reasons, partly because they avoid it (by taking it personally) and partly because they fail to pre-empt it. The best facilitators handle conflict more effectively because they work to minimise conflict before it arises. They are not afraid of conflict and they know

that they will save themselves time in the long run by 'putting it on the table' themselves.

Planning the agenda

A meeting is rarely a self contained discussion; it is usually a snapshot of a number of activities which are at different stages of development. Some will be early in their lifecycle, requiring scoping discussions. Some will be in their mid term with lots of actions and updates. Some will be winding down with status reports and reviews.

Therefore, planning the agenda for a meeting requires the facilitator to know about the life cycle of each discussion item so that they can allocate sufficient time to it. If the previous meeting worked well in terms of the time available for discussion, then the next meeting agenda can use the same times, adjusted for any changes due to the life cycle of discussion items.

The best facilitators don't worry about having the agenda timing perfect because they will often dynamically rearrange the agenda anyway. Their focus is on concluding the highest priority items so that they can achieve their goals for the meeting. By stating the objective of the discussion item upfront, the participants are able to focus on it.

It is important that the right participants will be present at the meeting to achieve the stated objectives, so if a key decision maker will not be present then there is no point including the item in the agenda. Ensuring the right people are present for the planned agenda items means that the meeting time is used more efficiently and more is achieved.

Objectives

High performing facilitators have clear goals, and their meetings are a means to achieving those goals. Their goal, which might be to see a standard adopted, or some research acted upon, or a change program implemented, serves as a fixed point like a star to navigate by, which makes it very easy for them to identify any deviations from the topic under discussion. They recognise that an off topic conversation may be interesting, but their meeting is not the time or place for it. Therefore, they do not undermine the value of the conversation, they merely refocus participants' attention on the matter at hand.

Conversely, poor to average facilitators hold the meeting itself as the goal and are therefore less flexible during the meeting. They are more likely to allow the conversation to go off topic because they don't have a clear goal as a point of reference. Because their goal is essentially 'to hold a meeting', the discussion can go off topic and they will still achieve that goal. They might even go as far as to consider the off topic discussion as valuable because it sounds interesting or useful.

Broadly speaking, we can identify the following traits relating to goals and objectives:

- Poor facilitators see the meeting as an end in itself
- Average facilitators see the meeting as a means to a short term end
- The best facilitators see a series of meetings as a means to a long term end

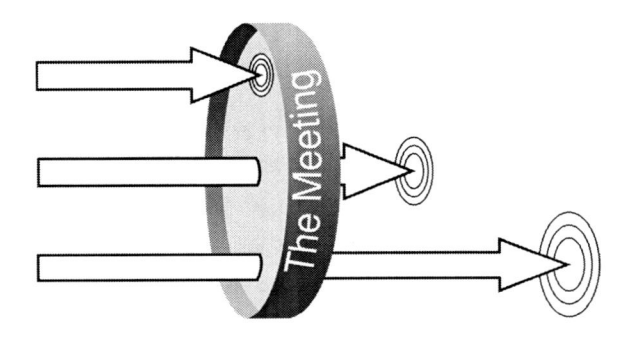

Process

The best facilitators are very process-focused when in a meeting. Paradoxically, they use the agenda to control the meeting, but the agenda does not dictate the meeting. Conversely, a poor facilitator will stick more rigidly to the agenda which increases the chances that the meeting will run over time and that participants will leave due to other commitments.

Time

High performing facilitators have a long term view of time, in that they will invest time in the short term in order save it later on during a meeting or in completing a project more quickly.

Conversely, a poor or inexperienced facilitator will save time in the short term with minimal preparation or an agenda sent out only the night before the meeting, and as a result their meetings last longer and more meetings are required to achieve the same results because participants are not adequately prepared.

High performing facilitators also value time within the meeting itself and will dynamically rearrange the agenda to adapt to changes and keep the group's focus on high priority items. As already mentioned, poor facilitators will tend to stick more rigidly to the agenda which means they're more likely to rush to fit the discussion into the time available and skip over items which need more thorough debate.

High performers will set the agenda based on two rules; the first is to place the highest priority items first, and the second is to make the best use of participants' time. They might group items that are relevant to particular participants who don't need to attend the entire meeting, and they might move important items back if key participants are late. Importantly, they will defer agenda items to a subsequent meeting in order to achieve their most important objectives.

High performers said that time management was perhaps their most important ability, which means managing the process of the meeting to ensure the highest priority items are dealt with first and that the time within the meeting is focused on the agenda items and decisions with minimal off-topic discussion. In fact, 'time management' is a generalisation and a result, what the high performers actually do is to manage a decision making process.

A poor to average facilitator will prioritise easy or quick items first to 'get them out of the way' and leave room for the more challenging items, which may be a by-product of avoiding conflict. However, the easy and quick items are rarely easy or quick and take up significantly more time than the facilitator had intended, leaving insufficient time to tackle the more important issues. This is more likely to generate conflict as participants do not have time to fully explore different perspectives, and is more likely to lead to superficial agreements, made just to finish the meeting on time, which are not backed up by genuine buy-in to actions and commitments. Therefore, by trying to avoid conflict, a poor facilitator creates it.

A high performer pre-empts and deals with conflict, with the result that conflict is less likely to occur because participants have had their more extreme views aired in a more collaborative way which 'takes the wind out of their sails'.

The meeting

Probably the single most important characteristic of the high performing facilitators is the way that they view the meeting itself. A poor facilitator sees a meeting as a time and place to get a group together and address any outstanding business such as project updates, presentations, decisions and actions. Whilst this may seem reasonable, it is a very inefficient use of participants' time, which has the following consequences:

- Since the participants' time is not valued, they don't give the meeting a high priority and are often late, leave early and 'multi-task' during the meeting

- Since multiple discussion types are permitted within the meeting (e.g. challenging, decision making, information gathering, knowledge sharing), it is much more difficult for the facilitator to keep the discussion on track, because it's impossible to tell what is a valuable discussion and what is not

- Because different activities are combined within a meeting, the participants are not always clear of their roles, resulting in decision taking longer to make and an increased chance of conflict

High performers see the meeting not as a discussion space but as a negotiation space.

This is a very important distinction, particularly given [Client]'s need to operate as a neutral facilitator.

Discussion (outer ring): Compromise, Change opinions, Save face, Think out loud, Ask silly or obvious questions

Negotiation (inner ring): Agree, Decide

By treating the meeting as a negotiation space, the focus is on making decisions. The only discussion which arises is aimed at reaching a decision, and this enables the high performer to keep the discussion on track easily.

The downside of this approach is that a negotiation is practically impossible when the parties have strongly opposing views, and this is where the discussion space is used outside of the meeting itself.

At the beginning of a discussion on, for example, a new standard, we might say that the most extreme points of view, represented here as A and B, are simply too far apart to reach a discussion.

(A)   [Agreement]   (B)

Any pressure on them in an open forum to change their views will simply entrench them more. Each [industry] representative is not a lone entity, they represent an entire industry sector or organisation, and they must be able to demonstrate that they 'hold their own' at industry meetings, otherwise they have no value to the organisation which employs them. They cannot be seen to be 'giving in' to pressure from their opponents, and so any pressure on them to do so will have an extremely counter-productive effect if done in front of other people, as the representatives have a strong incentive to protect their hard-earned reputations.

$$A \longleftrightarrow \boxed{\text{Agreement}} \longleftrightarrow B$$

A high performing facilitator spends time outside of the formal meeting to understand the relative positions of representatives. They do not try to change those positions, they merely seek to understand them so that they can build those different positions and expectations into the item under discussion, which may be something like a new standard or a project scope.

$$\boxed{A \Rightarrow \text{Agreement} \Leftarrow B}$$

They will then present the revised item at a meeting and clearly mark out the aim of the discussion as being an agreement or approval. By expanding the scope of the subject to get closer to or even encompass these different positions, the facilitator lowers the barriers to reaching an agreement and allows even the most intransigent representatives to show good faith in front of their 'opponents' and compromise on an agreement.

High performing facilitators therefore save the meeting discussion for the final agreement, mainly so that a public commitment to that agreement can be heard by all participants.

```
        Negotiation
    ┌─────────────────┐
   Lobbying    Forcing
            representatives
            into entrenched
              positions
         Discussion  Influencing
          Manipulating
```

If an [Client] facilitator were to attempt to move representatives from their positions within a meeting, they would likely entrench those positions further. However, if a facilitator were to conduct a negotiation outside of the meeting, perhaps asking for commitment or acting as a mediator, it would be seen as lobbying or even manipulation, with the facilitator 'picking off' participants in order to influence their views and behaviour.

A high performing facilitator therefore combines a number of skills in order to achieve the outcome of consensus, even though consensus is not their intention.

Preparation

The facilitator takes time to understand how each participant may view the subject under discussion.

The facilitator rehearses the meeting and those opposing positions, either mentally or with colleagues.

Discussion

The facilitator talks to participants to understand their positions and aims to encompass those, or get as close to them as possible, in the wording of the decision being presented.

Facilitation

The facilitator guides a negotiation between participants so that they move closer to each others' positions.

The facilitator does not engage directly in the negotiation, instead reminding participants that it is for them to reach an agreement, if one is possible.

Starting the meeting

The best facilitators start the meeting by reviewing the minutes of the previous meeting. This may seem trivial, yet it is intrinsic to the consensual decision making process.

This serves a practical purpose of approving the minutes, and participants may indeed offer corrections which are then incorporated into a revision of the minutes.

Poor facilitators might focus on the meeting at hand, perhaps reviewing actions from the previous meeting.

The best facilitators review the minutes of the previous meeting, not just the actions, and this enables them to lead the participants through a mental re-run of the previous meeting. Whether each participant agreed or disagreed on each point, they can now agree that the minutes are an accurate reflection of that discussion, so the meeting actually begins with all participants agreeing about a shared past experience. This creates a powerful state of compliance which makes the decision process much easier.

Packaging

The best facilitators break the meeting down into 'packages' or self contained discussions. Each package follows the same format:

1. Direction to the relevant section of the agenda or notes
2. Announcement of the topic under discussion
3. Announcement of the goal for the discussion
4. Request for decision
5. Management of the discussion – if necessary
6. Summary of agreement and/or actions
7. Document the discussion for the minutes

The meeting itself follows the same format and represents an overall package into which the agenda item packages are contained. Even if items are deferred to a later meeting or offline discussion, the meeting itself always seems 'complete' because of the packaging of the discussion.

A poor facilitator starts at the beginning of the meeting and keeps going, without clear delineation between agenda items, which results in blurring of the discussion, deviations and over-runs.

A good facilitator notices visual and verbal signals that the participants use to signal their readiness to move onto the next package, such as sitting back in their chairs to indicate they are 'leaving' the discussion.

Engaging

It is often said that good facilitators are highly attuned to the group and are therefore externally referenced, however this is not the case within the [Client] culture. The most likely reason for this is that [Client]'s position, whilst impartial and consensual, is in fact driven by the organisation's own purpose, namely "Where reasonably practicable, continuously improve the level of safety in the [industry]". If we consider a more neutral facilitation environment such as that offered by Relate, the facilitator has no agenda other than to help the participants reach a mutually agreeable conclusion. In this case, an externally referenced facilitator would be able to draw out sensitive issues and encourage all participants to engage in the discussion. At [Client], this could be counter-productive because forcibly involving a participant could lead them to withdraw from the discussion, and could be viewed as lobbying.

Good facilitators keep a close watch on the group and are able to see if any participants have a point to make but are reluctant to speak up.

The signs that they look out for include:

- Leaning forwards
- Making eye contact with the facilitator or current speaker
- Raised eyebrows, head up
- Clearing throat
- Raising a hand
- Tapping a pen or pencil on the table
- Agreeing in order to grab an opportunity to speak
- Interrupting

Some of these signs may be very subtle, however the best facilitators are not great masters of 'body language'; their secret is very simple. A poor facilitator will become involved in the discussion and their focus of attention is on the point they are making, not on the other participants. The best facilitators are not involved in the conversation directly, their position is more like an observer, so they are more easily able to notice any behaviours which are different to the majority, much like someone would see the differences in a 'spot the difference' puzzle. If 15 people in a group nod and one frowns, it's easy to spot the frown and draw that person into the conversation. The best facilitators will do this in a very informal, casual way so as not to put undue pressure on the individual. Remember, the best facilitators want every participant to have an equal opportunity to participate. Whether they do or not is up to them.

Poor facilitators want everyone to contribute, so they are more likely to poll the entire group, asking for view or feedback, and this formulaic approach is more likely to disengage participants.

The consequence of not watching the whole group, in the words of one role model, is "minority dominance".

The best facilitators will work to ensure that the discussion is balanced, so if the conversation is leaning to heavily towards a particular point of view and is not taking all possible positions into account, the facilitator will play 'Devil's advocate' and raise points that rebalance the argument. A good facilitator is careful to bring this up in a neutral way so that it doesn't sound like their own personal opinion.

Good facilitators openly offer the opportunity for participants to discuss agenda items prior to the meeting. Again, this offer is made in front of the whole group so that the facilitator can not be accused of singling participants out. This allows participants to air their more contentious or sensitive opinions in a 'safe' way prior to the open meeting. Often, in any negotiation, people will change or soften their positions once they hear themselves making a certain point, realising that it sounds perhaps aggressive or unreasonable. If they can only speak up in a meeting, they will cause a reaction from other participants which will often strengthen their position so that they can save face. Staying consistent to our stated beliefs and intentions is a strong driver for people (Robert Cialdini, Influence Science and Practice) and so forcing participants to discuss their positions in an open forum will make them adhere more strongly to those positions. Giving participants the opportunity to air their views in a more private setting makes it more likely that they will adjust those views to achieve a consensus position.

There are times when a facilitator will have a vested interest in the group reaching a particular decision, perhaps for the adoption of a standard or the approval of a project. In such cases, the facilitator is no longer neutral, yet they must maintain their neutrality or lose control of the meeting. When a good facilitator wants to gently nudge the group in a particular direction, they will conduct the meeting as they normally would, encouraging all opinions and positions to be shared openly. However, they will also offer additional encouragement to participants who are speaking in favour of the facilitator's goal, and give less 'airtime' to participants who are not supportive.

Not every agenda item is relevant to every participant, so it is unreasonable to expect every participant to be fully engaged throughout the entire meeting.

A poor facilitator wants everyone to contribute because their focus is on the meeting as a whole and as an end in itself, so their effectiveness is dependent on keeping all participants engaged, like a school teacher who wants their students to pay attention to every word they say.

A good facilitator thinks in terms of 'packages' and focuses on the participants who have an interest in the current package (agenda item). This gives the other participants some welcome time to 'tune out' and gather their thoughts.

A good facilitator also makes frequent breaks in the meeting, again to allow participants to gather their thoughts, amongst other more practical needs that they may have. A good facilitator would rather have participants engaged at the right times rather than sitting there worrying about important messages and not paying attention to the proceedings.

Focusing

The best facilitators have a number of ways of knowing that a discussion is going 'off track':

1. The discussion is not serving to achieve the objective stated by the facilitator at the start of the discussion
2. The discussion is becoming overly emotional, either in an adversarial way or because the participants are personally interested in the topic
3. The participants have raised the same points at least twice, indicating that they have not moved any closer to a conclusion

The problem for a poor facilitator is that the more animated the participants become about the discussion topic, the harder it is for the facilitator to get the group's attention in order to regain control and bring the discussion back to the topic at hand.

Also, a poor facilitator, because they do not have control of the group, is more likely to experience the problem of the group splintering into subgroups with several discussions happening at the same time. A poor facilitator will deal with this be asking everyone to focus on the discussion at hand, disregarding the fact that they were; it just wasn't the discussion the facilitator was focusing on.

A good facilitator will call the meeting to order but will also make sure that each splinter group has its say.

Influence

Neutrality and impartiality are vital to [Client]'s role in the industry, however the best facilitators are highly influential, using non-obvious methods to shape the outcomes of a meeting.

By clearly stating that the meeting is "your meeting", i.e. the participants', the best facilitators push accountability for decisions back onto the group. They cannot 'blame' the facilitator for influencing them, because he or she clearly stated that they are neutral in the decision.

By staying out of direct discussion as much as possible, the best facilitators encourage the participants to debate with each other. Therefore, any agreement or disagreement is made with another member of the group, not the facilitator. This also aids in conflict management, because the best facilitators manage the group such that they are arguing with themselves, not with the facilitator. This further protects the facilitator's neutrality.

By working outside of the meeting on the wording of agreements, papers, projects etc. the best facilitators are able to use resources such as documents to make a point for them. For example, a facilitator might refer a participant to the wording of a standard rather than debating directly. The participant cannot argue with the standard because the standard doesn't argue back. The facilitator protects their neutrality and further reinforces the point that, "these are your standards, not mine".

The best facilitators use the people in the room to exert influence, for example building on supportive arguments and also using government representatives to indirectly influence the group.

Handling conflict

When conflict does arise, it is directed either at another participant or at the facilitator. Conflict will often arise for one of two reasons:

1. A discussion has become heated because participants are focusing on being heard rather than on listening
2. A participant is playing out a role in order to gain control of the discussion or intimidate other participants

The best facilitators rarely encounter the first reason because it is central to the role of a good facilitator, which we can sum up as follows:

The participants come to a meeting to *have their say*, and the facilitator makes sure that they are *heard* by getting them to *listen* to each other.

This connects back to the sense of equality; in order for all participants to have an equal say, they must also listen in equal measure.

The second reason is something that the best facilitators preempt with their preparation. By understanding the relative negotiating positions of the participants, they are able to distinguish between a genuine objection and 'bluster' or positioning and deal with it appropriately. Probably the most important behaviour in this case is separating the message from the tone; valuing and including what the person has to say it irrespective of how they say it.

Once a valid point is made, though, the facilitator will deal with the way in which it is made by reminding the speaker that their behaviour is inappropriate and will not be tolerated; an approach based on the belief that all participants are equal and therefore deserve equal respect.

By pushing accountability back onto the participants ("it's *your* meeting", "these are *your* standards"), the facilitator is reminding them that the conflict is theirs to resolve, or at the very least they are disagreeing with their own standards or previous commitments, not with the facilitator.

One of the most important points in any conflict situation is to avoid the language of direct disagreement, which can always be paraphrased as, "you're wrong". Instead, the best facilitators use language such as:

- Yes, and...
- Yes, if...
- Perhaps, if...
- Not only, but also...
- I agree, and...
- And in addition to that...

By using such phrases, the best facilitators are able to build on the discussion, whereas negative language such as "no", or "but" will tend to stifle a discussion. The best facilitators therefore use conflict to flush out alternative options, which if not addressed in the meeting will come back later on and cause bigger problems.

Decision making

The best facilitators do not open each agenda item or 'package' with a discussion. Because they know what the purpose of each package is, they open each item in a way that allows them to achieve that purpose or outcome using the minimum time and effort. They also ask very specific, closed questions in order to guide the discussion quickly towards their desired outcome.

Having said that the facilitator has an outcome, they are also not attached to it. In a way, they don't mind whether the decision is 'yes' or 'no' as long as the group makes a decision, quickly. This is another aspect of their neutrality which they work hard to protect.

The best facilitators' decision making process is:

1. State the outcome of the discussion item i.e. a decision
1. Give the context to the discussion item
2. Ask for the decision
3. If everyone agrees, close the item and move to the next

Only if anyone raises a concern does the facilitator open up a discussion.

Most importantly, when the group agrees, the facilitator does not overtly acknowledge the fact that the group have made a decision, they merely close the item and move to the next with the minimum of fuss. This emphasises that making decisions is quick, easy, painless and most of all, completely normal and to be expected.

Closing the meeting

The end of the meeting is very simple; asking again for any AOB items, summarising any significant decisions or progress, stating the date of the next meeting, if there is one and thanking the participants for their contribution.

Beliefs & Perceptions

The operating principles and behavioural rules that form the foundation of high performing behaviour.

These are unconscious processes which shape the resulting behaviours and as such are not normally available at the level of conscious awareness.

Beliefs

Beliefs are rules. Most people think of beliefs as fixed 'truths', however they have been learned through life experiences, just like rules about social behaviour and train timetables. The only difference with a belief is that we are less likely to question it when experience contradicts it, instead discounting the experience or looking for some other factor to blame.

Behavioural traits

The following behavioural traits can be thought of as perceptual filters, colouring a person's view of the world and thereby influencing their behaviour so that they tend to react in consistent, predictable ways. These traits can be highly context specific, and of course people can adapt to situations which require a different way of thinking. However, by identifying these traits, we can produce a recruitment template which makes it easy to identify similar people, and we can also build content into a training program which makes it easier for other people to see the world as a high performer does, which naturally leads to high performing behaviours.

Options **Procedures**	Favours familiar processes and proven methods over new ideas
Towards Away	Goals based on achieving results rather than avoiding problems
People Task	Focuses on people and relationships rather than tasks and objects
Team Individual	Achieves results through a team rather than by themselves
Internal External	Bases decisions on their own internal frame of reference rather than on external benchmarks and comparisons
Difference Similarity	Notices differences and exceptions rather than similarities
Active Reactive	Takes action rather than waiting to react
General **Specific**	Detail oriented rather than generalising or 'seeing the big picture'

Purpose

The best facilitators believe that [Client] exists to help the industry to make decisions.

The best facilitators believe that a meeting exists to make decisions.

Therefore, meetings are not a time consuming non-work activity for the best facilitators, they are the fundamental way in which [Client] achieves its purpose, and they are therefore a core activity for a good facilitator.

Participants have to feel that they have achieved something in the meeting, otherwise they will feel it has been a waste of time and will be more difficult to engage in subsequent meetings.

Confidence

The different role models who we interviewed attributed their talents to different factors, for example their extensive [industry] experience which they used in one of two ways:

- They could understand technical points, or the history behind them
- They knew the 'personalities' and were better able to handle them

40 years of [industry] experience is hard to gain without spending 40 years in the [industry], so in order to replicate these talents in others, we must understand what this experience gives the high performer.

Firstly and most importantly, it simply gives them confidence. They have a sense that they have 'earned their place' and that they can deal with some of the more challenging representatives because they see them as equals. Therefore, confidence is relative to the position and behaviour of people in the meeting, so high performance depends on the facilitator seeing the meeting participants as peers or equals and are put off neither by status nor challenging behaviour.

However, it is impractical for other staff to spend a similar time in the industry just to gain confidence. Each individual has a different way of generating confidence which we will tap into during the training program, removing this dependency on [industry] knowledge.

Secondly, industry experience gives the facilitator an understanding of the subject under discussion which they say helps them to keep a discussion 'on track'. In fact, they were using other methods to achieve this which were discussed in the previous section.

In fact, industry experience can sometimes be a hindrance in that it can lead the facilitator to form opinions which could bias a discussion. In [Client]'s culture, neutrality is one of a facilitator's most valuable assets.

It is important to note that confidence is not an abstract feeling, it is part of a process that forms part of how the high performer achieves their results. Confidence is not an end in itself, it is a means; confidence to *do what?*

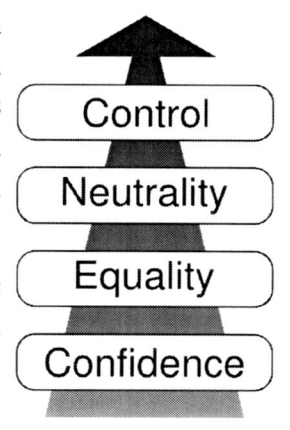

Control

Neutrality

Equality

Confidence

Confidence is the conclusion of a process of mental preparation, a state of readiness and for high performing facilitators it serves the vital purpose of levelling the playing field. A poor facilitator brings the perceived status of meeting participants into the discussion, allowing more 'important' participants to dominate the meeting and failing to earn the credibility and respect that would allow them to easily handle conflict.

An average facilitator tries to leave the participants' job titles out of the meeting because they know that each person has an equal right to be heard and an equal right to be treated with respect. However, they still feel some underlying sense of a 'pecking order' and this influences how they treat different participants.

The best facilitators don't need to try to remember this; they know what earns them the right to facilitate the meeting, such as years of industry experience, and it is easier for them to command respect from the participants, which in turn makes it easier for them to perform the most obvious tasks of a facilitator; keeping the discussion on track, keeping the meeting to time, ensuring that all participants have the opportunity to share their views and recording minutes and actions accurately.

Ownership

Good facilitators see the meeting as a means to an end, that end being the adoption of a standard, the progress of a project etc. In order to achieve that end, a number of people must reach an agreement, and a meeting is an efficient way to achieve that. However, especially when dealing with external stakeholders, the facilitator must protect [Client]'s neutral position, so they focus on the process of the meeting rather than the content, and guide the participants to focus on the content without having to worry about the process. However, by managing the process, a good facilitator is able to focus the participants' attention in such a way that the content leads the participants towards the facilitator's desired outcome.

If a facilitator allows themselves to get drawn into the content of the meeting then they risk losing control of the process.

The best facilitators regard the process of the meeting as theirs and the content of the meeting as belonging to the participants.

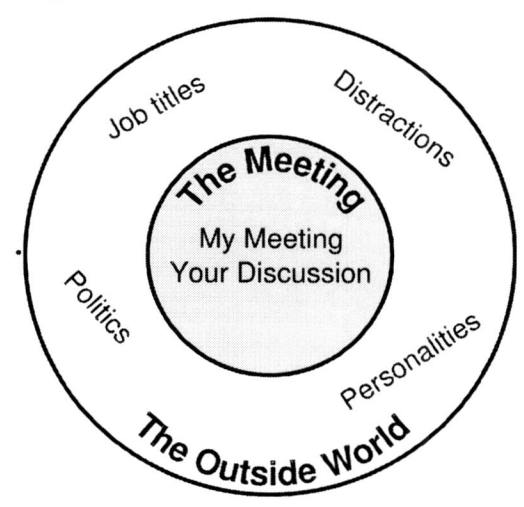

Diagram: concentric circles. Inner circle labeled "The Meeting" containing "My Meeting / Your Discussion". Outer circle labeled "The Outside World" containing "Job titles", "Distractions", "Politics", "Personalities".

With this perspective, the best facilitators essentially mark out their territory within the meeting room, and set out the ground rules that go with that.

They will also remind the participants where these boundaries lie, e.g. "remember, these are your standards, not mine", pushing the responsibility for the negotiation back onto the participants. This is useful if the participants start to make the facilitator the centre of the discussion.

A poor to average facilitator, in contrast, *tries* to control the meeting which signals to the participants that the facilitator is not in control, opening up the potential for participants to dominate the meeting.

Preparation

A poor facilitator will fail to send out sufficient information prior to the meeting and will therefore waste time during the meeting reading minutes, notes, papers etc. This teaches the participants that they don't need to prepare in advance.

A good facilitator assumes that the participants have read through any information that was sent to them in advance, even saying, "If they haven't, that's their problem, not mine". A participant only needs to attend a meeting once without having prepared, and they will likely not do it again.

Time

A poor to average facilitator sees the meeting agenda as constant and time as variable, whereas a high performer sees time as constant and the agenda as a variable. This attitude enables them to focus on getting their highest priority items resolved in the time available, or the time made available by participants as a result of travel problems, other commitments etc.

Equality

The best facilitators believe that everyone participating in a meeting is equal, in that they have an equal right to be heard and an equal right to share their views, irrespective of their job title or the organisation they're representing. This beliefs leads to three conclusions:

1. The facilitator is also equal to the participants and is therefore not influenced by job titles
2. The participants must treat each other with respect since none has superiority
3. A participant has a right to share their views or not

It's interesting to note that while a good facilitator does not respond to job titles, the participants do, and the atmosphere in a meeting is notably different when a government representative is present. The facilitator will sometimes use this to their advantage, asking the government representative to leave the room or arrive at a particular point in the agenda so that participants can have an 'off the record' discussion. This further strengthens the facilitator's ownership of the meeting space.

A good facilitator believes that the more senior the participant (in terms of their 'day job'), the more valuable their time is, therefore the more value they choose to invest in the meeting. Therefore, an 'important' participant does not daunt a good facilitator as they would a poor facilitator, they actually strengthen the role of the facilitator, because the facilitator knows that they would not give their time freely if the meeting wasn't worth attending.

Engagement

If all participants have an equal right to share their views then it must also be true that they may or may not choose to exercise that right. Therefore, the best facilitators think in terms of 'providing an opportunity for participants to share their views'. They believe that there may be social factors such as peer pressure, or personal factors such as uncertainty or confusion which may prevent an individual from engaging in a discussion, so they are aware of the 'body language' that indicates that someone has a view which they are not sharing. However, they do not 'push' individuals to engage as that would violate their belief about the individual's rights. The right level of discussion is preferably to discussion for its own sake, even if that means a "no comment" from every participant.

Poor to average facilitators measure their effectiveness by the number of people who *do* speak, rather than the number of people who have the *opportunity* to speak, because the discussion is an end in itself, therefore more discussion is good.

Conflict

The best facilitators' beliefs about equality determine how they handle conflict. In particular, because they treat all participants as equal, regardless of their job title or external status, they are able to apply the same rules of etiquette to all participants.

In contrast, a poor facilitator will fail to tackle inappropriate behaviour from someone 'important' and therefore treats the meeting participants differently depending on their perceived status, which may come from their job title or from their superior or intimidating behaviour during the meeting.

Furthermore, a poor facilitator will handle inappropriate behaviour outside of the meeting, essentially placating the perpetrator and encouraging discussion to take the group's focus away from the inappropriate behaviour, which:

- Shows the 'victim' that they are not respected or protected
- Shows the 'perpetrator' that they can get away with it
- Shows the other participants that inappropriate behaviour will not be addressed
- Shows the group that the facilitator is not in control of the meeting

The effect of this is that healthy debate will be suppressed, as quieter participants will fear conflict with the more bullish members of the group because they believe that the facilitator will not 'stand up' for them.

Influence

A good facilitator believes that they must understand a person's point of view, otherwise they cannot help them to find a solution.

They also believe that if they allow a person to talk freely, that person will often talk themselves in to or out of a particular position or point of view.

These beliefs make it easier for the best facilitators to influence a group whilst maintaining their neutrality.

Culture

Cultural rules provide the foundation for the individual high performing behaviours. They provide the environment which shapes and dictates which perceptions, thoughts and behaviours will lead to average results, and which will lead to exceptional results.

These cultural elements describe the environment around the role being modelled and are in addition to the corporate cultural elements described elsewhere.

The [industry]

[Client]'s culture is largely defined by the [industry] that it serves. Neutrality is important in every activity, with some staff being almost paranoid about not being seen to be influencing the [industry]. This can lead to staff being overly cautious at times, particularly when presenting research which they fear will not be well received by [Client]'s members. Rather than 'tell it straight', there is sometimes a tendency to 'tone down' information rather than risk offending a member. This opens the door for political behaviour from the members, with some representatives actively working to develop a "fearsome reputation", designed to make it easier for them to get their own way. Managing these 'strong characters' is a concern for many [Client] staff.

Many [Client] staff exaggerate this neutral position into a sense of powerlessness, saying that [Client] has no regulatory powers to impose standards and is therefore subservient to its members. However, if [Client] had regulatory powers then [industry] operators would have no accountability for safety standards. They could always blame [Client] for making them introduce changes and improvements, and they could, for example, blame increased passenger fares on the cost of introducing [Client]'s unnecessary and over-protective standards. By taking up an advisory position only and introducing standards through industry consensus, [Client] is actually in a more powerful position because it can recommend what is right or best and leave its members to debate how to introduce change. By achieving this through a consensual process, members must accept responsibility for the decisions that they make and the standards that they agree to implement. The [industry] therefore relies on [Client] as a source of expert knowledge, and [Client]'s value is therefore greatly underrated by many of its own staff.

Support

Overall, the culture seems to be participative and supportive, however some pockets of political activity cause frustration for some staff who are outside of those power circles.

Organisational size

[Client] has now grown to a size that means that staff no longer recognise all of their colleagues. This can lead to the development of 'silos' where staff focus on their own roles and teams and forget how their purpose connects to the rest of the organisation. Networking sessions would be a good way to add to the lunchtime learning sessions that are currently in place, with the focus being on getting to know people across the business rather than focusing on technical knowledge.

Change

One of the most important features of [Client]'s culture is that it is changing rapidly. Since [Client] was established, it operated in much the same way, with its culture and its people emerging from that of organisations such as [industry]track and the train operating companies.

However, a number of factors are converging to change this culture.

- The move to a new office meant a new corporate identity and a new working environment
- The change in [Client]'s constitution signalled a change in its thinking
- The imminent departure of the Chief Executive creates uncertainty
- The retirement of staff who have spent a lifetime in the [industry] shifts the focus away from that as the primary source of value
- The attraction of staff with technical skills but not [industry] skills

The last point is important because it also opens up the culture to change, as fewer staff are attached to the ways that the [industry] has worked in the past and perhaps look more objectively at how it might work better in the future. [Client], and therefore the [industry], must begin to value generic technical skills over historical industry knowledge. However, both are vital to [Client]'s operation, and therefore the loss of that historical knowledge to retirement must be very carefully managed.

The Difference

General features of high performers

They have a goal which is greater than that of the task which they are recognised for excelling at, so the task becomes a means to an end and not an end in itself.

We observed high performers setting long term goals, such as "to build a coherent change strategy", for which meetings were a means to an end, not an end in themselves.

Their intention, attitude or methods are counter-intuitive and not obvious to an observer.

High performers do not set out to build consensus within a group, because this would be contrary to their neutral position. Building consensus implies influencing the group towards a particular decision, and whilst the high performers did indeed use covert influence methods to achieve this, it was not their primary goal.

Preparing from the participants' points of view is not obvious, as it looks exactly like preparing from any other point of view in that the external behaviour simply involves reading.

High performers avoid conflict by tackling it head on, whereas a poor facilitator tries to avoid conflict, thereby causing it.

They appear to get results easily because they actually do make it easy for themselves by implementing short-cuts or methods which are not obvious to an observer.

High performers make it easy to gain agreement and manage conflict within a meeting because they do the majority of work outside of the meeting. When a group gets together, they are focused on making a decision which then happens quite efficiently.

High performers therefore excel at gaining consensus within a meeting because they have already stacked the odds in the favour prior to the meeting. However, at no point do they lobby or try to influence any participants, as this again would conflict with their need for neutrality.

Specific differences

	High Performers	Average/Poor Performers
Purpose of a meeting	To make decisions	To discuss or debate
Ownership	The facilitator owns the process, the participants own the content	The facilitator owns the meeting

Equality	Sees all participants as equal	Is influenced by job titles and status
Preparation	Extensive, ensures participants have enough time and information to prepare thoroughly	Minimal, focuses on own preparation and may not give participants enough time or information
Preparation perspective	As if they are the other participants, considering all positions	As if they are a participant or chairman
Objectives	The meeting is a means to an end	The meeting is an end in itself
Direction	Has clear goals for the meeting and keeps the conversation on track by checking against their goals	Does not have clear goals, therefore tends to value any discussion, even if it is off topic
Opening	Invests time in reviewing previous minutes, building group compliance through shared experience	Reviews minutes where necessary but mainly focuses on the current agenda
Process	Packages the meeting into agenda items	Treats the meeting as a single entity

Agenda management	Dynamically rearranges the agenda to achieve its objectives	Sticks to the agenda and works through from start to finish
Time	Time is fixed, the agenda is variable	Time is variable, the agenda is fixed
Negotiation	Works outside the meeting to resolve differences, making it easier for participants to compromise	Debates within the meeting, causing participants to become entrenched in their positions
Personal involvement	Not directly engaged in conversation, therefore easier to spot	Gets involved in the conversation so doesn't always notice
Engagement	Knows that not all participants will be engaged in each agenda item and focuses on those who are involved, allowing the others to gather their thoughts and maintain concentration	Wants all participants to be engaged throughout the whole meeting, causing participants to become disengaged when they are realistically unable to maintain concentration

Contribution	Gives all participants an equal opportunity to contribute, whether they choose to or not	Wants all participants to contribute equally
Neutrality	Protects their neutrality, pushing accountability onto the participants	Becomes directly involved in the debate
Decision making	Presents a decision at the start of each agenda item and only opens up a discussion by exception	Opens agenda items as discussions and then concludes them with a decision
'Strong personalities'	Separates the message from the behaviour and doesn't take it personally	Discounts the message because of the behaviour and takes it personally
Handling conflict	Reminds the group that their conflict is with each other	Becomes involved in conflict
Inappropriate behaviour	Tackles it directly in the meeting	Smooths over it in the meeting and tackles it outside of the meeting, if at all

Recommendations

The following recommendations are organised around the 'people cycle' illustrated below.

```
┌──────── Attraction ────────▶┌──────── Development ───────▶┌──────── Retention ────────▶
│ (Attract)(Recruit)(Select)  ││ (Induct)(Perform)(Develop) ││ (Align)(Succeed)(Exit)
◀──────── Person ─────────────┘◀──────── Behaviour ─────────┘◀──────── Culture ─────────
```

The people cycle breaks down the lifecycle of the people in an organisation into three phases. Each phase feeds back to itself so that successful selection refines the attraction of new employees, successful development refines the induction process and exit management drives team alignment. The overall cycle enables an organisation to evolve while protecting the unique culture which makes it successful.

Attraction

A good facilitator prepares thoroughly and is procedures oriented. The language of a job advert should reflect this and should avoid words like 'freedom' and 'challenge'. They are also 'towards' oriented and seek results.

All external communication serves to attract the right people to [Client]. [Client] may not be well known outside of the industry, however with the culture shifting away from industry knowledge and towards technical skills, it would be useful to explore the role of social media in building a brand for [Client] as an employer of choice.

Recruitment

The most notable quality which can be tested for at interview is the high performer's practice of preparing from the other person's point of view. A simple test would be to ask the candidate to set the agenda for the interview. A poor performer would not thoroughly prepare for the interview, but both the average and high performers would. The agenda would enable you to see how they prepare. You can expect an average performer to create an agenda biased towards them 'selling' themselves, whereas the high performer would bias an agenda towards the interviewer's needs. Having set the agenda, you would also expect the high performer to 'manage' the interview.

Selection

Overall, the selection process needs to give successful candidates a good understanding of [Client]'s culture. Any candidate who thrives on being in the limelight and driving change is probably not a good choice as they will struggle with [Client]'s neutral position in the industry.

Good facilitators achieve results through a team, which may be their colleagues or their meeting participants. Once a candidate is past the first stage of the recruitment process, an assessment centre would therefore be a better test of team behaviour than an individual interview.

Induction

The most important part of any induction process is a cultural alignment. New recruits should attend a wide range of meetings to get a 'feel' for the [Client] facilitation style and the unique working environment.

Performance

Performance management of new recruits needs to be structured to support high performing behaviours.

Regular reviews of meetings should be held, with colleagues acting as observers who are able to give useful, objective feedback to a developing facilitator.

Development

Aside from a formal training program, we recommend that staff occasionally attend meetings which are outside of their normal work area. In particular, attending any standards meetings as an observer would give staff a valuable insight into one of [Client]'s core activities.

Alignment

Any team that has to participate in, chair or contribute to meetings must have an understanding of how to support the facilitation process. Freeing up time to prepare for meetings is one of the most valuable things that a manager can do to support their team.

Succession

The most obvious succession planning activity is to have staff attend regular meetings to get to know the people involved, and to stand in for regular meeting chairs to develop their skills, confidence, and their understanding of the topics under discussion.

More broadly, it is important to manage the transfer of industry knowledge to younger staff. In a software company, the methods and working practices can be totally different today than even ten years ago because there is no 'real estate' to manage or protect. [Client] has to build modern operating principles on an infrastructure whose roots go back hundreds of years. Therefore, lunchtime storytelling sessions, where industry veterans can talk about 'when I was a lad' would be of huge value in passing on that deep industry knowledge, and would be hugely entertaining too.

Exit

The key consideration when managing a high performer out of the business is to manage the handover of the relationships that they have created. It is very important that their replacement does not try to step into their shoes and instead makes a committee their own, establishing their own ground rules, expectations and standards of behaviour.

...

From this research, I created a three tier training program to install the attitudes and behaviours of high performers into all stakeholder facing staff. Outlines for these three tiers of the program follow on the next few pages.

Workshop Outlines

Overview

Level 1 – Presenting with Confidence

One of the most important skills in any organisation is the ability to stand up and present your ideas or achievements to internal colleagues and external stakeholders. Yet this is also one of the most often avoided activities. Whilst some people will go to great lengths to make sure they never have to do it, others relish the opportunity to present at anything from project reviews and team meetings to research debates and industry conferences.

In this one day workshop, we'll be exploring and practising the qualities and behaviours of the best presenters, giving you new ways to structure and deliver your presentations, whether you're a new presenter or an old hand. Most importantly, any nervousness that you might feel will be gone, and if you find your presentations have gotten stuck in a rut, you'll definitely leave with fresh inspiration and new ways to engage your audience and get your message across.

Level 2 – Chairing Meetings Effectively

Meetings are an important activity in any organisation, because people need to get together to share ideas and make decisions. Yet, without structure, meetings can easily become disorganised and frustrating, resulting in disengaged participants and missed project deadlines.

The best facilitators can structure a meeting and keep the participants on track with only the lightest touch, enabling everyone to get on with the discussion at hand and not worry about timekeeping or staying on topic.

In this one day workshop, we'll be working through the most important characteristics and behaviours of the best meeting facilitators, learning and practising both their methods and their 'secrets'; the things that aren't obvious yet make the difference between having to wrestle a meeting into line and gently keeping everyone focused, on track and productive.

Level 3 – Achieving Consensus in Challenging Situations

[Client] has a unique role within the [industry] and in fact a very unusual role for any industry. A vital skill for anyone in a stakeholder-facing role is the ability to position [Client]'s strengths, convey the value of [Client]'s service and engage with multiple stakeholders who each have different views and different needs.

On the surface, it seems an impossible task to build consensus in such an environment, yet some people achieve this easily. Following an in depth analysis of [Client]'s culture and working practices, we have developed a unique, two day workshop which will enable you to practice and develop an approach which combines your own personal style and experiences with the innate, hidden talents of expert facilitators.

We'll be exploring challenging situations and the individual barriers that you face so that you'll be able to manage complex groups and further strengthen the credibility of [Client] within the [industry].

Level 1 – Presenting with Confidence

Workshop Purpose

By the end of the workshop, each participant will have the skills to stand up, any time, any where and present any subject to any audience.

Workshop Duration

1 day, 09:00 to 17:00

High Level Content

Introduction

What is a Presentation?

Excellent Presenters

How do you Design a Presentation?

Your Outcome

Share your Outcome

When Does the Presentation Start?

Getting Ready

Planning Outcomes for the Audience

Communication Channels

Credibility

Questions

Narrative Communication

Framing your Communication

Question-Story-Question

Structuring the Presentation

Framing

Outcome focus

Timeframe

Frame/Story/Question

Six Questions

STAR

Association (shifting referential index)

Reflecting current experience

Getting the Timing Right

Using Presentation Aids

[Client] Style Protocol

Handling Questions and Answers

ERR

When Should you Take Questions?

Closing the Presentation

Putting it all Together

Level 2 – Chairing Meetings Effectively

Workshop Purpose

By the end of the workshop, each participant will have the skills required to chair a meeting so that it achieves its purpose.

Workshop Duration

1 day, 09:00 to 17:00

High Level Content

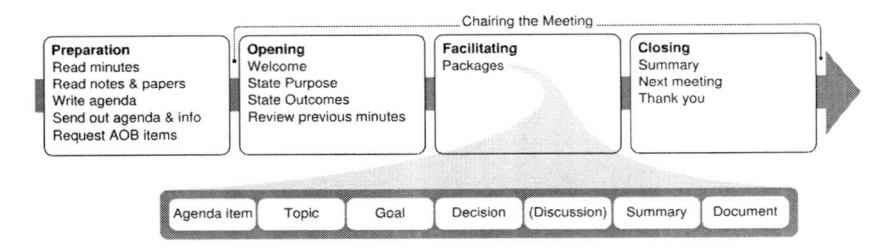

```
                              ──── Chairing the Meeting ────
┌──────────────────┐ ┌──────────────────┐ ┌──────────────┐ ┌──────────────┐
│ Preparation      │ │ Opening          │ │ Facilitating │ │ Closing      │
│ Read minutes     │ │ Welcome          │ │ Packages     │ │ Summary      │
│ Read notes &     │ │ State Purpose    │ │              │ │ Next meeting │
│   papers         │ │ State Outcomes   │ │              │ │ Thank you    │
│ Write agenda     │ │ Review previous  │ │              │ │              │
│ Send out agenda  │ │   minutes        │ │              │ │              │
│   & info         │ │                  │ │              │ │              │
│ Request AOB items│ │                  │ │              │ │              │
└──────────────────┘ └──────────────────┘ └──────────────┘ └──────────────┘

     ┌───────────┬───────┬──────┬──────────┬──────────────┬─────────┬──────────┐
     │Agenda item│ Topic │ Goal │ Decision │ (Discussion) │ Summary │ Document │
     └───────────┴───────┴──────┴──────────┴──────────────┴─────────┴──────────┘
```

Meeting Planning & Design

What is the purpose of the meeting?

What is the shortest route required to achieve that purpose?

e.g. Decisions, Discussions, Debate, Knowledge sharing

Build the necessary agenda items into packages, each with its own purpose

Prioritise the packages

Write the agenda

Meeting Preparation

Send out the agenda and accompanying notes in time for the participants to prepare

Plan the meeting, thinking about the different participants' positions on each agenda item

In the Meeting

Keeping the meting on track

Time management

Handling conflict

Taking minutes

Closing the meeting

After the Meeting

Follow ups and reminders

Managing actions and deliverables

Managing regular meetings

Level 3 – Achieving Consensus in Challenging Situations

Workshop Purpose

By the end of the workshop, each participant will have the skills required to enable a group to reach a consensus decision.

Workshop Duration

2 days, 09:00 to 17:00

High Level Content

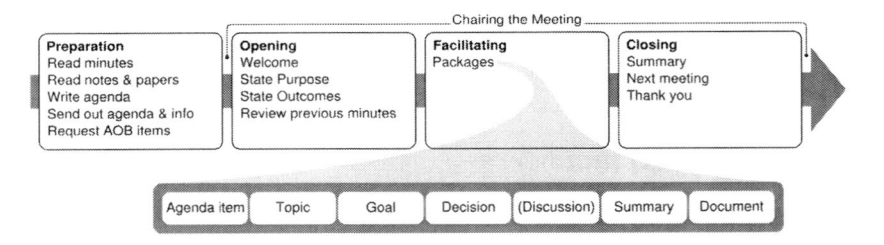

```
                              Chairing the Meeting
┌──────────────────┬──────────────────┬──────────────┬──────────────┐
│ Preparation      │ Opening          │ Facilitating │ Closing      │
│ Read minutes     │ Welcome          │ Packages     │ Summary      │
│ Read notes &     │ State Purpose    │              │ Next meeting │
│   papers         │ State Outcomes   │              │ Thank you    │
│ Write agenda     │ Review previous  │              │              │
│ Send out agenda  │   minutes        │              │              │
│   & info         │                  │              │              │
│ Request AOB items│                  │              │              │
└──────────────────┴──────────────────┴──────────────┴──────────────┘

  Agenda item | Topic | Goal | Decision | (Discussion) | Summary | Document
```

Meeting Process

Participants already know the basic process above

Excellent Facilitators

What more do the best facilitators do, over and above the average?

Equality and confidence

Neutrality and impartiality

Meeting Preparation

Pre-meeting research and communication

Creating an environment where participants can rethink their positions

Mentally rehearsing extreme positions

In the Meeting

Opening the meeting to build group compliance

Packaging

Advanced conflict management

Dealing with inappropriate behaviour

Dynamic agenda management

Accountability

Maintaining neutrality

Maintaining the right level of participation and engagement

Using breaks and other resources to manage the meeting

After the Meeting

Communication

Managing regular meetings

25 Further Reading

Books

The NLP Practitioner Manual	Peter Freeth
Change Magic	Peter Freeth
Structure of Magic, vols 1 & 2	Bandler & Grinder
Patterns of the Hypnotic Techniques of Milton H Erickson MD, vols 1 & 2	Bandler & Grinder
Modelling with NLP	Robert Dilts
Strategies of Genius, Vols 1 - 3	Robert Dilts
The Brain that Changes Itself	Normal Doidge
Growing Up With Lucy	Steve Grand

Articles and Papers

Mirror Neurons and the Simulation Theory of Mind Reading, Gallese and Goldman, Trends in Cognitive Sciences, Dec 1998

Recalling Routes around London: Activation of the Right Hippocampus in Taxi Drivers, Maguire, Frackowiak & Frith, The Journal of Neuroscience, Sept 1997

Differential Consolidation and Pattern Reverberations within Episodic Cell Assemblies in the Mouse Hippocampus, Oşan, Chen, Feng & Tsien, PLOS, Feb 2011

Websites

merzenich.positscience.com

www.cgwpublishing.com/genius

www.genius-at-work.co.uk

www.geniuslearning.co.uk

uk.linkedin.com/in/peterfreethexpertauthorcoach

Reader's Offer

As a reader of this book, you get a 15% discount when you reserve your place on training courses organised by the author[16] – just forward your receipt email to **learn@nenlp.com** and save 15% off the total course fee.

For the latest news about upcoming courses, visit

www.nenlp.com

Conditions:

1. You'll get a 15% discount on the list price of the courses listed above for the purchase of any of the following books, in any format:

    The NLP Practitioner Manual

    The NLP Master Practitioner Manual

    Genius at Work

    The Unsticker – all by Peter Freeth

2. This offer is subject to availability of places, so if a course is already full then you're too late. You can use this offer for the following year's courses, though.

3. One receipt, one discount, one course.

4. Discounts are transferable, so your friend can use your receipt to get a discount, but you can't both use the same receipt.

---

16 Currently, this includes courses running in the UK and Spain. The courses running in Goa are organised by someone else and are not subject to this offer, although other discounts may be available.

Lightning Source UK Ltd.
Milton Keynes UK
UKOW02f0246040616

275582UK00006B/375/P